VOFM
Library

*f*P

Gonville

A Memoir

Peter Birkenhead

Free Press

New York London Toronto Sydney

FREE PRESS
A division of Simon & Schuster, Inc.
1230 Avenue of the Americas
New York, NY 10020

NOTE TO READERS
The names and identifying details of some individuals
portrayed in this book have been changed.

First Free Press hardcover edition March 2010

FREE PRESS and colophon are trademarks of Simon & Schuster, Inc.

For information about special discounts for bulk purchases, please contact
Simon & Schuster Special Sales at 1-866-506-1949 or
business@simonandschuster.com

The Simon & Schuster Speakers Bureau can bring authors to your live event.
For more information or to book an event contact the Simon & Schuster
Speakers Bureau at 1-866-248-3049 or visit our website at
www.simonspeakers.com.

Manufactured in the United States of America

1   3   5   7   9   10   8   6   4   2

Library of Congress Cataloging-in-Publication Data

Birkenhead, Peter.
Gonville: a memoir/Peter Birkenhead.
p. cm.
ISBN-13: 978-1-4165-9883-1
ISBN-10: 1-4165-9883-9
1. Birkenhead, Peter. 2. Actors—United States—Biography
3. Fathers and sons—United States—Biography. I. Title.
PN2287.B45465A3 2010
792.02'8092—dc22
[B]
2009023790

ISBN 978-1-4165-9883-1
ISBN 978-1-4391-0127-8 (ebook)

For my mother, my brothers, and my sister.
And for Jenny.

PROLOGUE

My father is Gonville again.

That's not beatnik slang for crazy, although he is behaving quite strangely at the moment. My father is doing one of his favorite impressions, which involves wearing one of his favorite outfits: faded red bikini briefs, circa 1975, and a genuine British army officer's pith helmet, circa 1879. Now, this is December 1992, and I'm trying hard to stay focused here because I'm on a mission that couldn't be more important or frightening to me, but I just can't get over the fact that a pair of bikini briefs can *last* for twenty years.

Gonville was a real person. Gonville Bromhead was his full name, and he was a leftenant in Her Majesty's Service, a winner of the Victoria Cross for his valor at the Battle of Rorke's Drift during the British Empire's subjugation of South Africa in the mid-nineteenth century. But more importantly, he was a character played by Michael Caine in my father's favorite movie, and the first one I ever saw, at age five—*Zulu*, a film about that battle, which was the bloodiest of the war.

Bromhead is a slightly foppish stiff-upper-lipper who keeps his red tunic buttoned all the way up to the neck and who, along with a hundred and fifty other Englishmen, fights off four thousand Zulu warriors during the horribly violent siege depicted in the movie.

My dad and I are standing in the middle of his apartment, which means the helmet is competing with dozens of rifles, bayonets, Zulu fighting sticks, and other helmets for a place on the list of Things that

Make You Go "Help." My father is an avid gun collector, and his "pieces," as he calls them—not in the gangster kind of way, but in a *curator* kind of way—fill just about every available inch of wall space in the tiny Hell's Kitchen one-bedroom where he's lived for twelve years, since my mother divorced him.

The mainstay of his collection is the Martini-Henry, the rifle that brought whole subcontinents to their knees and our family to its senses. The Martini-Henry protected and served the British Empire and her colonies for over thirty years. It was the most advanced firearm of its day, and the orphans of British soldiers built the cartridges for it.

Dad is getting deeper into character, and it becomes impossible for me to look him in the eye. I try to focus on his mouth, but that's even more disturbing, since he's pursing his lips in that way that English men over sixty do when they want to be witheringly ironic, but only succeed in reminding us all how much Paul McCartney looks like an old woman now.

So I open the always-handy eyes on the side of my head and take a little tour of the room to check out the arsenal. Six of the twelve rifles in the gun case to my left are Martini-Henrys. The fact that I know this at a glance makes a little bubble of acid pop in my stomach.

This gun case is the smallest and least impressive of the three in the apartment, but they're all pretty imposing. They're tall and made of oak, with locked cabinets at the bottom, and when I was a kid they emitted a dark and scary force field. They were deeply frightening and unbearably tempting. After all, having a dad who's armed and dangerous offers few benefits, but bragging to your friends about handling weapons is one of them.

Guns are kept in cases to keep them away from moisture, and touching my father's guns was always discouraged. I'm very tempted to grab one now, as I stand here on the veldt with Gonville, but I've just come from the bathroom and my hands are still wet. My father hangs his ratty old towels right over the cat's litter box, where they've soaked up years of crap fumes, and whenever I'm at my dad's place I spend six or seven minutes with wet hands because I'm so afraid to use the towels.

So I keep my hands at my side and my feet to the floor, despite a very strong urge to leave.

Not because I'm brave, but because I'm scared. Scared of a lot of things, especially my father, and I don't want to be scared anymore. It was only two weeks ago that I had my eyes re-opened to all the reasons he scares me—my mother, my brothers, my sister, and I have only recently started talking about Dad and the past—and since then I've thought about nothing else but coming here, about what I would say when I got here, and what my father would do. If I leave here now I'll only be back in an hour, at least in my mind. I'm here because I need to get away from this place. So I stay. I stay even though I've reached the forty-minute mark—a time limit I gave myself years ago for visits to the veldt, as a way of avoiding the humid guilt that would cling to me after seeing the look on my father's face if I left too early, making the walk back to the Upper West Side feel like trudging through molten rubber; and also of avoiding the rage that would stiffen my neck if I stayed too long, making the walk home not just difficult but dangerous because of my inattention to looking both ways when I crossed the street. So I may be risking death by Columbus Circle to stay, but that would be better than being crushed under the wheels of what's been heading my way for as long as I can remember.

PART ONE

1

Okay, I'm flying. I'm three years old and I can fly. Who knew?
But I'm always full of surprises and today's is that I'm flying. Not in an airplane, but like Superman, with my arms stretched out in front of me and the wind in my face. There's a lot of turbulence, but I'm not flying through the sky. I'm setting what must be the indoor air-speed record, flying down a long stairwell without touching the stairs. The turns are very tight, really scary, and as I approach each one, I sense that I'm flying too fast, and that I'm going to crash into the wall. I don't know how I'm doing it—what's propelling me, or holding me up, but my thoughts seem to play a role. Just as I think, "I need to slow down if I'm going to make this turn," I do, and I keep going.

Years later, when I was eight, and sensing that this was not just a dream but a memory, I would spend hours trying to reconnect with my super powers, which by that time had apparently gone into remission. I was especially interested in that thought-controlled steering system; it implied that I could make things happen just by thinking about them and that was particularly appealing to me.

So I made up concentration exercises that I would do in bed at night, hoping that the next day I'd be able to steer baseballs to my bat and turn Rebecca Lowenstern's face my way. I would stare and stare at the illuminated face of my Sony clock radio and try to stop the second hand from moving, or at least slow it down a little bit.

I really hated that clock. A clock radio had been the must-have gift for the pre-teen set at Glen Cove Middle School the previous year, but my parents were always way behind the curve with these things. We didn't have a color TV until long after NBC had stopped doing that peacock-spreading-its-wings business. One day I begged my friend Ben to come over after school because I knew Dad was finally going to bring home a toy I'd been asking for for weeks—a Billy Blastoff like Ben and all the other kids had. Ben's family had lived next door to us in Brooklyn, and they had moved to Glen Cove the same week we did, but the similarities pretty much ended there. I always felt like Ben was a hundred degrees cooler than me, which was borne out when we got to my house that day and what was waiting for me wasn't a Billy Blastoff, but a halfhearted knockoff called Tommy Takeoff. That was the moment when Ben dubbed my father The Man Who Won't. I said what do you mean? And he said whatever most people do, he won't; whatever they're for, he's against; and even as I was telling Benny to go to hell I knew he was right.

The only thing I was sure of when it came to my dad was that he was the center of my universe. After that it was all questions. I was eight years old, the eldest child in our family, and I wanted to get a bead on Dad so that maybe I could get a bead on me, but whenever I tried I just felt confused. Is he a proud member of the National Rifle Association or a guy who leads anti-war marches? Absolutely. Is he a guy from Brooklyn who wears a torn old T-shirt to Thanksgiving dinner or a professor of economics who decorates his house with little blue Wedgwood plates commemorating the birthday of Queen Elizabeth? You betcha.

I caught my father in glimpses, heard him in fragments. He was a collection of fleeting pieces and parts, and sometimes it seemed like each part was opposed to the next. He loved being The Man Who Won't—the looks from other peaceniks when they saw his gun collection, or the cringing faces of the neighbors as they walked by our proudly unmowed, Addams Family crabgrass lawn.

So I was relentless with my demands for a clock radio, hoping that it might help elevate me to at least non-weirdo status with the other kids, or maybe even make me the kind of kid that nobody noticed, which I knew was probably too much to hope for, but I thought, why not dream big? And when I saw the word "SONY" on the top of the box through the Christmas wrapping that year, I felt like I had made it, like my dream of uneventful anonymity might be within reach. And then I opened the box, and I pulled out something that was, yes, technically a clock radio, but that lacked the one and only reason everyone wanted a clock radio in the first place, which was, of course, the digital clock. I didn't even know they made clock radios with old-fashioned clock faces on them. You'd have to go pretty far out of your way to find one, I thought, and I have to admit being very impressed with my father's resourcefulness. My mind-over-matter experiments began that night, and while I never succeeded in actually stopping time, I did learn that I could slow my heart rate pretty much at will. As I stared at that pitiful clock I would fall into a kind of trance, and eventually into fitful sleep, during which I would dream about running down flights of stairs.

I seemed to improve my skills with each dream, getting to the point where I could take two stairs at a time, and then three, and eventually I would basically be in a long, controlled free fall, keeping my hand on the banister and whipping myself around the turns without my feet touching a single step. I always managed to get away—whatever was chasing me never caught me—but it did literally scare the piss out of me. Any delusions I had about being a superhero were very well humbled when I woke up wet, to a sound like one of those self-destruct alarms in the movies. A pad of tinfoil under me was attached by wires to a big green box next to my bed that would howl with derision as soon as the first drop of pee hit the sheets. I guess the idea was to humiliate me into continence, but of course it just made things a whole lot worse.

I can't imagine who came up with the idea that kids who wet their beds are *just not nervous enough*, yet someone had, and I fantasized about smacking him to death with a rolled-up newspaper. But until that day came, I would have to deal with the mess I was in. I'd fallen asleep practicing to be a hero, and I woke up wondering what kind of explanation I could give to my mom that would make her believe that I wasn't an eight-year-old, bed-wetting baby. In fact, I was getting very good at the art of the explanation, spinning stories about mischievous gerbils and glasses of Tang, and I was starting to think that maybe I had found my ticket to the big time. I mean, even though the only super power I seemed to be developing was the ability to bend truth in my bare hands, I thought it might be enough to build a decent super-hero career on.

My newfound power was awe-inspiring. Lying was almost as thrilling as I imagined flying would be, and it felt very heroic. It didn't seem like "lying" to me so much as creating a new and improved truth, and I could do it whenever I wanted. It was like having a genie in a bottle—my wish was my command. I pretty much *could* make anything happen just by thinking it: "I think these kids might accept me a little bit more if I were royalty." *Shazzam!* "My great-grandfather was an English duke who was famous for giving away his fortune to the people of his, whaddayacallit, dukedom." And my powers only increased when I became an alleged adult. "I think this girl will be more likely to sleep with me if the scar on my leg was caused by a knife-wielding mugger instead of a beach umbrella." *Shazzam!* "I was stabbed! I am a brave and dangerous character! Thank you, me. Thank you very much."

The best thing about my power, though, was that I could lie to myself and make myself believe it. This came in handy at night, when there was no one else around to fool. During the day, I could fake my way through anything. I just kept moving so I wouldn't have to be alone with myself. Like the Sundance Kid. When Robert Redford said, "I'm better when I move," and then rolled on the ground and fired off six perfect shots, I knew exactly what he meant. As long as

I was in motion I was okay, sometimes even impressive. But when I was stationary I was in trouble, and it was very hard to stay in bed all night. My parents had vicious fights on the other side of my bedroom wall, and sometimes I'd press my ear to it and try to figure out what the fights were about, or I'd bury my head in a pillow to drown them out. It wasn't until I discovered the malleability of truth that I learned to live with them. The noise on the other side of the wall became a prison riot, or miners trapped in a cave, or the Bolivian army waiting for Butch and Sundance.

One night, as I was lying in a state of suspended animation necessitated by the fact that I was Charlton Heston in a spaceship heading for, little did I know it, the Planet of the Apes, I detected a strange noise outside my frozen astronaut sleeping pod, and believing that something might be wrong with the ship, I allowed my ears to open a little bit more than they had been. I was right, something was wrong. The other astronauts had somehow broken out of their sleeping pods and had burst right into the middle of—holy shit—my room.

There they were, right next to my bed, screaming like hell at each other. My mother must have been pointing at me. She was saying, "Look what you've done, he's trembling!" I don't know if my father looked at me, because I couldn't see him. My eyes wouldn't open because I was in suspended animation.

There was nothing I could do about that. Everyone would have to wait for the duration of the journey, however long it took until we reached the planet that was actually Earth, even though we wouldn't recognize it. They would have to wait until we got there for me to open my eyes, and stop shaking.

Twenty-three years later I started dreaming about the stairs again for the first time since I was a kid. I asked Mom about the dream one day, over lunch in her apartment. I had recognized the stairway as the one in the building we lived in when I was three, so I wasn't surprised to learn that my dream was in fact a memory, and that my mother had been the motor of my flight down the steps, that she was the one thinking about speed and controlling it. I *was* surprised to learn that Mom was carrying my younger brother David under her other arm, which must have made her flight that much more difficult. I imagined what it must have felt like for her not to have a hand free to grab the banister, to have to slow down more than she wanted to in order to make the turns. I wondered if she considered dropping one of us to give the other one a better chance of making it. But I didn't ask her about any of those things. For some reason I was fixated on what kind of gun was involved. I realized as she began the story that one had been, and I wanted to know if it was a rifle or a handgun. Mom said, "He pointed a gun at me, then you, and I just snatched you and David up and started running." "Right. Right. Mom, what kind of gun was it, do you remember? I mean, was it—" "Oh it was one of those, those old ones. Those big, horrible old ones." "Not a pistol?" I said. "Oh no, no," she said, "no. Not a pistol."

My mom has played the piano all her life, and now she let her hands fall onto the table as if she were resolving a chord. She looked at me steadily, and I felt like saying, "Wow, it's great to meet you." I placed my hands on hers. I felt her fingers twitch, and I took a slow breath. Eleven years before this conversation, in 1980, my mother's friend Barbara had driven her to the emergency room, my mother's hands still being bruised from injuries my father had done to them during a long and horrible evening. Mom had escaped to Barbara's house, where Barbara put her in the car and called the police, and that's all I knew about that day. As I felt the pulse in my mother's hands, I felt my own heart racing, and new questions catching in my throat.

2

Between school years, my father used to manage a summer stock theater on Cape Cod, in Hyannis, which is like the tacky kid sister of Hyannis Port, just a couple of miles up the road. The theater was pretty upscale as these kinds of places go—these kinds of places being enormous circus tents on the edge of town. Back in the sixties and seventies, big tours of Broadway shows would come through and play the Melody Tent for a week or maybe two, and I'd watch every performance.

The actors would make their entrances from outside the tent. They'd come down one of the narrow, sloping aisles of the theater and step onto the stage, and then climb back up the aisle when they exited. Sometimes I'd sit on the grass outside the tent and eavesdrop on them as they waited to go on stage, puffing on cigarettes and joking about the way someone in the audience was dressed. I couldn't get enough of the moment when an actor would mumble something out of the corner of his mouth, stamp out a cigarette, and burst into the tent, disappearing into a kaleidoscope of light and leaving his colleague laughing to himself outside. It was like watching someone step through a portal into another dimension.

I would get the same feeling in reverse when I sat in the empty tent in the mornings. Without the lights and the rapt attention of the audience, the scenery would seem hokey and insubstantial, the folding canvas chairs a little tired, but the atmosphere was quiet and cool in there, and everyone who worked at the theater liked to come in and sit for a while when nothing was going on. My dad used to sit in the front row with the theater's maintenance man, a big salty guy named Chappy who wore a Red Sox cap and who could've been forty or sixty-five and had been there forever. Chappy was the kind of guy my father struck up friendships with wherever he worked, the kind of guy who probably grew up in a place like Bedford-Stuyvesant, the tough, old neighborhood in Brooklyn where Dad had been raised.

I sat in the back row of the theater one morning, a month or so after my night of suspended animation, and watched the backs of their heads as they sat quietly with each other. Dad was talking about his brother Donald, the first person in his family born in America, who had been in the navy during the war. Dad took long pauses as he spoke. He and Chappy sat a little slumped in their chairs and stared at the stage, and Dad said, "Submarine." And Chappy said, "Yeah." Then Dad said something with lots of numbers and letters and Chappy came back with numbers and letters of his own and they paused again. Chappy asked, "How are Susan and the kids?" and I leaned all the way forward. But all Dad said was, "Fine, fine." Every once in a while a rogue current of air would lift a big, untethered panel of orange canvas and flop it back down with a crack, or send a Dixie cup skidding quickly down one of the aisles, but mostly it was quiet.

Dad spoke a little differently when he spoke to Chappy. As he was packing his pipe he shot his eyebrows up and said, "Right under the bridge," but it sounded like "undah de bridge." It made Chappy laugh, and my dad beamed and lit his pipe. He took something small out of a pocket and showed it to the older man, who seemed impressed, and Dad told him about one of his guns. He said, "The workmanship is out of this *world*, something you just don't see anymore. The name of the soldier it was made for is engraved on a brass plate on the stock. Just gorgeous." Except he pronounced it "gaw-geous."

* * *

Dad's childhood, when I pictured it, looked like one of the gangster movies on channel nine, all shadows and rain and men with scars from the corners of their mouths to their ears. Dad called it "the mark of the squealer," and said that "a kid in Bed-Stuy" had one. A kid!

Dad had been a fat kid, but a pretty kid, and he'd helped support his family by working as a child model until he was twelve. While his recently immigrated, devotedly Communist parents were taking any work they could find, Dad was doing magazine ads for Bosco chocolate sauce and Buster Brown shoes. And, I imagine, getting beat up for it by the other kids in the neighborhood on a pretty regular basis.

His father, Tom, worked as an operator of photostat machines, the precursors to Xerox copiers. Dad's mother, Florie, briefly worked as a retouch artist for movies, but mostly took care of the house and everyone in it, including Dad, his brother Donald, his sister Pat, an older aunt, and a cousin. And they were all still living with Florie and Tom, on and off, as adults, all these years later. I dreaded every trip to their apartment. It had big sinks and clocks and doorknobs from The Olden Days, and everything smelled of bad breath. There were no pictures on the walls, but there were doilies on the tables and elaborate Victorian lamps in the corners. It was dark and contradictory and confusing and scary. Everyone there drank a lot and fought all the time, about everything. And when they weren't fighting they were talking about fighting, about the Battle of Stalingrad or the Chicago convention or last week's bar brawl.

Dad and Chappy sat in the quiet tent, breathing lightly together and smiling to themselves. Dad was still talking about his gun. At home, whenever Dad took a new rifle out to show me I would freeze up, and I could tell my fear was not only a disappointment to him but an insult. I promised myself I would try harder not to be afraid. After a few more minutes Dad and Chappy made their way up the aisle and out of the tent to start their day, and the whole place filled with a muted, reddish light that felt contemplative, almost religious.

* * *

One of my favorite shows ever at the Melody Tent was a production of *Fiddler on the Roof* starring Leonard Nimoy as Tevye. It's still hard for me not to measure any experience I have against the surreal thrill of watching Mr. Spock dance with Cossacks at his daughter's wedding, but even that wasn't the best thing I ever saw on that stage. And it wasn't Robert Goulet in *Man of La Mancha* either, although my all-time favorite was presented on the same set where he was courting Aldonza every night at 7:30, no bathing suits allowed.

Every Sunday morning the theater would stand in as a church for a small group of elderly Catholic parishioners from the neighborhood, and I used to sneak in as often as I could, just for the chance to see a priest sermonize from Stanley Kowalski's apartment or Snoopy's doghouse. I was particularly eager to see the *Man of La Mancha* mass because it would of course take place in a dungeon of the Spanish Inquisition. I was a little kid, and my knowledge of the Inquisition was pretty limited, but I knew from the show that it wasn't the church's finest hour. Since I identified completely with my mother's Jewish side of the family and not at all with my father's lapsed Anglican atheists, I was hoping that the priest might be inspired by the set to apologize to all Jews everywhere, and that I, as the only one actually present, would be available to accept his gesture on behalf of a grateful people.

But my hopes of being the star of The Mass of La Mancha were dashed that Sunday morning when I saw Teddy Kennedy walk into the Melody Tent wearing his Chappaquiddick neck brace. There was some explanation at the time as to why he would leave the sanctuary of The Compound to commune with a gaggle of bingo-playing locals in a circus tent, but like most of the other stories coming out of Hyannis Port that summer, it was made of pretty flimsy stuff.

By 1969 Ted Kennedy was a hero in our house, but it hadn't always been that way. Just a year before, during the early primaries of '68, my parents were insisting that they "weren't Kennedy people," they were "Eugene McCarthy people." In 1968, "Kennedy people" meant Robert Kennedy people, but Robert Kennedy hadn't come out against the war early enough, and apparently he was something called an "opportunist," which made him sound to me like some kind of musician, or maybe a doctor. But I knew who he was—I probably knew more about Robert Kennedy and Teddy Kennedy and Eugene McCarthy than most kids knew about Mickey Mantle. I could quote LBJ's dropping-out-of-the-race speech verbatim, and often did, to the endless nonamusement of my Glen Cove friends. I went door-to-door, alone, gathering signatures, or more accurately, signature, on a petition to Stop the Bombing Now. I wore a MCCARTHY FOR PRESIDENT button on my paisley shirt to my third-grade class, and I patiently explained to the pitcher on my little league team why he and his family were fascists.

As it turns out, they were among an unusually large number of fascists in our neighborhood. And "hardhats," and Nazis, and just plain, unaffiliated evil people. We were frighteningly outnumbered in 1968, but Dad wasn't afraid. He cared even more than I did about all the little Vietnamese children who were being killed every day, and these people, these people with the LOVE IT OR LEAVE IT decals on their big ugly American cars—they were directly responsible for the suffering of every one of those napalmed kids. Dad wasn't the kind of phony who would bother being polite to these people, or pretend that just because they smiled when they talked to you, they weren't the baby burners they were. So when some short-haired waiter would tell him he was out of roast beef, or some crew-cut store manager asked him to keep his voice down, Dad would be on to him. And every time he smashed a coffee cup against a wall, or threw a chair across a restaurant, I managed to hold out a few minutes longer against that crampy feeling in my legs I at first thought was fear but that I now, at the age of eight, understood was weakness. The waiter would cower and shuffle away, mumbling words like "crazy" and "insane," but I was old enough to know that all the Great Men had been considered crazy at some point. They were ridiculed, persecuted, tortured. Even killed. We lived in the kind of world that required great men like my dad and Don Quixote, men who felt deeply and fought with their last ounce of courage for what was right, and who would be vindicated by history and the love of a fair damsel.

The damsel in question needed some convincing, though. And first I had to find her. Mom was always just outside the margins of things back then. At dinner every night she would stand off to one side and hover in the corner making busy noises, picking at the occasional noodle, and when dinner was finished she'd disappear behind the bathroom door. I don't know how I made a mystery out of that, but it took me years to realize that what I'd heard coming from the other side of the door had been the sounds of her throwing up. She had four kids by that summer: Me and David, three-year-old Richard, and one-year-old Alison, and the same husband she had married at nineteen, and her eyes always looked like they were trying to remember something.

But I was trying to figure out which way was up, and I needed Mom to settle the issue for me. I desperately tried to help her see the Knight Errant in my father, to see the dragons that Dad saw and to enlist her in the good fight, whatever that was. I can't imagine what it must have been like for her to have to listen to an eight year old's rambling, passionate, ice cream–induced speeches about why Republicans were stupid, but eventually she did come around. And of course the person who actually brought her into the fold wasn't me. He was on our television on a windy night in April, looking very sad, running his fingers through his hair and quoting Aeschylus—something about drops of pain giving shape to a life the way water shapes stone. My mother's eyes became focused again and wet, and the ash on her Kent 100 was defying gravity, and the next day when the sun came out we were all on a mission together, marching behind the flag of Sir Robert of Hyannis Port. Turns out Robert Kennedy wasn't a doctor, he was a magician who brought my parents together in a way that was less like a compromise than like alchemy. They seemed taller and lighter on their feet for the rest of the spring. While they were marching for Kennedy, Dad was his noble self.

The month of May, 1968, was like a brief, shining moment of peace in our house, and I dared to believe that it might last. The walls of the room I shared with David had always been bare, but now I started taping photos of heroes next to my bed. George Harrison playing guitar. Muhammad Ali in the ring with Floyd Patterson. I was sleeping at night, and waking up on dry sheets, and becoming a very big fan of the routine. So when my father opened our door at five o'clock one morning in June, and he looked like the pictures I had seen of him from when, believe it or not, he was once a boy, too, I got scared. He looked scared. I thought he was going to ask if he could climb into bed with us, but he was fully dressed, and looked like he'd been awake for a long while. He held tightly to the knob on the bedroom door, and he said, "Boys, they shot Bobby Kennedy last night."

It was one of the happiest moments of my life. My father was tender and baffled. It was sad and thrilling for me, and comforting. I turned to George Harrison to see how he was taking it, and he looked sad and tender, too. I felt older, and Dad looked younger, and everybody seemed to be the same age all of a sudden. Dad was calling Robert Kennedy "Bobby," like he was a friend. Everyone would start calling him Bobby, and a couple of nights later, as Dad and I were riding in his orange Austin Mini, we would stop right in the middle of the highway, just stop moving right there along with everyone else, to listen to the description of the funeral march over the Potomac to Arlington, where Bobby would be buried next to Jack. My father was crying. A fat woman in a blue Valiant next to us was sobbing and smoking ferociously, smearing her face with black ash and mascara. The whole world seemed to be crying together, and it was sad the way *Man of La Mancha* was sad, in a noble and inspiring kind of way, a hopeful way. That Christmas we looked at the Earth from space, and when the astronauts quoted the Bible my father didn't even sneer. How could we not be okay now? We were dreaming the impossible dream, and the world was starting to dream it with us, starting to see how right we were, how noble, how good. Don Quixote wasn't crazy, he was a sad and righteous hero—the Knight of the Woeful Countenance, and the beautiful Dulcinea would be his forever.

A year later Teddy walked into the tent, and I quickly ran to my usual seat for Sunday mass. When the tent was used as a church, the parishioners would fill only one side of the theater-in-the-round, and I would take what I thought was an inconspicuous seat on the other side of the stage. I did this so I could watch people take Communion, which was of course my favorite part of the show. I loved the blood drinking and big capes, and the added bonus of getting to watch grownups stick out their tongues at an authority figure. But the priest wouldn't be the big shot on stage that day. Ted Kennedy was a mythological figure by then, even in our family. Seeing him in the flesh was like seeing a unicorn.

As 1969 had dragged on, all the remaining goodness and hope from the year before, from before Bobby was shot, seemed to me to be resting on his shoulders. The fact that he was the same age as my father, and looked like him and confused people in the same "is he good or bad?" way, hadn't occurred to me yet. But Dad had been losing his lightness from the year before, little by little, and he'd reached a point where it seemed like he could go either way. I didn't know that a lot of people were feeling like that in 1969. I certainly didn't know they were feeling like that about Ted Kennedy. But something was going on and even an eight-year-old could feel it.

I was trembling with excitement in my red canvas chair as Teddy Kennedy walked stiffly down the aisle to the basement dungeon where Don Quixote would be tilting at windmills later that night, and where a plaster crucifix had been temporarily rigged amidst the shackles of blasphemers and Jews. I was trembling the way I would when I was lying in bed at night and heard my father's car pull into the driveway—the only time of day when, because I couldn't move or go anywhere or do anything to distract myself, I couldn't avoid the truth about him.

I don't know what I expected to see that day, but I know I wanted to see it clearly. A lot of borders had been blurred for me—between theater and religion, family and country, Camelot and La Mancha, truth and mythology, truth and lies. I was dizzy and buoyant, walking in space but desperate for someone to pull me in and get me back to the good, good Earth. Everyone had been talking about Teddy's accident for days. I couldn't understand why they seemed so full of swirling, complicated, grown-up feelings when they did. "Accident" was the word for "nothing to be angry about," but there was anger and suspicion all over the place at home, especially when Mom talked to Dad about this supposed "accident." I badly needed things to be different, to be the way they were the year before. I needed plaster Jesus to climb off the cross and have Robert Goulet join him on stage and testify to Teddy's heroism and goodness and have everything be right where it should.

No one on the other side of the stage pretended to look anywhere but at the back of Teddy's head as he knelt on the painted floor. We were all running the same tapes in our minds. The water, the girl. Dallas, Hyannis, "on to Chicago and let's win there." Back braces, neck braces, "sending a man to the moon and returning him safely to the Earth." "Some men see things as they are and ask why?" "Ask not . . ."

Teddy knelt with his son, who looked about my age, and when his turn came he stuck out his tongue, and it wasn't forked, and the priest placed the wafer on it and it disappeared into his mouth and I wanted to jump up and yell to everyone on the other side that everything was going to be okay. Then the priest brought the cup of wine towards his mouth and Teddy turned his face just a little, refusing it, and the priest moved on to Teddy Jr. and all of a sudden there was quicksand under my feet. Teddy was lying. I don't really know how I knew, but I did. He couldn't drink the blood, couldn't face it. He didn't do what he was supposed to do, what everyone did every Sunday, whether they wanted to or not, because it was the rule. He was the Man Who Wouldn't, pretending to be a good guy. He was lying to everyone sitting behind him by not shaking his head and refusing the wine vigorously enough. He probably just couldn't take a drink with the neck brace on, or he was keeping a brand-new promise to stay away from wine, but it didn't matter—whatever he had done that day, I would have been on to him.

After dinner that night my brother asked if I wanted to have a catch. I grudgingly followed him outside with my mitt, and started to toss the ball in the usual high lobs that David had yet to get under consistently. I told him the story of Teddy and the wine, but he didn't believe me. I don't think he was even old enough to comprehend that a person from television could actually exist anywhere other than *on* the television, and it seemed to be not just unbelievable, but troubling to him. The more I insisted that I'd seen Teddy, the more upset he got, and soon he was barking the words "Not true" over and over, all the while keeping up his flaccid game of catch. And then, when he spit out the word "Liar!" I'd had enough. I waited for his throw to come down for what seemed like a minute, and I waited the way a major leaguer would, a couple of steps behind the ball, so I could meet it on the run and put momentum behind it. I stepped into the catch and made the throw all in one motion, and David didn't even have time to flinch. He was an experienced flincher, and the only thing good about that throw is that it reached him before he knew it was coming. The ball seemed to go right through his head, but that was because he had started to tilt it back, in anticipation of a different kind of throw. A large pink tumor was already growing on his forehead when I got to him, and he wasn't making a sound. I yelled at him to get up, but he didn't move, and I screamed that he was full of shit and that I was sorry, and he rolled on his side and started to cry, and I ran inside to hide in my room.

The knock on the door never came. I stayed awake all night waiting for my father's footsteps and the punishment that would follow, but nothing happened. David never said a word. He must have made up a story about the bump on his head. He didn't even seem very angry at me. He just got kind of quiet, even quieter than he always was, and I don't remember seeing much more of him that summer. When we got back to New York in September, David started doing a lot of push-ups, and then, over the years, lifting weights and hitting a heavy bag he hung from the basement ceiling, but his muscles were meant to deter an attack, not to defend against it. Once, when he was fifteen, he left fingerprints on one of my father's guns, and I watched as my father pounded his fists into him and he crumpled to the floor at my father's feet. I had just taken a bite of an apple, but I didn't chew. Moving my mouth to chew would have meant I was capable of speaking, of maybe forming the word "Stop," and the beating went on for as long as it took the un-chewed fruit to turn to mush in my mouth. As David drooped under the blows, his big shoulders, which I'd seen him lift a hundred and fifty pounds with in one straight shot, closed around him until they almost touched. It seemed like the punches were flattening him into the floor, but it wasn't Dad's fists that were doing that work. His hands were only punctuating his words, which were: "You're not my son! You're not my son! You're not my son!"

I sucked the warm apple muck through my teeth and swallowed.

3

Mom was on the phone, smoking. "That's not true," she said, "Mother, that is simply not true." I loved her when she was like this. Steely. With her back up. When Mom was alive like this the world made more sense to me. She stepped from the kitchen into the foyer and took a forceful drag on her cigarette. Dad was sitting at the kitchen table, which had six or seven black, oily rifle parts scattered over it, each one resting on a separate sheet of *The New York Times*. It was Saturday morning so he was cleaning a gun, pinching a cigar with his teeth, and holding a disconnected rifle stock, almost black with linseed oil, straight up between his legs with his left hand, and a greasy old cloth with the other. David was sitting there, too, walking an Incredible Hulk action figure back and forth across an exposed patch of table. Mom moved the phone a bit off her ear, her eyes darting to the ceiling then to mine, like we were in this together. "Mother!" she said, and David's Hulk roared. Dad stopped rubbing the gun stock and glared at him, holding the cigar tightly in his teeth. Before he could say anything I barked, "Hey!" and David shot me a look that said, "What's your problem?" and went downstairs to the basement.

Mom was winding things up. "Well, I'm sorry, it couldn't be helped. When are you leaving Brooklyn? Okay, so, we'll see you whenever you get here. Well, Mom, if you've got a headache I wish you'd take an aspirin. What are you afraid of? . . . All right. Okay, yes, okay." She hung up the phone, sighed, and said to me, "Grandma and Papa are coming to visit for the weekend. They're staying overnight. Will you get the Little Ones into the car and come to the grocery store to give me a hand?"

Dad closed and opened his mouth around the cigar—*pah!*—releasing a puff of complaint but keeping his eyes on the gun stock.

"But we're going to the boat pond today."

"When Dad's finished you'll go but right now I need you to help me."

I ran upstairs calling, "Kids! Guess what?!" as if we had just won the lottery. "We're going to the store!" and Richard came running out of his room yelling, "Yay! Yay!" I couldn't understand why Mom didn't make more use of this amazingly simple method for getting them to do anything we wanted.

As our car rolled into the parking lot at ShopRite, Mom turned to me and said, "Are you okay?" and I froze.

Where the hell did *that* come from? Jesus. What had I done to deserve the third degree? I made sure Mom got a good look at the "Why the hell wouldn't I be okay?" expression on my face, but before I could answer she said, "Because you were sleepwalking last night. You came into our room and just stood there for a minute, then you turned around and walked out."

Whoa. Okay wait, what?

Sleepwalking? I'd gone from bedwetting to sleepwalking? Seriously? How could anyone be so bad at *sleeping*, for God's sake?

I wasn't even sure if this was a step up or a step down. I turned to Mom and said, "Sleep—" and suddenly there was a big, jangley, *SMASH!*

Mom gasped and hit the brakes hard.

"Hey!" A man was standing right in front of our car, his shopping cart almost tipped over.

"Lady! Huh? Watch where you're going!"

I tensed up. But then the man looked at Mom and smiled. She put her hand up and silently moved her lips to say, "I'm so sorry," and the man smiled bigger and pointed at her the way parents do when their kid does something adorably bad.

I'd started to notice that people would lift their heads a little when they met Mom. They'd say, "Oh," and smile. Even some people in the city did it, but everyone did it in Glen Cove. She was tall, thin and straight, with long, dark brown hair that she wore the way Katharine Ross from *The Graduate* and *Butch Cassidy* did, and she walked the way a movie star would, like she'd done an hour of ballet in the morning and was heading to lunch with an old friend, and then home to curl up with a good book. And I think these things were happening in her head as I helped her load the back of our Ford Falcon station wagon with bags full of chopped ground round and orange juice. She seemed almost permanently distracted by a sense of missed possibility.

The night before Mom got married, her mother sat her down to tell her about sex. Grandma Gert wasn't happy that her nineteen-year-old, piano prodigy daughter had chosen to marry the twenty-four-year-old, gun-collecting son of semiemployed British Communists, but she'd apparently resigned herself to it and needed to warn Mom about the birds and the bees. She began an obviously rehearsed tutorial, but my mother interrupted her before she got very far and said, "Mom, but, Mom, I'm not a virgin,"—and Grandma kept going. She just kept on talking as if Mom had never said a word.

I think it's possible that my mother married my father just to experience that moment.

She'd met Dad in a theater. She was a senior at the High School of Music and Art in Manhattan when she was invited to a show at Brooklyn College by a friend, who introduced her to my father later that night. Dad was a graduating senior, an economics major and a big-shot "producer" in the college theater group. He followed Mom around for weeks afterwards and she was flattered by the attention, thrilled at the prospect of a relationship that might get her away from what had become a stifling home life in Boro Park, a middle-class Jewish enclave in Brooklyn.

Grandma Gert had been listening in on her telephone conversations for years, and Mom's grandmother, who lived in the house with them, had been searching Mom's mail, reading it, and reporting the contents in Yiddish to Mom's mother at the dinner table every night. Mom would sit there dying from embarrassment and wanting to say, "Please pass the bread I have sex. With gentiles the chicken is wonderful. May I be excused to have sex now?" Her parents' unease about Dad and his family, who couldn't have been stranger to them, only fueled Mom's curiosity about him.

And for Dad, visiting this quiet, bookish girl in her kosher home, or bringing her into his parents' chaotic, equally orthodox household, where she would be pounced on for every apolitical slip of the tongue, must have represented the perfect opportunity to have one foot permanently outside every room he was in. To become The Man Who Won't.

In addition to playing piano from an early age, Mom was a gifted soprano, and when Dad heard her sing he invited her to try out for his theater group's latest production. She took him up on his offer and got the part, and they were married two years later.

"Mom, can I get some chocolate cigarettes?"

A weary look. "Sure. Here's a dollar. Get one for David, too, and something for the kids. Hurry back, though."

"Wax lips!" Richard barked from the backseat, peering through his Beatle bangs at a plastic Dracula. "I want wax lips!"

"I know what you want," I said, and got out. Alison, two years old and made almost entirely of blond ringlets, looked up at me and giggled a hiccup. "Lip," she said.

By the time I was eight I was pretty sure that the Little Ones had been placed in a rocket and sent to Earth just as Planet Adorable was exploding. I had already perfected my Clark Kent hairstyle and developed eye bags worthy of a Norwegian priest, but David looked like John John Kennedy, and Richard and Alison, well, they had hair the color of straw and eyes like opals. They looked like living watercolor.

Running back to the car I could see their little heads swaying in time to music. Mom's, too. Something on the radio must have caught her ear, and she cocked her head like a bird's toward the sound, like she was getting a message in music from somewhere. Through the window she looked a little bit like the girls at school did when a song they liked came on the radio. Seeing Mom get excited about something was exciting for me, too, and unsettling.

I flopped down onto the big vinyl front seat. The music was The Who's "We're Not Gonna Take It," from *Tommy*. This caused a small wave of pre-mortification in me, as it meant that Mom would almost certainly be singing "We're Not Gonna Take It" in a perfect soprano within earshot of my friends sometime in the near future. And then the feeling of embarrassment turned tight and hardened.

This was happening a lot lately. Anger at Mom, coming on like a sneeze, for no apparent reason. I gripped the chrome door handle.

"Did you get something for David?"

"Yop." My mouth was full of chocolate.

"You know, when I was your age I wasn't allowed to eat most kinds of candy."

I gripped the handle tighter. "Who the hell cares!?"

"What? What did you just say to me?"

"Nothing. I was kidding. How come they didn't let you eat candy?"

"Don't you ever talk to me that way again, do you understand me?"

"Yes, Ma."

"I mean it."

"*Okay.* How come Grandma and Papa didn't let you eat candy? Cavities?"

"I suppose. Maybe. I'm not sure. Grandma and Papa forbade me from doing lots of things."

Forbade. Yes, I could see that. They could definitely be forbidding. Dad's parents didn't forbid anything. Except for "believing one single word those commercials tell you."

"Like what?"

"Like Eskimo Pie ice cream."

I made a noise. "*Pfff.*" It was the noise Dad made when Mom told him things like that.

After we got home and put the groceries away and Mom started cooking, I went up to my room, flopped onto my bed, and put it all in my notebook:

THINGS THAT WERE FORBIDDEN
Eskimo Pie ice cream
penny candy
"The Shadow" radio show
"The Inner Sanctum" radio show
comic books (except for Disney ones)
Italian ices
marshmallows
germs!

ENCOURAGED
weekly trips to the library
piano lessons
practicing the piano
Hebrew school
reading

TOLERATED
ballet lessons
riding lessons

I made the Dad noise again, in my head. But part of me wished that the list was my list, that my mail was being read. I was hungry for a little more intrusion into my life. And I could see myself in Mom's childhood, which weirdly felt to me like some kind of possible future even though it was a long time ago. In my mind it looked like the home movies Papa, Mom's dad, had taken with his big, noisy camera from Switzerland, full of bright, deep colors and laughing people in funny bathing suits.

Downstairs, Dad started singing one of his favorite songs. It was from his *Greatest Hits of the British Army Collection, 1860 to 1927: The Imperial Years.* His voice came marching up the stairs.

> So here's to you, Fuzzy-Wuzzy, at your 'ome in the Sudan:
> You're a poor benighted heathen but a first-class fightin' man;
> We sloshed you with Martinis, it weren't 'ardly fair, but
> You big black boundin' beggar, oh you broke the British
>   square!

He stood in my doorway, hands crossed flat over his crotch. He narrowed his eyes in mock suspicion. In an Oxford-ey, suffering-fools-ish accent, he said,

"You were supposed to be ready."

"I am ready. Let's go."

Then, as a cartoon Nazi, slightly clicking his heels, "Vat are you writing?"

"Just junk."

"Junk?" The lips pursed. The accent got Kipling-esque.

"We don't write *junk*, old boy. We're Birkenheads."

I let out a little laugh and grabbed the boat from its special shelf. Dad had brought it home for me, along with one for David, from a trip to England the year before. It was a beautiful little sailboat with an iron keel, made in the city of Birkenhead, as a matter of fact, the name of the town printed across its hull under two canvas sails and a polished hardwood deck.

As we came down the stairs into the foyer Mom said, "You'll be back before they get here?"

Dad's cheek throbbed a little bit. "I love how they take *all* priority," he said. "I'm sorry, I'm not going to adjust my schedule because they need attention."

Mom sighed. "What? They don't need a—"

"We'll be *back in time.*" Which meant "Fine, we'll follow the hobgoblins of your little mind, but you and I both know that they are leading you to all things evil."

My nerves were buzzing as we got into the Mini. Dad closed the door hard but without slamming it, backed the car out of the driveway fast but without scraping the bottom on the pavement. We'd get away okay.

With pained exasperation Dad said, "Peter, for God's *sake*—please don't put the *boat* on the *dash*."

I secured it in my lap.

We were quiet through Glen Head, Glenwood Landing, Sea Cliff, Brookville, all the way to the expressway. Dad really let the Mini air out on the highway, as usual, and brought it up to the edge of its unsuspected capabilities. The engine struggled desperately to roar as we forced ourselves past cruising, incredulous Cadillacs and Fords. A man on the radio was talking about a writer who was running for mayor of New York. I was pretty sure I'd heard the writer's name before, Norman Mailer, and that he was on Our Side, so I said something like, "He's for peace, isn't he, Dad?" and Dad turned his head away from me. "The reality is he's a *monster*. I mean, here's a guy who stabs his own wife, and suddenly he's the darling of the Left." He said it as if there were other people in the car with us, as if he was saying, "I'm sorry, but you all need to let go of your fancy illusions and face up to the brutal truth."

"Wow," I said, and nodded like I was thinking, "Yeah, uh-huh, I figured as much."

I was going to say more but I noticed we were approaching Mount Bump. I'd tried everything over the years to make it bearable: holding my breath as we crested, talking to Dad, closing my eyes on approach—but nothing worked. It was only thirty feet of warped expressway, but hitting it felt like a moon shot. It felt like the wheels moved right up into the car with us, just like my testicles did in my abdomen. We actually caught air at the peak and left the road, momentarily losing control and lifting out of our seats a bit, which Dad didn't seem to notice. I always got a small buzz of adrenaline just as my butt left the seat, and it would stay with me the rest of the trip, making me feel sour and jumpy. I gulped for air as we headed for splashdown on the pavement, my balls doing zero gravity cartwheels, stirring my breakfast into an anxious froth.

There was a moment after we bounced back to the road when I almost said, "Wow, you know, you drive really fast," but I was tough enough to keep it to myself, again.

The drive into the city felt like a journey from birth to afterlife for me. The trees by the road grew older and fewer as we moved through Nassau County and approached the border of Queens. We passed the aluminum-sided, single family town houses at the edge of the borough, then the squat, two-family bricks, the big old faceless apartment buildings, the department stores, warehouses, and roller rinks that seemed to sag and buckle like an old man's knees right in front of my eyes, and then the super-modern "World of Tomorrow," the 1964 World's Fair buildings, the oldest looking of them all. Finally, suddenly—always a surprise even though I knew they were coming—the gravestones, the endless, stoic acres of faded gray crosses and slabs that fill the cemeteries at the edge of the city. The car got quiet, the traffic slowed.

And then, just as suddenly, there was the New York skyline, fountaining up behind the graves, filling the horizon with life, taking over the sky, and proving once again that Manhattan was in fact heaven on earth.

When the cemeteries came into view I asked Dad about his father. Or, rather, I asked about a word Dad had been using when he talked to Mom about his father.

"Dad, what's 'cobalt'?"

He grimaced. "Cobalt is something the doctors are using to help Grandpa get better."

I didn't know Grandpa was sick. Dad had been saying "cobalt" for weeks, but I didn't know why. I immediately pretended I did, though, like we'd talked about it before. But we hadn't.

"Is it working, the cobalt?"

"Well, he's feeling better. You'll see him next weekend. But he's got a blue spot on the side of his head. That's where they put the cobalt gun, so they can aim it right at the cancer."

It was cancer. I knew all about cancer. It was always on "Medical Center." And I knew that the picture of Grandpa with a blue spot on his head wasn't something I was ready to deal with.

Dad's parents were old before their time and very weird, like gnarled old trees that didn't get enough water. Nana would chew with her mouth wide open, spitting Yorkshire pudding clear across the table so she wouldn't waste any time that could be used to rant about the evils of advertising and religion. She was totally bewildered by the world, and she drilled into her kids that their mission was to change it.

"It's a gun?"

"Not that kind of gun, dimmy. It's a cobalt gun, a big machine that shoots radioactive medicine at the tumor, like an X-ray machine, only instead of taking pictures it shrinks the tumor. *C'mon, fellas.*"

He laid into the horn. The "fellas" were slowing us down again, the idiots in the other cars who drove like little old ladies.

As the traffic slowed to a smoggy crawl for the Queens Midtown

Tunnel, Dad got quiet and started breathing heavily through his nose. We listened to the news in silence, a reporter talking about Nixon and economics, my dad's field. I tried to think of something to say about economics. Dad heard the reporter say something that made him lift his hand a little off the steering wheel and turn it palm up. He made the *"pfft"* noise.

I said, "God, I *hate* Nixon," but Dad didn't reply. The reporter kept talking, and then his voice broke up into static as we entered the tunnel. Dad turned the radio off. I turned my head slowly back and forth, like I just didn't know what I was gonna do with this Nixon guy.

We hit the zoo first. At the seal pool, Dad helped me up onto the flaking wrought-iron railing that had been there forever, that I knew had been there, like all of New York, since he was a kid. I thought of the city as a place for dads, where every boy would live when he wasn't a boy anymore. There was wrought iron and copper and brass all over the city then. Automats and aftershave.

I considered the zoo the southernmost border of GoodDadLand, a little country that encompassed the entire southeast corner of the park and included the armor room at the Metropolitan Museum and the model boat pond in between—its main attraction and emotional capital. It's possible that we'd only made this trip one or two times before, but in my mind it felt like dozens. At the park my dad was the nicest man I'd ever met.

We hit the armor room after the seals and I loved Dad in the cool, quiet gallery, reading the inscription beside an old battle flag, lingering over a shield depicting St. George and the Dragon, examining medals under glass. He was reverent, awestruck, in his element.

I was pretty amazed, too. I liked seeing the swords and shields and lances again, imagining pulling Excalibur from a rock and riding into battle with long trumpets blaring.

But this time I was stopped short by a suit of armor on a red pedestal, its visor up, exposing an open helmet with nothing in it. Dad saw me staring and stood next to me, clasping his hands in front of his crotch again, tipping on his toes, and raising his eyebrows to impart privileged information.

In his pretend British accent he said, "From the Royal Workshops at Greenwich," and normally I loved it when he told me things like that, but I was transfixed by the head-shaped emptiness in the helmet, afraid of the space left by the person who used to be in it and of what it implied about my own temporariness. I felt scared of how incomprehensible it was. I was already well into my project of trying to know absolutely everything, and the fact that I couldn't wrap my brain around all that gone-ness made me feel like I was at the mercy of it. I thought about Grandpa's blue spot.

I had a couple of doughy bites of hot pretzel with mustard from the snack stand as we sat on a hill by the pond. It turned out the girl who worked at the stand attended Brooklyn College, Dad's school, and he gave her all kinds of advice about what classes to take and where to eat lunch and buy books. They talked for a while and laughed at some things Dad said that I didn't understand, and I could tell she thought Dad was really, really nice.

We sat down and Dad took sips from a plastic cup of wine while untangling a line on my boat. He wasn't usually good at things like untangling, but the peaceful period that had begun a year and a half ago, when Bobby was shot, was still holding (although lately tensions had been running high) and he was getting better with knots in shoelaces and kite strings.

Dad told stories about World War II, about how some of the English guys who flew Spitfires against the Germans in the Battle of Britain were only sixteen years old and had just learned how to fly only two weeks before, and how some who went down in the English Channel had actually started to drown before they were rescued. He said that they actually enjoyed the experience of taking water into their lungs, that it made them feel relaxed, even "euphoric." He took a huge bite of my pretzel and, still chewing, he said that his brother told him that every morning at five o'clock an ensign would come into the room on the submarine where he and all the other men slept and yell, "Let go of your cocks and grab your socks, it's time to get up!" and he let out a big bark of a laugh. People turned toward the noise.

Dad was wearing a thick, red plaid wool coat, and he'd brought a scratchy, green camping blanket for us to sit on. It was cold for October, but I was feeling like there was no cold cold enough to get to us. The other dads were wearing trench coats, and some of the sons were wearing caps. One was even wearing a white captain's hat, "If you can believe it," Dad said.

I loved this place. We would set the boat's rudder to just the right angle so it would circle the pond, then put it in the water—my hand on one side of the hull, Dad's on the other—and, "One, two, three!" set it off on its journey with a little push. It had two real canvas sails, and they'd catch a bit of wind you didn't even know was there, and float in and out of the shadows made by the trees. The only time you could affect its journey was before you put it in the water, when you set the rudder and the sails. After that it was at the mercy of the currents and the wind, and it would collide with other boats sometimes, or run aground on an old sneaker near the edge of the pond, and then you'd have to lean out over the water as far as you could to retrieve it, maybe holding a stick right at the ends of your fingers, or maybe even being held right out over the water by your dad if you were lucky enough to have a boat in serious danger.

My father held me around the chest and, even though I was nine and too big to be picked up anymore, managed to extend me over the water (maybe he stepped into the pond), and I got to work freeing the good ship *Birkenhead* from its mooring. He talked me through it: "Put the end of the stick between the mast and the sail. Now move your arm slowly to the right . . ."

But the stick kept slipping. I couldn't seem to get the boat loose, and I laughed from the strain and the picture I knew we were making.

I was in heaven. We were a team, a good one, involved in important work that would take time and carefulness to do well, and he never once got impatient. Two Christmases ago Dad had picked up the tree and thrown it across the room because the job of balancing it in the stand was too much for him, but something about the boat pond made him a different guy.

It had the same effect on me. It was a civilized place, a refuge, a long concrete pool embraced by a patio and gently climbing steps that led to a "boat house." I always felt like I should be wearing a monocle when I was there.

On the sunny side of the pond was a big copper statue of the Caterpillar's Mushroom from *Alice in Wonderland,* surrounded by the Mad Hatter and the Cheshire Cat and all the others. On a day like that they were hot to the touch, but I would keep placing my hand on the mushroom, for a little bit longer each time, until I was acclimated, like I was getting into a hot bath. I would slowly warm my body up or cool the metal down enough to make it bearable to sit on with the rest of the inevitable throng of kids, and become part of the scene.

I almost felt like I was inside a book there, and not just the Alice books, which were like sacred texts in our house (when my mother was pregnant with her fourth child she asked me what they should name the baby if it was a girl. I said, "Alison, like Alison Wonderland," and so she did) but my astronomy books, with their illustrations of tandem stars circling each other so closely they "locked arms" made of flame. Or my books about the Constitution and dogs and the Beatles—I had the same experience of things revealing themselves in an orderly progression, staving off confusion with beauty, exposing the rational, complicated, considerate something, that was—that had to be—at the heart of everything.

And because I read so much, if Dad started getting upset, I could bring him back with a few well-chosen bits of arcana. I didn't share his interest in war, but I had tried to read enough of the World War II entry in the encyclopedia that, if he was beginning a rant about, say, the Bataan Death March, I could cite something a little less fraught, like the amazing accomplishment of the Japanese marine engineers who designed the first bulbous ship's bow, for the battleship *Yamato*, significantly decreasing its hull resistance. An even tone, a wry observation or two, and a few obscure, very boring facts like that would noticeably calm the waves in the kitchen or the car, and keep plates on the table and hands on the wheel. They were the tools of peace, and I was learning how to master them.

I sat on the mushroom, beaming *Who. Are. You?* thoughts at each passing person for the rest of the morning. Dad was sitting at a round metal table in front of the snack stand, having some wine with the girl who'd sold us the pretzel. She was wearing a poncho now and laughing. He was smoking his pipe. It made me feel proud that he was so charming, that he could make a stranger laugh.

I must have fallen asleep in the car on the way back. And apparently my face oozed Super Glue when I slept. I peeled it off the backseat, and it sounded like duct tape on a raincoat. I lurched up and to the right and saw Dad, hunched over at the wheel and leaning towards the passenger-side window, growling, "You fff*uck*! You fff*uck*!"

The car to our right was dark and shiny, so close I could have climbed up into it. The man driving it was wearing a tie and no discernable expression. There was at least one kid in the backseat, a six-year-old girl with a big book in her hands. They made the most put-together picture, a diorama of the way things were for other people. Our cars were almost touching. Dad screamed, "I'll blow your fucking head off!!"

The other car veered sharply to the right and the Mini whined loudly as we followed it onto the service road, Dad swerving in and out, coming closer to the other car each time. The man in the car never turned his head, but after about ten seconds he turned sharply and abruptly away from ours and slowed almost to a stop. Dad cut into his lane and accelerated for another fifty yards or so, and when he turned to look back for the guy our car careened to the right, scraping hard against a curb. I slid sideways and slammed my shoulder against the door as the hubcaps screeched wildly and threw off sparks. At last Dad jerked the car back onto the road and finally eased off the gas himself.

He was breathing heavily through his nose again, his eyes fixed straight ahead. I relaxed and leaned my cheek against the cool window glass and tried to breathe with him. We got back onto the highway and I watched the squatty little houses of Queens give way to the trees of Long Island.

When we got home Papa Ken, my mother's father, was standing right by the front door as if he'd been waiting there, and I think he stood for the rest of his visit. He never seemed to take a seat. Even in the living room, with Grandma sitting on the couch biting into something on a cracker, he stood with his hands in his pockets, jingling change and looking concerned.

But his eyes lit up when he saw me, and Grandma smiled like she could melt Siberia. *Peter! Oh, Peter!* She threw her arms open like she was beholding the messiah. I was tired and woozy from Mr. Dad's Wild Ride, but I felt straightened up and out of place, a little unprepared when I saw them, as I always did. Papa wore a sports jacket. Grandma was in a dress. I was mumbly and unsteady in the face of all their affection and realness. These people weren't kidding around. They *meant* everything they did. It made me very uncomfortable.

They were so different from my father. I don't mean just in the particulars, in their habits or tastes, although they shared none of those with Dad. It was more than that. Dad was angry and sweet, warm and detached, capable of bursts of terrible violence followed by months of none at all. But while Dad could seem like a hundred different people, Papa was never more, or less, than one. As much as my father embodied contradiction, Papa seemed in agreement with himself and unified. Grandma did, too. It's not that they never surprised me. But their surprises always made sense. I had a feeling that I knew them better than I knew my dad, even though I barely knew them.

Most of what I did know I'd gleaned from dinner conversations with Mom. Grandma was a teacher, a bad cook, a "grammar maven," whatever that was, a poetry memorizer who was "liable to burst into Byron or Shelley at the drop of a hat." She was also the youngest of four children; her brother Max Feller was an executive at Playtex ("I do most of the heavy lifting and separating around there," he told me) and her brother Abe Feller was one of the authors of the Charter of the United Nations, and was its original General Council. Her sister Molly was riding a bike and acting in plays on the Upper West Side when she died at age ninety-nine.

Papa was a jewelry designer, a sculptor, a chess fanatic, and the hero of the family for quitting his job during World War II rather than going along with a partner's profiteering scheme. He grew up two houses to the left of and behind Grandma's in Boro Park, Brooklyn, and was the eldest of four—all brothers—whom he had supported as a young man, paying their tuitions at art school and college by working seventy hours a week. The story of his life could be told, if it needed to be told quickly, which it usually did, like George Bailey's in *It's a Wonderful Life*, with a recitation of the accomplishments of others. His son Steve is a bluegrass and "old time music" banjo virtuoso who played with Bill Monroe. His brother Sandy flew fifty missions over Germany in the Army Air Corps, and went on to own a string of hotels and raise three children; while his brother Dave went on to become an accomplished painter and writer.

Dave's biggest claim to fame with us grandnephews and nieces, however, was his son, Alan Arkin, who was one of the biggest stars in Hollywood when we were kids. Going to see him in *Catch-22* or *The*

In-Laws was a source of the same weirdly conflicting emotions that seeing other members of my mother's family was, but heightened by the size of the screen and the presence of strangers watching along with us.

After a late dinner everyone went to bed, except for Papa and me. I had begged Mom to let me stay up to watch highlights from the World Series, which the Miracle Mets had won just a few days before. I was a freshly minted baseball addict, already spending hours a day throwing into a chalk strike zone against a wall at school.

Dad hated sports, so I was teaching myself to play and had some serious catching up to do. We were all developing a knack for catching up quickly, becoming a family of fast learners and late bloomers. I had just played my first full season of Little League (a couple of years after my classmates had started), making contact exactly once, when I fouled off a pitch in my last game. I was obsessively working my way towards hitting .500, "*Five friggin' hundred*," Coach Parrisi would say, "like one and a half Yastrzemskis," the following year. I'd thrown myself into baseball with the same semiautistic commitment I was already giving to collecting the world's knowledge and lying, and it was paying off well, most importantly in a marked decrease in schoolyard witticisms hurled my way. (Hey, Brokenhead!!)

Papa was in the dining room playing chess against himself, using a pen-and-paper method he'd devised years before. Like Dad, he had no interest in baseball. Or basketball or Hot Wheels or *Abbey Road*. But unlike Dad he did have some interests I was actually interested in. While I watched the Series highlights I flipped through a beautifully illustrated book of Greek mythology he and Grandma had given me earlier as a belated birthday present. They'd written, "Beware of gifts bearing Greeks!" on the inside cover, and signed it "Much, much, much, much love." I decided right away to make it the centerpiece of my Library of the All-Knowing.

Papa had also brought us an album full of photographs he'd taken on other visits, and over the next few days I spent a lot of time looking at them. My favorite was a picture of Mom, David, and me on the living room floor of our Brooklyn apartment. Mom is sitting; David is an infant, lying on his belly with one hand on her knee; and I'm standing on shaky, two-year-old legs and wearing a diaper. We're all smiling. I loved looking at the picture even though—or maybe because—it gave me a nasty little jolt whenever I did.

Mom looks especially young in the photo. She's wearing her hair in an old-fashioned style and seems curious about the alien creatures clinging to her. But the main thing is that her face is different, not yet the face I knew as hers. I had a sense that I couldn't quite put my finger on, that the photo was evidence of some sort of disturbance in time, some event in the past that had altered our future.

Papa came to the den and said, "Peter, do you think I could interest you in an ice cream soda?" Like everything else he said and did, it created a feeling in me like I was stepping on the gas-pedal and brakes at the same time. Yes, yes you could interest me in an ice cream soda, what, are you kidding? And chess and photography and sculpture and egg creams—whatever they are—and gifts bearing Greeks, and all the rest. I'm interested, okay? I also don't want to hear another word about it, not any of it. I want to bury myself under this blanket and listen to the muffled television through three layers of wool for the rest of my numb, dumb life.

This was happening a lot lately, too. Everything about Grandma and Papa—the careful way he polished his glasses, his patience when he taught me photography, her attention to language, her long, long hugs—was so full of promise, implied responsibilities, and hard truths I could barely stand it. Papa's eyes never narrowed or darted the way Dad's did, and his steady, wakeful gaze felt like a gravity beam, pulling me towards an eyes-wide-open future that I wasn't equipped for, was deeply afraid of, and wanted more than anything else in the world.

"Yeah, sure. I love ice cream sodas." (I'd never had one.)

So, the secret to a great ice cream soda, my grandfather said, as if it was the secret of life, which of course it is, was packing the ice cream down at the bottom of the glass, rather than letting it float at the top. That way, the ice cream can be enjoyed at the end, like a reward for your patience. It maintained its structural integrity, and absorbed the soda without being destroyed by it.

I almost swooned with appreciation. And I wanted to call him a phony and run away.

Boy, it was good, the soda, even though I didn't want to like it. The whole scene, standing there in the kitchen with Papa, felt "queer, like a dumb commercial" as Lenny Gussman, our second baseman, put it when a photographer made us form a human pyramid in the outfield for the team picture. It felt Cracker-Jack-ey, ice-cream-soda-ish. But Papa was not wrong, the soda was really good. And he liked it even more than I did. His eyes were shining as he made it, his hands moving with a jeweler's precision, a chess player's deliberateness, and a world-class frivolist's knack for drama. He got so much pleasure out of watching me drink it that he teared up a little.

"It's terrible, isn't it?" he said. Then he went on, "I just went upstairs and said good night to David. He's a wonderful boy, your brother. A gentle soul. We're pretty fond of you both, you know. I think he's pretty fond of you, too."

More gas-and-brakes, wobblyness and straightness. Taken out of my reality by reality.

"Yeah," I allowed.

"Geez, when you two fight it breaks our hearts."

I looked down into my glass and watched the soda sink. David and I had shared bunk beds for years, talking in the dark every night. As far as he was concerned, I was a font of unlimited information, doled out on a need-to-know basis, all of which was of course bullshit—like how it was safe to eat oak leaves and how dead dogs could still bark for two days after they died. We were so different temperamentally that we never had to bother with the I'm-this-and-you're-that struggle that other, more similar brothers went through, but it made us more suspicious of our parents' preferences, questioning why the other guy got the bigger slice of pizza or bowl of Lucky Charms. At supper that night, David had freaked out because I had more mashed potatoes than he did. We took it outside, like Dad said to, and I guess we'd gotten a little muddy. He'd sure given me a hard shot in the thigh when Dad barked, "The leg, the leg!" And I guess I'd probably hurt him pretty badly with that elbow to the ribs.

Papa and Dad talked about it in the living room later. Dad had his voice raised a little and his arms crossed, and I think he said, "It's called sibling rivalry, it's *natural*. It's what kids *do*."

"You think I could convince you to take a day or two off from fighting with him?" My sticky mouth opened just a bit around the straw. "Yeah," it said, without actually making a sound.

I didn't know it at the time but Dad had done everything he could to keep us away from Papa and Grandma—I would later learn the words "intrusive" and "bourgeois" when he used them in connection with my grandparents—and by the time I was three and David was two, Papa felt like we literally might not ever get to know them.

He began writing a letter to us that year, a letter of introduction, the beginning of a family history, telling us who he was and who we were. "My name is Kenneth Arkin. My wife is Gertrude Arkin. Her last name used to be Feller . . ." It was found in his papers when he died at the age of one hundred.

That ice-cream-ish goo at the bottom of the glass was a mucky, thick, gooey, delicious mess. It was slowly revealed to me as I kept my eyes down and the soda disappeared up the straw—a pile of treasure at the bottom of the sea. I was surprised that it wasn't white anymore, and wasn't exactly the color of cola, either. It was dark, light, and wonderful. When I finished, Papa took me up to bed.

The image of my grandfather standing in my room, leaning in towards the wall to get a better look at my life-size poster of Mick Jagger, will stay with me forever: both of them with their eyes wide, Mick's mouth agape, like he's going to eat Papa's head, Papa looking like he might let him. He crinkled his eyes, put his hand on his head, and said, "Sheesh!" He was completely delighted by his own ignorance, astonished at how much the world was changing, and loving every disorienting minute of it. I almost asked him to read me a story, the way he would when I was younger.

"Good night, Peter; don't let the bed bugs bite," he said, letting his thick lips linger a bit on each *b*, relishing the phrase with a smile, as if he had just made it up. I took out the photo album and stared at the picture of Mom from The Before Times, and fell asleep.

I woke up standing in the middle of the driveway, looking back at our house. It must have been around five in the morning. The grass on the front lawn was wet. My bare feet were cold on the pavement. Everything was bathed in indigo. The street was quiet and deserted in a deep, full way I had never seen or heard before—no lights on in the houses, no crickets chirping, the air completely still. The end of the world. I thought about what Papa had said to me after I'd gotten into bed, just before I went to sleep. He'd sat down and tucked me in, and as he started to get up I screwed up my courage and asked him what happens when we die. He stopped, and looked at me for a moment and said, "You remember what it was like before you were born?" "No," I replied. He smiled a little. "It's exactly like that."

4

David was saying something to me, something urgent, but I couldn't make it out because I had blood in my ears. Not real blood. Ketchup. I was lying in the middle of the street, my arms sprawled out beside me and one leg bent as twistily as I could manage. I coughed, "What?! I can't hear you," and disturbed the splatter we'd arranged on my chest. Enough sticky Del Monte spilled out of my right ear for me to hear David say: "She's coming, shit!"

David was seven—finally old enough to be my partner in crime once in a while, although his sense of humor ran more to quiet, vengeful bon mots than the elaborate pranks I preferred. Just recently, when I'd introduced him to the classic Charlie Horse, a quick, one-knuckle punch to the mid-thigh, he'd returned the favor the next day with a jab to my upper arm. When I yelped, "Ow, geez, God! What the hell was that?" he said in a soft voice, "That, my friend, was an *Irving Cow*."

We were teaching each other the ancient arts of the deadpan, the arched eyebrow and the slow burn, the double take and the triple take, performing a stealth vaudeville for each other at the dinner table every night.

I plopped back down onto the pavement and re-held my breath. Mom was due home any minute. She and Dad had been visiting Grandpa Tom, Dad's father, in the hospital. The blood would have to do. Maybe in her upset Mom wouldn't take the time to do the physics.

Maybe her brain would short-circuit from how much she loved me and she wouldn't notice that the splatter pattern made no sense, not if I'd been hit by a car.

Do. Not. Breathe. Not at all, I thought. This is gonna be good: She's gonna rush to my side and scream, "No, no, no, not Peter, no!! Take me, God, oh, take me! Take *me*! Leave my amazing precious perfect firstborn son, God, please! Please, no!!!"

Wait. Okay, wait, no. That wouldn't be good. I mean it would, it would be great, but she would actually feel, you know, bad. I decided to abort the mission.

"Peter, would you please get up? Come on, I have enough to do without you horsing around like this. You're on the dirty pavement, for God's sake!" My mother was leaning her head out the car window.

"What the hell were you thinking? Boys, please . . . Jesus, go inside and clean yourself up this *instant.* Enough."

"O-*kay.* God!"

David and I sat at the kitchen table, shooting glares of blame at each other over toasted pizza bagels. Mom sat down and fired up a Kent.

"How's Grandpa?" I said.

She looked at me. Not in the usual Mom-doing-a-thousand-things-and-she's-only-gonna-say-this-*once* way, but really looking. For just a picosecond, which was the shortest period of time ever measured, which they had to figure out before sending men to the moon and which, by the way, none of my classmates knew. (The teacher didn't know, either, which made me really worry about the quality of my education.) And it only took that one picosecond of Mom looking at me to know Grandpa had died that day. "We'll talk about it when Dad gets home," she said. "He'll be just a little while." And I was even surer. Grandpa was dead. Dead. This was what having someone be dead was like. It felt just like five minutes ago, except now I thought I should be crying.

David put a big rubber mastodon on the table and growled, "Braawaha, brawwa!" I pulled it sharply out of his hand and said, "David, cut it out, this is serious." He looked at me with the desperate grief and rage that only toy theft can elicit, but as soon as he did he must have caught something in my look that made him shift into a quiet, befuddled, lower gear. He gently kicked his legs back and forth against his chair, nervous about whatever was going on, and frustrated about not understanding it. I awkwardly put my hand on his shoulder, in a gesture of big brotherhood I had been trying to pull off ever since seeing it on *My Three Sons* a few weeks before.

When Dad got home Nana was with him. He had to help her up the front stoop to our door, which I'd never seen him do.

I veered wildly back and forth in my feelings about Nana. Sometimes I'd sit with her in front of the television and enjoy how in tune we were with each other, both driven crazy by how the plots of the shows made no sense, how the commercials were so blatantly manipulative. She never seemed to find my critiques tiresome the way Mom did—she even joined right in with me. She took long walks every day, and I joined her even though she always complained about her phlebitis, especially when Mom and Dad wanted to go somewhere later without her. She showed me the proper way to walk, reminding me to swing my arms back and forth and keep my back straight, all in her chewy Scottish accent, which I loved.

But also, if you had told me she was the Grand Witch of Glasgow, who ate chunks of coal formed by the decaying, thousand-year-old bodies of dead children, I wouldn't have asked for proof. She wore very old thick, gray wool skirts and jackets, and she was always saying creepy things at the dinner table, referring to Mom as "in trouble" when she was pregnant with Alison, and telling me when I was eight that a woman's period was a "horrible, horrible thing to endure." She was short but her bearing was haughty, her complexion somehow ashen and dark at the same time, like chalk dust on slate. Her hair was a stiff gust and her eyes were black tunnels to China. At night, before going to bed she'd take her teeth out and leave them in a glass filled with water, baking soda, and bits of dinner, which, on the occasions I came across it, filled me with revulsion.

Nana limped as Dad escorted her into the house. Alison must have been napping upstairs, and Richard was on the swing set in the back-yard, but Mom didn't ask me to call him in. In a highly unusual move that instantly created an air of gravity, Mom and Dad and Nana sat down in the living room, not the kitchen. David and I joined them. I could almost hear organ music playing under the whole scene. Appropriately, our living room was furnished with a couple of small, velvet, funeral-red love seats instead of full-fledged couches or sofas. Dad and Nana sat very close on one of them, Nana gripping his hand. Mom sat in the other.

David's T-shirt was riding up over his belly and he was making fart noises, spraying me with spit. "C'mere," I said, and pulled him close. He rocked back and forth, his eyes on the love seat upholstery, clearly wishing hard for whatever this was to be over. I made myself look right at Dad, right in his eyes.

"Well, boys, Grandpa died today," he said, and Nana let out a high-pitched, broken little moan and her head tilted to the side and started shaking very slightly.

"He did?" I said, and David looked up at me, scared.

Mom said, "Yes, he did. He was just too sick to get better. But he didn't feel bad when it happened, he didn't suffer. He was very calm and peaceful, very relaxed."

"From the cancer?" I asked, and Dad said, "Yes."

I don't remember if that's when Dad told us about his father's last breath, but at some point he told us that Grandpa had put an imaginary cigarette to his lips with two pinched fingers, pulled it slowly away, and blew imaginary smoke just before he died, which is probably why I've still never taken more than a couple of puffs from a cigarette.

Then Nana stood up, hugged me tight, and said, "You're all I have now," and I was frozen with dread. The truth is, I only had a few memories of Grandpa, even then. He used to do a magic trick with a quarter. He had kind, droopy eyes and a head full of white hair. A Manchester accent. Once, when everyone was talking about a book he was reading, he said he liked "the dirty parts," pointing to a spot on a page and showing it to Mom. When he was at the house just a couple of weeks before, with half his head shaved and the blue spot above his ear, he fell out the back doorway, pushing the screen door open and cutting his forehead on the stoop. Dad and Nana reacted with a fury, grabbing him and pulling him up very quickly. And that was about it. I didn't have much of him, not enough to feel what I wanted to. I wanted to feel bereft, but I was only nervous.

That night, as Dad put us to bed, just as he turned out the lights, he said, "Remember, boys, I lost *my* daddy today." I badly wanted to feel sympathy for that instead of being secretly creeped out by it.

But the creeping-out was just beginning. Nana stayed for a long time—a few weeks, I think—and I started to notice how strangely intertwined yet estranged she and Dad were, at once cold and too close. She asked him more questions about where he was going and what he was doing than Mom asked me. And he answered them. They finished each other's sentences and sometimes just communicated in gestures. And they would completely freeze each other out when they felt insulted, like a couple of graying eight-year-olds.

After just a couple of days Dad was snapping sharply at her, with Nana usually responding by assuming a wounded superiority and pointing her chin up very high. Many of their fights were political, of course, with Dad, incredibly, taking the rightward or at least less-lefty point of view, clearly annoyed and embarrassed by his mother's old dogmas.

One afternoon she even scolded Dad for buying us Hershey bars—not because of the sugar, but because she'd heard somewhere that Barry Goldwater had a connection to the Hershey Company. Late at night I could hear her and Dad drunkenly tearing at old family scabs that were completely mysterious to me, blurting insults and half accusations that hinted at unhealed resentments and sexual secrets. I would usually catch only stray words, never as much as a sentence, but they were enough to make an impression.

One night at dinner, after Nana had been staying with us for about two weeks, Mom was feeding Alison, who was sitting in her high chair opening her mouth for spoonfuls of something or other, and Nana said, "Thank God the nursing is over, eh, Susan?" Mom kept up her rhythm and said, "Oh, Florie, I loved nursing my children. It's really the most wonderful sort of experience." "Oh, it's an experience, yes." Nana chuckled. "I was cursed with quite an abundance in that area. Uch, my breasts would ache so. And when the milk came it was so thick it came in bloody clumps."

David and I perfected our Jack Benny deadpans at that moment. Dad glared, I'm not sure at whom. Mom stopped her spoon and said, "Florie, I'm sorry . . . Kids? Kids, if you're finished can you please go downstairs and finish cleaning up your toys like I asked you to? Please? Right now."

And so we did. The rumblings from upstairs were like faraway thunder and never grew louder, but they lasted a good long while.

Sometime later in Nana's stay Dad cooked a big meal for us, spending half the afternoon broiling steak, hand-mashing potatoes, and sautéing Brussel sprouts. It all looked massive when he placed it on the table. I don't remember if it was for a special occasion, but I'm guessing it was an attempt at a peace offering for Mom or Nana.

All four of us kids were at the table, Alison in the high chair. The food was perfect—fresh, hearty, full of flavor—and it put everyone in a good mood. The steak, the sprouts, and Dad's Scotch created a buttery aroma that filled the room. Richard, who was four at the time, was very hyped up, banging his feet together, playing with his food, and quacking out strange noises and made-up words. We were all trying not to laugh but failing, letting little bits of sweet potato spill out of the corners of our mouths as we surrendered to a sudden squawk of

"Doodashooflam!" or "Boogershnot!" I'd been out all afternoon playing with friends and I really went after the steak, barely catching my breath between the gorging and guffawing.

Dad was laughing, too, but eyeing Richard strangely over the top of his Scotch glass. He often had this kind of skewed reaction to laughter, like he didn't trust his own amusement, or the source of it. He was still smiling as he put his glass down, but warned, "All right, dildo, that's enough. Pay some attention to the food on your plate, mistah." We all put our heads down and went back to eating, and Rich suppressed a smile. He had a natural performer's killer instinct, and in the quiet after Dad's remark, he could sense he had his audience right where he wanted them.

I was side-eyeing Rich closely, and as a tiny smile crossed his lips, I opened my mouth to stop him, but I was so tickled by how full of mischief he was that instead of a warning a weird half-laugh came out of me, and startled everyone.

Dad flinched a little and glared at Rich, and as he put his glass down I said, "Wait," but no one heard me. Dad said, "Okay, dildo, that's—" and I realized *I* hadn't heard me either and that I couldn't breathe—not at all.

I bent my head down to try to re-open my throat but nothing would move. I tried to stay calm, stood up slowly and walked around the table like I was carrying a hot bowl of soup to Mom. There was some noise but I couldn't make out what anyone was saying. Mom's attention was divided between Alison, Dad, and Richard, as I pulled on her blouse—lookatme, lookatme, lookatme—pointing to my throat.

"What is it, sweetie, what?" I pointed again, opened my mouth, an icy stiffness hitting my calves and hands.

Everything went reddish, and I was suddenly upside down, my mother holding me by the legs, my father pounding on my back, harder and harder. I was watching Richard's bare, motionless feet, one on top of the other, their toes curled in. They were touching the ceiling. Nothing moved in my throat. I opened and closed my mouth, over and over, but nothing happened. I struggled with my shoulders and my waist and my mind but I couldn't get any air.

Dad hit me with all his might with a balled fist, right between the shoulder blades. I wanted to move my hands to my neck but I couldn't—everything was stuck. Then Mom was prying my mouth open—it had frozen shut—and reaching right into it with her hand, her whole hand, filling my mouth, right through it and down into my throat, moving her fingers around and grabbing, and then she pulled her wrist and hand back out, and eeeeeeaah air air air air air air air oh eeeeeeeaaah. An acid burn in my throat. Hohaahoooo. Hhaaaaa.

Mom's fingers were covered in goo. They were holding a little hunk of brown steak. I wheezed a roomful of air sharply into my lungs and Dad laid me down on the floor and I started to cry.

I was covered in red spots, hundreds of them all over my face, shoulders, and chest when I woke up the next morning, broken capillaries from Dad pounding on my back. And I couldn't swallow my breakfast. I chewed it for minutes and tried not to think about choking, but everything just stopped and closed down as soon as the food neared my throat.

Mom let me stay home from school for a few days, sparing me for at least a while from freak-show-dom. I watched reruns of "Adam 12" and drank milkshakes for lunch, and on Saturday Mom took David and me to see a production of *The Sound of Music* at a local community theater.

The two of us spent most of the time making fun of the child actors in the cast and their ridiculous lederhosen, and then when the lights came up afterwards Mom said the show was going to be produced at the Melody Tent that summer with some old movie star in it and that they needed to cast a bunch of kids, all of whom would get paid lots of money to be in the show. My position on lederhosen evolved instantaneously and I made a silent promise to myself that I would learn to yodel by June.

On Monday morning I was still covered in spots, and Dad asked me if I wanted to come in with him to Brooklyn and watch him teach a class, which I had never done before. David and I used to spend a lot of time at Brooklyn College when we were younger—Dad would take us to see the goldfish in a little pool on the campus, or just set us up in his office with a legal pad and a box of colored pencils and we'd go to town—but we'd never actually seen him teach.

So I forgot all about my red-speckled misery and practically flew from my bed to the car. In the years since I'd last been there, Brooklyn College had become a place of great drama in my imagination, the arena where Dad performed feats of valor and fortitude every day. The stories had grown especially dramatic in the last couple of years as all the tensions of the times had ratcheted up. Dad was very quiet on the drive to Flatbush, probably thinking about Grandpa, and one of the Brooklyn College stories that I'd thought about a lot since I'd heard it came back to me again as we made our way in. It was practically haunting me by the time we got there, one line in particular: "They dragged her by her breasts."

I was running the words through my head, over and over, trying to lessen the weird buzz they gave off, or maybe get a mental picture from them that made some sense. "They dragged her by her breasts." But that's impossible, right? How could that happen? And what *was* that buzzing around the words when Dad spoke them back then, like they had little zigzag lines drawn over them? Dad said one of the cops, one of the policemen who had come to the college because the students were protesting, had done this, had dragged one of the students by her breasts—down a flight of stairs, no less. And that the other cops had done things just as bad.

I was sitting in an aisle seat at the back of Dad's classroom now, which wasn't really a classroom at all, he said, but a "lecture hall," and

Dad was writing on the blackboard at the front. "Capital," he wrote, in big letters, fast, and then he threw the chalk into the well at the bottom of the board with a loud clink. The students got quiet. They seemed excited, like an audience at a play. Their faces were lit by leaf-filtered light pouring in through two enormous windows that Dad stood in front of. They all looked up at him, some of them smiling. But I didn't look at Dad. I looked at the girls.

Even though none of them looked like they had been dragged down any stairs lately, I couldn't stop staring at them and wondering, "Was it her? Is she the one? Oh man, what if it was her? How much did it hurt?" Dad said it would be unbearably painful for a woman, that it was like the things the Nazis did. And yes, it had happened a year and a half ago, in May of '68, but I knew that if I was still thinking about it, the person it happened to must be also. When we were driving in that morning I'd figured there was probably a fifty-percent chance I'd see the stairs girl that day, and that I would know it was her because she would be crying.

The students had wanted more black people and Puerto Ricans admitted to Brooklyn College, and Dad thought that was a good idea—the college was still ninety-nine percent white and eighty-five percent Jewish, just as it had been in the fifties when Mom and Dad were students there—but he also thought that some of the protesters were "loony tunes" and "whacko" because they said they weren't opposed to the use of violence if it was necessary.

My father and six other professors had signed a letter to the president of the college asking that the police not be called in to break up a sit-in as they had been the week before at Columbia, where the cops used tear gas and batons against the students. In a *New York Times* article about the protest, Dad and his six colleagues come across as sane, moderate lefties trying to calm a volatile situation, and that's just how Dad painted the picture to us at home. But there was an energy to his movements, a quickness to his words, and an abundance of whiteness in his eyes when he told the story, and the experience of listening to him embedded itself immediately in my memory as if I were hearing the sound of something fundamental, as if I had gotten a few steps closer to the engine room of a big ship where a furnace was being noisily stoked. Especially when he said "breasts."

His role in the protests had clearly made Dad into a minor celebrity in his own mind and, as I could see from the looks on his students' faces, in their minds as well. I knew Dad was a popular teacher because his friend Sam, who also taught economics, had told me so ("Your dad is everybody's favorite teacher—go figure"), but as he began his lecture, I saw that he was more than popular, he was a star. All the students laughed at the first thing he said. The girl next to me with long dark hair like Mom's and the bell-bottoms and the lap I just wanted to crawl up onto turned to share a laugh with me. Her eyes opened a little, and I remembered that my face was covered in red specks. I wanted to die. She cooed, "Hey, are you okay, man?" Oh. Oh. Oh. Did she just call me "man"? Oh God. I felt like I had just grown a mustache. "Yeah, yes, I'm okay. I have these dots on my face 'cause they're broken capillaries. I was choking and I almost died. But my dad saved my life and he had to hit me on the back. That's my dad." "Hey, that's amazing—you look just like him. I'm glad you're alive, little man! My name's Sheila."

Little?

Sheila opened her notebook. Dad sat on the edge of the table at the front of the room. Sheila looked back at me, excited. The show was about to begin. I was so proud and nervous. *I know, he's like Poseidon or somebody, isn't he? What, you don't know Poseidon? Oh, he's the greatest—you gotta read this amazing mythology book I have, I'll tell you about it later, after class—but seriously, wait till he starts teaching. You won't believe how smart he is. You know he hasn't changed his underwear in two days, right?*

Then he started teaching.

Have you ever wondered what it would be like if someone made a movie about your life? How you'd feel watching people who were just a little bit handsomer than you, wearing slightly shinier versions of your clothes and actually saying the things you wish you could go back in time and say? And what if you got the chance to be the actor who played you? Brooklyn College had cast Dad as Professor Birkenhead, and at first I barely recognized him. Someone had taken Dad and filed him smooth, rounded him off, and polished him up. They'd closed all the spaces between the things he said, airbrushed the wariness out of his eyes, and used only the takes where he wasn't eating or farting. His asides were spiced with just the right amount of what, in this context, seemed like playful bitterness, and his digressions were few and funny. There were no sighs, no barks, no eruptions. No interruptions. There was no us.

There was no us. Nobody pulling at his sleeve or shouting from the other room, certainly nobody challenging him, when he was so clearly and seductively *right*. Without interruptions about mucus and baseball practice and mashed potatoes, Dad was free to be as gloriously authoritative and quietly cogent and grudgingly brilliant as he imagined himself to be. And as he genuinely was. I was almost hypnotized by the play, back and forth, between his professor self and what I had always thought of as his real self. I felt like maybe someone was under the desk, with his arm up Dad's coat, making his mouth move. The Professor walked and talked just like Dad, but as if someone inside him was thinking, *"Now bend the arm just a little bit . . . and . . . point!"* Yet there was no one up there but Dad, and there was no denying the realness in the room.

As he spoke, I could see that the students were doing even more than Dad was to endow him with the regal-but-roguish qualities of Professor Birkenhead, looking at him like they expected to be enlightened in a way they could relate to, and I could see that he was grateful for that and enjoyed living up to their expectations, coloring in their impression of him as tweedy-but-streety with nuanced flourishes of his own. They were eating it up.

I remember Dad saying something like "So your work is turned into a thing on a shelf, your creativity is put up for sale."

I thought, wow, maybe if David and Richard and Alison and I could just—like Dad was always saying—shut up for one minute at home; if we would just *listen for Chrisakes*, then maybe we'd get some time with The Professor, this other Dad, who had such an easy way about him, and who clearly had a hell of a lot to teach us.

There were dozens of Dad's familiar gestures and tics in The Professor, but they somehow added up to a different person. The Professor used the word "unfortunately" a lot, and moved his eyebrows up and the corners of his mouth down when he said it, just like Dad did. The same sad notes came into his voice. He tipped up on his toes like Dad, but now it seemed more jaunty and Johnny-Carson-ish than apologetic and foppish. Dad had a habit of starting his sentences with the word, "Again," which sounded creaky and fusty in the kitchen at home, but here in the lecture hall, it sounded helpful and deliberate, even though he pronounced it "Agayn."

He listened to the students with a look of real concern on his face, and he said, "Good point," to a couple of them when they asked questions, and "I'm not sure I follow," with a friendly squint, to the others.

So I was a little pissed off. I looked down and studied my Keds. I mean, this Professor guy was great, amazing even, but either he was a little full of it or my dad was, right? I slumped down a bit lower in my seat. The Professor kept talking about things I didn't understand, and doing it well. I didn't need to know what "the fetishism of commodities" was to know that he was helping other people understand it, and even *enjoy* understanding it.

Or so it seemed. For all I knew he was improvising, making all this shit up right here on the spot. I looked around at the students. None of them seemed bored. A few seemed enchanted. By the freaking fetishism of commodities. Jesus H. Kee*rist.* He was good, no doubt about it. Did these students understand they were getting Boat Pond–level wisdom and attention and patience from my dad? God, I was jealous as hell.

He wasn't even teaching economics, really. He was teaching Marxist economics, and that meant, especially in 1969, especially the way it landed on my ears, that he was teaching right and wrong. Which was very cool. There was a giddy hum in the room, the same hum I felt at the peace marches and moratoriums Dad had taken me to. It was the sound of the fun of righteousness, and it was totally intoxicating. Walking to class that morning, Dad had an almost cocky spring in his step as we passed groups of students sitting in circles on the grass, listening to The Zombies' "Time of the Season," and The Turtles' "Happy Together," all accompanied by the rising hum of the right-on.

I looked up. Dad was speaking in a tone of voice he used at home, the one that said, *I apologize for being infallible,* and it sounded less out of place than it usually did. So, did that mean he actually *was* infallible and that Mom needed to lay off a bit? He was saying words that, when he said them at home, made Mom hold her breath. Did this mean he didn't deserve that? Or did it just mean these students needed to know about his underwear?

And why couldn't I just be excited? Why did I have to be excited *and* uneasy and proud and resentful and jealous and tired and doubtful and certain and confused and wary and blue and lost and cocky and cranky and lonely? Why couldn't feelings come one at a time and stay in one place?

There was movement behind Dad, outside on the path that ran by the window. A couple of students in big wool peacoats were tossing a football. One of them yelled something and jumped on the other's back and the two of them spun around until they fell to the ground. They looked like all the kids sitting around me, but different. The way the students around me would look in a few minutes, when they got back outside, when the teacher wasn't around anymore. Apparently college was a lot like fourth grade in that way.

You know what? I knew what Dad was up to. I knew what this was, with the voice and the funny lines and all that. This was New and Improved Truth; this was something I knew about. And this was something, I realized, that maybe I didn't invent. It was definitely something I wasn't as good at as I thought I was. And I think I could see what Dad was after.

When he slipped into Brooklynese, the tough guy stuff, when he held his arms out from his sides a little bit and narrowed his eyes, the feeling in the lecture hall was, *Yeah, uh-huh, this guy is cool, he gets it. He hasn't forgotten where he comes from. He's one of the people.* When he paused to pack his pipe with tobacco some of the students crossed their legs and looked at Dad wistfully, their heads slightly cocked.

The sound of Dad's voice coming out of The Professor started sounding less like ventriloquism and more like singing. Like when Mom sang, but with a beat. He wasn't just teaching now, he was preaching—-I could see it on Sheila's face. There was a slight flush on her cheek and she was nodding with sympathy, alive with sadness. Dad was saying, " . . . *real* people, with *real* lives and *real* problems . . ." He was driving a train now, building a rhythm, and a lot of other heads started nodding in time to it. Even a couple of kids who had seemed bored were sitting up straight. *"The means of production . . . the inevitable . . . dialectic . . . fundamental . . . corrective . . . historical . . . momentum . . ."*

Bwauumm!

My arms went up, elbows out. Dad ducked and recoiled. Sheila flinched. The window shook, and the two kids in peacoats were staring through it from outside, into the room, mouths agape. The ball had hit the window, hard. But nothing was broken, everyone was okay, no one was hurt. Wow, that was loud. But everything's okay. Sheila turned to me and quickly patted my hand and because she was smiling, I did, too. We all breathed a collective, chuckley sigh. Dad looked up at all of us and then back through the window. A couple of kids laughed. But as he turned back around I saw the blackness of his mother's eyes in his, and a familiar flash of discombobulated rage. My whole body went cold. At home, a sound like the one made by that football against the window was a prelude to an explosion. Dad's eyes vibrated. His cheeks did that flutter as a wave of something moved up from his neck to the top of his head. He said something, first to the guys outside, then to the class, but he sounded like he had food caught in his throat and his words came out all mashed together, two or three at a time, overlapping each other. "Ar fufell. Sothafine, whyco." And he put a piece of chalk in his jacket pocket and started putting papers together. His face grew red and he looked up. He said, "That's all." He smiled a little. "I shall see you all on Friday."

Sheila put some papers in her book and got up without looking at me. I realized that I was deeply in love with her. I wanted to walk out with her and spend the rest of my life looking at goldfish with Sheila. I stayed in the chair waiting for everyone to clear out. The whole football incident had lasted just seconds and outwardly almost nothing had happened, but I felt like crying.

When we walked to the car there was more shuffle than bounce in Dad's gait. His confidence had faded. His shoulders were rounded with weight.

I loved saying the word "capillaries" to my friends at school, but I still couldn't swallow any food. At first I'd pretend to be eating, spitting pieces of PB and J into a napkin, but I couldn't keep it up and after a while everyone at school knew I was "eating" only fluids. The embarrassment was more than balanced out by the cool story about my parents saving my life, though, and after a few weeks I forced down some egg salad and everything was okay.

Nana left a couple of days after I saw Dad teach. She left early in the morning when I was still in bed, so I didn't get a chance to say good-bye. But that was actually fine with me. The night before, I had gotten out of bed to go down to the kitchen and get some juice, and when I opened my bedroom door in my pajamas Nana was standing across the hall in a very long, very old-looking, faded nightgown. She didn't see me. She stood completely still by the entrance to Mom and Dad's bedroom, her hands clasped tightly in front of her, and her ear pressed right up against the door.

I took two steps backward into my room, slowly, rolling my feet to the floor, toe to heel. As I did, I pulled the door gently closed again, and turned the knob quietly back into place. I stood completely still, wondering if my bare toes were visible from the other side. I didn't move. I didn't breathe. But I did turn my head to the side, and listen hard.

5

I started the seventies by going on a sort of sleepover tour, spending
almost every weekend at friends' houses, and as far as I knew confining all peeing and walking to the daylight hours. I must have been
feeling either unusually confident or especially desperate to get out of
the house, or probably both. Sleepovers were always dicey, like foreign
travel without a phrasebook, and they were especially disorienting
after Nana's long stay with us. I had to squint at everything, like someone who'd been living underground and was now poking his head out
into the sun for the first time. As I watched my friends' fathers make
good-natured jokes about spilled glasses of soda or unfinished homework my mouth would start to open in preparation to laugh, and then
I'd realize that they weren't doing wacky send-ups of normal people,
they were *being* normal people.

I couldn't believe how quiet it was, how well everyone slept. In our
house, quiet like that meant things were about to get noisy. And I was
amazed at how consistent the personalities of the families were, each
child a variation on a central theme. Whether that theme was Upscale
Hippie Ski-Bum Audiophile Jewish (the Meeds), Doctor with Many,
Many Borders Jewish (the Adlers), So Assimilated We Drink Vodka
Martinis and Have Not Merely a Christmas Tree but an Aluminum
One with White Plastic Pine Needles Jewish (the Aaronsons, Ben's
parents), each family seemed to have sprung fully formed from a different patch of Brooklyn and moved to Long Island on the same day.

As far as I could tell we didn't have a family personality—not just one, anyway. If we had had a family crest it would have been a crest of crests. Each sibling was already in the habit of adopting the character traits of whomever we were standing closest to, trying on the tics and tastes and accents of every friend and acquaintance, performing all the same identity experiments other kids were, but without the control group.

And Glen Cove was chock full of identities. You wouldn't know it from attending a party with my parents and their friends, but unlike every other town on Long Island, Glen Cove was racially, socially, and economically integrated, as an optimistic outsider might have put it back then, or roiling with the tensions of a hundred-and-fifty-year-old personality disorder, as I would put it now. The nature of Glen Cove's identity was confused right from the beginning, when the Matinecock Tribe named it "Musketa," which British settlers decided to keep and amend as "Musketa Cove," even though many people naturally heard that as "Mosquito Cove," a name that tended to discourage investment. It apparently took the British a couple of hundred years to figure out that they might as well have named the place New Vermin and change its name to Glen Cove, but the identity crisis continued on into the nineteenth century, when Glen Cove became two things: a company town for a cornstarch maker, complete with first-generation Irish and Italian employees living in shabby, company-owned apartments and buying food from the company store; and a summering-place for Gilded Age magnates and robber barons like J. P. Morgan, F. W. Woolworth, Henry Clay Folger, and Standard Oil's Charles Pratt, all of whom built extravagant estates there.

The middle of the economic spectrum wouldn't be filled in until the influx of professionals and middle managers in the time period that included my parents, and that would help make Glen Cove seem like the angriest place on Earth to many of us.

But my friends and I didn't know it was angry yet. We were ten, and still had about year and a half left of being relatively nice to each other. After that we would split off into ethnic camps, which I wouldn't realize until twenty years later when Papa pointed out that a lot of my old high school stories featured friends with Jewish last names getting beaten up by kids with Italian last names.

In Glen Cove, Dad was perfectly situated for getting along with either everyone or no one, and the relative peace of our first years there tells me he must have sensed that. Maybe he was just enjoying the new distance from his parents, or the promising trajectory of his career at the time, but the period from 1966 to 1970, our first four years in Glen Cove, was his solidest. After a while, though, he seemed like a man without a country, never quite fitting in at either the baked ziti dinners down at the VFW Hall for the opening day of Little League, or the impromptu folk music jam sessions at the Meeds'. No matter how well things seemed to go at the beginning of an evening, and they sometimes went very well, it would eventually include a too-loud, too-belligerent, or just plain too-strange remark from my father, and someone would suddenly remember they had a big day tomorrow.

Dad's serious flare-ups usually wouldn't happen in overtly social situations, though. He struggled most with the mundane exchanges and negotiations of daily life. He could render gas station attendants and hotel desk clerks speechless with his flame-thrower reactions to casual remarks about credit cards not going through or rooms being delayed. Disagreement was an assault on his dignity. Every challenge was an offense and every offense a humiliation. Barricades were manned at the slip of a tongue. Truths were revealed, jigs were up, and ends were nigh when someone thought Dad was mistaken.

And even when things went well they'd go strangely. Dad would assume an overly "serious" voice; for example, artificially lower, flatter, and grimmer—almost robotic—when making a mere doctor's appointment or dinner reservation.

The inside of Dad's head was a lot like Glen Cove, actually: old working-class resentments, aristocratic fantasies, and a new middle-class identity at odds with both. A neighbor who worked for Pepsi was, according to Dad, an "amoral corporate fuck"; the pearl-wearing high school principal, he said, was "an entitled bitch"; and once, when Dad and I got on a bus after a long wait in the rain, and the bus driver explained impatiently that he couldn't make change because the company didn't let him carry any, Dad spat out, "No, it's because you're a moronic, fucking mick." No race, address, profession, or hobby was exempt from his wrath. It was as if his anger was sparked by the fact of identity itself. He scrupulously scrubbed his life of anything that might signify affiliation with any group, except for the two of which he could usually be sure he was the only representative in any room: English Car Lovers and "Gun Nuts." His life in Glen Cove was marked by missed opportunities to make some peace among the estranged pieces of himself, and between himself and the world. It's possible my father's fractured nature somehow led him to such a fractious place. But in the end it wasn't a happy fit. It was like everyone in the town reminded him of some part of himself he didn't like.

My own sense of identity was shaky enough that when I slept over at my friends' houses I felt like I was entering enemy territory, even though some of those houses felt homier to me than my own.

I started my tour with a couple of nights at Ben's, my first and still most frequent home-away-from-home, despite the fact that his parents and mine didn't seem to spend much time together anymore. They had been joined at the hip in Brooklyn, the mothers sitting with the kids around the small pool at our apartment complex during the summers, and the dads building snowmen and snow forts with us in the winter. But now my mother would drop me off at the Aaronsons' without coming in to say hi, and Ben's mom, Liz, would do the same at our place. I had no idea why, and I imagine Ben didn't, either, but for some reason we never addressed the mystery of our parents' falling out. Instead we played Battleship and Risk and pondered other great questions, like how quickly an astronaut's body would explode in space if his suit had a hole in it, and who in the hell had come up with this whole "French kissing" thing we'd been hearing about, easily the most troubling development of the new decade.

Ben was the best athlete among our group of friends, with the unflappable nature and laconic speaking style of an NFL quarterback, even in fifth grade. He was even more into constructing long, tedious trains of logic than I was, calmly holding forth on how to build a tunnel like the one in *The Great Escape*, or how statistically improbable it was for a Jew to become an astronaut. When he said, "You sunk my battleship," he said it like he was wearing a white lab coat. He was a very cool cucumber, real Secret Agent material, many of us thought; and in this way he was a lot like Arthur, his dad, who seemed to have an inner climate control system like the one in his big new burgundy Lincoln Continental. The Aaronsons still bought American cars. They still listened to Miles Davis and Sinatra; Arthur still kept his hair cut above his ears and Liz shellacked hers into a helmet. They had a color TV with a remote control and they let their kids watch "The F.B.I."

On this first sleepover, Liz Aaronson took one look at me and said, "Peter, your hair is as long as a girl's." I said, "Yeah, Liz, and yours still looks bulletproof." To myself, of course. To her I just said, "Heh." She was sitting at the kitchen table having a cigarette, and Ben was in the bathroom, so she told me to have a seat. The wicker chair squeaked as I tried to seem relaxed, a hard thing to do around Liz. She looked at me, blew a very long, straight stream of menthol-scented smoke, and purred, "Tell me how you're doing in school." The greatest mystery in life was why grown-ups bothered asking this unanswerable question. I almost said, "Shitty. Really, really shitty, because I don't give a shitty shit about anything my shitty teachers say." But instead I went through the time-honored motions. "Good."

"Good? Don't you mean 'well'."

Oh, Jesus. "Yeah, yeah, I mean well."

"What are you going to do this summer? Are you going away to camp?" We didn't do camp in our family. She knew that. This was now officially a hostile interrogation.

"I'm auditioning to be in *The Sound of Music* at the Cape Cod Melody Tent." (I hadn't even asked my parents if this was within the realm of possibility.)

Liz smiled her peroxide smile, blew another stream of smoke, this one curly from her laughter, and said, "Really? My goodness. They don't hire professional actors for those shows?"

I looked down at my shoes, back up at her.

"Well, if they hire you then you're a professional, I guess."

One of her eyebrows went up.

Yes, that's right, Liz. I just sunk your battleship.

Both eyebrows went up. "Well, I guess you're right about that. Good luck to you. Okay, here's Benny. Why don't you two go downstairs."

On the second night of my stay Ben and I sat on their stairway, spying on a party that I was very surprised to see my own parents at. It had been at least a year since our folks had seen each other, but everyone seemed to be getting along pretty well. The party was for a couple who had just moved to town, the Lyons, Lee and Nancy, who were radiant with confidence and tallness and wealth. Everyone in that group sounded like they were wondering about something when they talked, but Lee Lyon talked like he wasn't wondering about anything.

Ben and I were crouched on the stairs because we had run out of smarty-pants excuses to intrude on the festivities and show off, so we were hiding just out of sight, doing running commentary under the adults' conversations.

Dan and Barbara Kind, who had also lived at the complex in Brooklyn and moved out to Glen Cove with us, were there, too. Dan was a big guy, and he was holding forth in a big voice about one of the teachers at our school. The hair on my arms stood up as he said her name, *Mrs. Gallo,* and then again when he mentioned his son, our friend *Matt,* and our principal, *Mr. Jensen.* There was something illicit about hearing a grownup talk to other grownups in an unfiltered way about our world. He was talking about these people as if they were just people. Even his own son. Making jokes about them, or at least saying things that made the other grownups laugh in a way they didn't when we were around.

They all started talking about their kids, some of them openly mocking their son's speech patterns or their daughter's painting skills, to the great amusement of the others. So this was what it was like when we weren't around, I thought. We were figures of fun—lisping, pigeon-toed, giant-headed, drooling monkeys who made everything difficult. Ben and I looked at each other, making an instant, unspoken pact to lead a worldwide, underground kid's resistance movement, and also to use the information we'd just gathered to blackmail our friends' parents into an endless series of concessions over toy sharing and "shotgun" riding. And then it came time for my parents' turn and I got nauseous with nerves. Arthur said, "Peter's gotten so much bigger. He looks great!" But before either one of my parents could say anything, Liz jumped in with, "I hear he's auditioning for a professional production of *The Sound of Music*."

The world stopped spinning and we all skidded off into space, along with every building and car and animal and mountain on Earth.

Then I heard Dad say, "Yup. I'm gonna get Scott Sloan to bring him in—he's the GM up at the North Shore Music Theater, the guy who's putting together the package. And there's a part for him in *Mame,* too. I think he might have a real chance. He's pretty damn talented."

He never even broke his stride. Ladies and gentlemen, welcome back to Planet Earth. Now let's have a big round of applause for the Dad of the Century and the Savior of All Humanity.

Oh, and holy cow, I was gonna get an audition for a professional play.

It wasn't just what Dad said that made me feel so much love for him at that moment that I could bust, but the way he said it. He spoke quietly, and there was a small shake to his voice, like he was keeping a lid on his feelings.

And this was the always undeniable, best truth about my father—
he was more emotional than the other dads. Sometimes over the years
it seemed like every guy on Earth had an aloof, cold, unfeeling father,
but I never felt that way. To be sure, I often wished I did. When I was
old enough to see that Dad let his emotions push him around and
that what he was keeping a lid on that night at the Aaronsons' might
not have been love, but envy and defiance and insecurity, I started to
wonder what it would be like to have a dad with no feelings at all. But
that night I believed it was love, and sometimes I still do.

Everyone at the party bragged about their kids a little more,
and told some more jokes at their expense, and at some point Mom
started playing the piano, and a few people started singing along with
her to "Try to Remember." Arthur Aaronson got out his flute and
played along, and then he and Mom began a free-form duet, something very jazzy, slightly cheesy, Dave Brubeck-ish, that they gradu-
ally built from a simple theme to a multilayered back-and-forth, like
three distinct but related conversations all at once, and then slowly
took apart, peeling off one layer at a time until they were back to the
simple original theme, now completely cheese-free and much less
simple because of the ghost notes swirling around it. I snuck glimpses
of Mom through the stairway banister and saw a familiar picture, her
head bent over the piano, her face taut, and her eyes a darker-than-
usual brown. Ben and I just sat there on the stairs completely slack-
jawed and jokeless.

Mom knew Arthur from college. They had been in a few music
classes together. As I watched them play, I imagined Mom back then,
before she met Dad. I pictured her walking down a street in Brooklyn,
and then Dad walking on some other street just a few miles away.
I imagined them stopping at corners and watching the streetlights
changing, and I wondered how many hundreds of lights would have
to be green, or red, for them to end up together, or with different
people, or with no one.

Mom looked beautiful. Music always brought her to life, like a

blood transfusion. The earliest memory I had was of my mom singing "Soon It's Gonna Rain" on the stage of the Melody Tent when I
was three years old. For me her playing and singing were fountains
of her pure, unfiltered self. As gorgeous as they were, they were never
prettified, but conversational and full of feeling. When she sang, she
told the story of the song. She'd bail out on a note to save the phras-
ing, sacrifice tempo for dynamics, teaching me, intentionally or not,
what matters. Listening to her sing was a lot like listening to her read,
which she never did by rote but always, as she urged me to do, *with
expression.* She was unbound and real when she sang. She even danced
that way, maybe because she always danced with someone other than
Dad, who refused, through all the weddings and bar mitzvahs and
birthday parties they attended over the years, to ever once join her for
a spin around the floor.

After Mom and Arthur finished, everyone was quiet for a minute,
and then they slowly started talking again. I noticed that the conversation somehow came around to the war, which was an unusual topic
at the Aaronsons', not because they supported it or anything—that
would have been a total deal breaker—but because they were the least
political of all the parents. Politics didn't go with the cool jazz and the
Lincoln Continental.

Everyone was speaking a little slower than they had been. They
were talking about some event, something terrible that had happened
in Vietnam, something worse than all the other terrible things, and it
involved children being killed.

Mom and Barbara Kind talked about what the mothers of the
children must have felt like, and they sounded as sad as I'd ever heard
anyone sound. I started to feel like I wanted to stop listening, like I
wanted to run down there and stop them from talking and hug my
mom. The dads were talking about who did what, and how there was
going to be a court case and what this meant for future wars. Ben did
a very quiet, dead-on impression of Lee Lyon, the way he spoke like
he had too much spit in his mouth. He kept saying "court martial,"

and it sounded like he was going to drool all over himself. I barely succeeded in not laughing out loud.

Dad said a couple of things that started with "Unfortunately," and
the other dads sounded a little surprised or unsure about those things.
I noticed that his voice was getting louder. He talked about a man he
had mentioned at home before, someone who worked at Brooklyn
College who had been in the Green Berets in Vietnam, but who now
was against the war because he had seen such awful things. Every time
Dad talked about him he used the phrase "the truth" in this really
sharp, hard way, and got a look on his face like he was watching a little
movie in his head.

Dad was talking at the same time as other people now, and their
voices started to sound a little sharper, too, and annoyed. He said that
the man he knew had cut the ears off of the people he had killed,
that "they all did" over there. He said that American soldiers wore
the ears of the Vietnamese people on strings around their necks. The
more he spoke, the more people interrupted him, and the more he
said things like "unfortunately" and "that's why . . . ," and then he said
that the American soldiers put grenades in people's mouths, and that
they stabbed women with bayonets and raped them and put grenades
in their vaginas and blew them up. He said "vaginas" the way he said
"the truth," the same way he had said "breasts" when he told the story
of the Brooklyn College protest.

There was a feeling in the room when he said it, a feeling like everyone had just caught a disease at the same time. Ben looked over at me
and made a face: *Oh man, gross!* and I tried to make one back at him.
The grown-ups kept talking, but it was weird—their voices actually
sounded a little nicer now. They were starting sentences with the word
"Well," and someone was picking up glasses and plates. Lots of little,
quiet conversations were starting again, and not long after that everyone started saying good night to the Kinds, who had to get home.

* * *

Danny Meed lived in one of the fancier parts of town, on Morgan Island, as in J. P. Morgan; and there were definitely no gun nuts or Mini owners there. Danny's dad, Sherman, was a shrink who apparently had a membership in the Porsche of the Month Club, and his mom, Cammie, was famous for her Earth Motherish mane of stunningly uncolored, uncut, and uncombed salt-and-pepper hair. I was in love with her. She called me "Pete," like we were friends, and she was thrillingly generous with glimpses of the sides of her ample breasts. The Meeds had a ski house in Vermont and a thirty-five-foot-long teak sailboat that they shared with the Aaronsons; and Sherman was always bragging about the latest cold fusion turntable with kryptonite-alloy stylus or whatever the fuck stereo system that he'd just bought and forbidden his children to so much as *think* about touching; but the family still managed to exude a hipper, hempier version of the shabby old-money esthetic, complete with torn topsiders, no air conditioning, and a bombed-out, ancient Woodie as their second car. It all added up to a slow-motion aneurism for my father.

When I would tell Dad about a weekend spent sailing or skiing with the Meeds, he would purse his lips, pick up his chin—his neck tightening from the strain of biting his tongue—and force out an "Oh, that's great," then nod slowly with amused indulgence at my naiveté. It's not that he was way off the mark with his critique of the Meeds, or anyone, really. He caught the scent of authoritarianism in Sherman Meed right off the bat, and over the years predicted a lot of the guy's awful behavior, like the time he forced me to hold a bladder full of pee for an entire five-hour drive to Vermont while sitting in the shoe-box-sized "backseat" of that month's Porsche ("The schmuck wouldn't brake for his own grandmother in that thing"). It was just that Dad made these observations obsessively. It was unnerving. After a while they would achieve a critical mass and there would be an explosion. It would usually happen in a fight with Mom, as a quiet, slow, reluctant-seeming climax, an ace in the hole he was sorry to use. "That's because therapy is bullshit. Do you need any more proof than the fact that

Sherman Meed is a shrink? Your friends Sherman and Cammie are shallow *cunts,* who like to pretend they're changing the world when all they really care about is themselves." And then, continuing as Mom fled the room, quietly crying, "Just. Like. *You.*" Bathroom door slams.

This was why the relatively paltry state of our material life was beginning to bother me so much. One of the common denominators among our family friends was stuff. They all had a lot of stuff. We didn't have stuff. Dad was the only academic in the group, and even though he was nominally an "economist," he didn't seem to know how to handle money calmly at all. So we had even less stuff than we might have. And to me, our sparsely furnished rooms and roll-down car windows seemed to be evidence of contradictory truths. *Things* were what shallow people cared about, after all. And nice things could only be bought with blood money. Success was a symptom of corruption. That's what Dad taught us anyway. But, boy he taught us that a lot. So much so that it was clear he cared about things a lot.

When he took David and me camping in the Catskills we slept side by side in a tiny, army-surplus, World War II "pup tent," a hunk of green canvas designed to keep one underfed GI at a time from being drowned by a rainstorm in the forest (and that I scrupulously inspected for blood stains) while the families around us pitched highfalutin' contraptions you could actually roll over in. Not because we couldn't afford nylon—even a City University professor could spring for a sheet of colored plastic every couple of decades or so—but because we would have been betraying something, or someone, by not sleeping under secondhand burlap. The bullet-making orphans of London. The tougher-than-we-could-ever-dream-of-being soldiers at Rorke's Drift. The angry homunculus that lived in Dad's chest and forbade him to join the human race. Something.

But hey, look, Dad was right. The guy with the fancy stereo was mean, okay? Case closed, end of story. But then again, *Dad* cared about things. Maybe those things were guns and knives instead of stereos, but they were just as expensive, so didn't that blow the theory? But wait—aha!—Dad was mean! So maybe he was right after all . . .

When I slept at the Meeds' or the Aaronsons' I couldn't help connecting the presence of a modern stereo system with the presence of a family personality. It seemed that one was a reward for the other—I just wasn't sure which led to which. Maybe all our family needed to do was be the kind of people who bought the latest speakers and then we'd also be the kind of people who brought a little world with them wherever they went, like these other families did. Or maybe if we had Family Rules, like the Meeds' rule that no one could wear a T-shirt to the table, not even to breakfast; or if we had regular family traditions, like the Adlers' Matzo Brie Sundays, we would develop heretofore undiscovered reservoirs of discipline and organizational skill, the kind that created nest eggs and portfolios and quadraphonic Pioneer surround sound systems.

But the Meeds could be pretty schmucky. When Danny and I were being towed by the boat that afternoon, spinning and plowing through gentle waves while holding on to a thirty-foot line attached to the stern, he'd told me he was going to be attending a new school in September and that it was a private school, which meant it was "much, much better" than Glen Cove Middle School, and that all the kids there were "very, very smart." He said, "You should tell your parents to send you there. It really is much, much better." I didn't even understand what he meant by "send," but I had to admit it sounded good. So of course I told him I would be attending a fancy private school myself the following year, called The Long Island School. When he later got me to admit there was in fact no such place I said, "So what—you're still a fucking idiot," and punched him in the arm, which years later I realized was exactly the right response.

The push and pull between the outside world and home was getting stronger. After my day with Danny Meed I was almost eager to hear Dad go on about the charge of the Light Brigade. But I also knew that, after just a couple of minutes at the dinner table with Dad I would be tempted to stow away on Danny's boat forever. So I came home with a project in mind. I was going to help all of us, especially Dad, calm down and get in touch with our inner private-school-attending boat-owners. I would start small, and smart.

I would start at the dinner table. Beginning that night I would take Adler- and Meed- and Mom-size portions of food, and I would chew them slowly. I would drink water instead of soda, as Mom was always urging us to do, and like the Aaronsons' did, even if it meant sneers of contempt from Dad. I would eat with my mouth closed, as Mom was always pleading with us to at least *try*. I would set an example by not testing the load-bearing capabilities of my plate. I would. And I would speak in an even tone and sit up straight and—but here's the thing: when I actually did these things, they all felt pretty weird. It felt like I was capitulating to the girl side of things, the Mom side. I didn't want to be in the business of taming my father. That felt seriously askew. I didn't want to be learning how to eat perfectly; I wanted to eat well enough. Good enough. Enough to satisfy the girls but messy enough to balance things out.

I kept one elbow mannishly on the table as I said, "Mom, can you pass the green beans?" She smiled and said, "Yes, honey, here you go."

The problem was, Dad was all mess and no balance, all impulse and no control, especially at dinner. He brought his head down to his plate and got the dirty job done. His mouth was amazingly, enormously open and made all kinds of barks and wheezes while wood-chipping his food into a blur. Richard would imitate him sometimes but Dad couldn't even slow down enough to be insulted, that's how far gone he was. He ate so fast and so hard that his nose would run, like it does when you play basketball non-stop for forty minutes or run a marathon, so he was forever sniffing and wiping the heel of his palm up against his nose between shoe-size bites. And there was clearly a link between the chaotic fury of Dad's eating and the ferocity of his anger, which was so easily detonated at the dinner table. He got the dirty job done when he ate and when he raged. He laid waste to the village. I wanted to be taught the manly art of the controlled burn, but Dad only knew how to torch the town.

I tried to will Dad's mouth shut with my brain, tried to slow his hand like the one on my clock. Stop the noises coming out of him by eating slowly. Nothing worked.

I blurted, "David, could you stop eating like a goddamn pig?"

"Screw you! You're a pig!"

"*Watch* it, mister," said Dad, to David.

I felt bad for saying the thing about being a pig to David. Probably should have kept that to myself.

Alison started crying.

"Hey, David," I said, "what are you guys doing in Mrs. Boyce's class? Are you gonna do a play like we did? I played Perseus in the play when she was my teacher. Do you know who Perseus was?"

"I don't *care*. Dad, why does Peter have more french fries than I do? It's not fair."

Through a blizzard of french fry chunks, Dad said, "Eat what's on your plate and keep your mouth shut. I don't want to hear another word."

"*But—*"

I kicked David lightly in the shin to try to get him to abort the launch sequence.

"Ow! Anus!"

Mom grabbed his forearm gently. "David, please, that's enough. Let's just have a nice dinner, okay?"

"O*kay*, but—"

"Please. Here. Here are some of my french fries. And can you get me a spatula from the drawer, please?"

"Okay," David said, and jumped out of his chair towards the utensil drawer, barely grazing his tall glass of Coke as he did. He'd already pulled his hand out of the drawer by the time the soda spilled.

The sound of the glass on the table was loud, but the fizz of the coke as it spread over everything seemed even louder, like the table was a hot skillet.

"Jesus Christ, you *fuck*ing klutz!" said Dad. "What the fuck is the matter with you?!" His face was red. "Get me a goddamn napkin. Hurry up!"

"I will," said David.

He stood on his toes and grabbed at the paper towels with his free hand and pulled. A quarter of the roll unspooled on him, spilling over his head and shoulders. Some of it was already pooling around his feet when he said, "Wait," and turned towards Dad with a ladle in his hand. "Here."

Dad slapped it out of his hand, hard. "That's a ladle, you fucking moron. Go upstairs. Get the fuck out of my sight." The ladle clanked against the wall, then the floor. David's eyes went dead.

"Don't—" Mom said, and Dad turned on her.

"Don't? Don't what?"

Mom let out a little breath and said something like, "C'mon, kids, let's clean up. Richard, please stop playing with your food. Please. Give me a hand, honey, okay?"

We all silently busied ourselves with whatever we could grab. Mom took Alison upstairs and Dad started to wash a couple of pots in the sink. David and I got down on the kitchen tile and quietly, quickly picked up the sprawl of paper towels, gathering them up into a big, crumpled pile. Richard wobbled over to us with a smile on his face and a plate in his hands and dumped all his french fries right on the floor between us. He released the high-pitched squeal of laughter he'd been holding in, and bounced back and forth from one foot to another like a little four-year-old Jimmy Cagney. My eyes went straight to Dad's back. He was still scrubbing away, the hot water streaming loud and hard out of the tap, apparently obscuring the sounds of the french fry bombing and the bombardier's evil jig of celebration, very luckily for him. David and I grabbed madly at the fries and the rest of the towels and I bolted into the garage to dump it all into one of the big, metal garbage cans.

* * *

I went up to the bedroom David and I shared, weighed down by the feeling that I should have seen that one coming. It wasn't that bad, hadn't turned into that big a deal, but I should have stopped it when I could. It was the first in a long time. It was bound to happen, but I didn't have to start it, for crying out loud. I was better at keeping David from making mistakes then I was at stopping myself. I was sixteen months older than him, and better at spotting and avoiding *his* trouble, so when I'd watch him walking towards a lamp cord while drinking a glass of milk everything would start to move in slow motion, and I could jump into action.

I wasn't as good at seeing myself in this way, despite my constant state of alertness. Here's the thing about being deathly afraid of the next falling lamp: when you're five or six, or nine, to be afraid of knocking things over is to be afraid of yourself. I mean, there's no way you *can't* knock things over. It's what you do. You try to think of the part of yourself that bumps into lamps as the bad part, the dark side that you will do battle with and conquer, but that's a fight you can't win, and you end up convinced of your own defectiveness, afraid of your own shadow. So then you develop great peripheral vision and quick reflexes, a high metabolism and insomnia. Or, as in David's case, a hide thick enough to hunker down in until the storm had passed. And the storm almost always passed quickly and completely, like a thundershower in the tropics. The sudden, quiet aftermath of one of Dad's fits was sometimes more disconcerting than the fit itself. He had an uncanny ability to disconnect quickly, completely, and unsettlingly. There was never any acknowledgment of what had just happened.

Half an hour after the ladle slap Dad sauntered into our room, picked up a Hot Wheels Jaguar, slowly turned it around in his hand, and admired aloud how accurate the body design was. We enthusiastically agreed. He said, "Of course if it was really authentic it would have the steering wheel on the right. They've put this one on the *colonial* side."

There was a little pause, and David said, "Heh."

Dad assumed his hands-over-crotch pose and narrowed his eyes. He stood completely still, and paused for effect.

"What would the two of you think about us all living for a year . . . in the mother country?"

We were silent. David probably because he was still young enough to be clueless about what Dad meant, or surprised, or intrigued. I, on the other hand, knew that Dad was going to drag this out, doling out tiny bits of information with a cocked eyebrow, in short phrases, each one ending in an elongated last word ("Eeenglaannd") and that it was our job to pretend to be on the edge of our seats.

So I did my best to play along until he finally got to the point: He was going to take a sabbatical to write a book and he wanted to write it in England, so we were probably going to move there for a year. He wasn't sure exactly when, or even if we were going, but he was "talking to people" about making it happen.

When he finally made his dramatic exit from our room, David looked over at me with undisguised sadness and worry. He hadn't even been able to force out a perfunctory "Wow" when Dad was breaking the news. He pretty much didn't like going anywhere, not even down the block, and England was a lot farther away than that. I didn't know what to tell him.

It probably took us a long time to get to sleep. Sometime after we did, though, the sounds of a fight suddenly bubbled up out of the dead night silence. It was never gradual. It took about three or four quick beats to rise from low conversation to the bang of Dad's voice cracking the air like a whip. At first I thought they were fighting about David and the ladle, but then I realized it was something else. I heard the sounds of physical struggle, wrestling sounds that, if they came at all, would usually come much later in a fight. And this struggle didn't sound like the others. I definitely heard Mom say, "No!" at least once. It wasn't a frightened "No," it was a refusal, and a reprimand. And I don't know if it happened that night or a week or two later, but at some point around this time, during a fight like this one, my father came out of their room and, in a full, sharp voice dripping with contempt, he said the word "repressed," for the first of many, many times over the next several years.

I finished my sleepover tour at the Adlers, my favorite family. Josh Adler was short, scrappy, and funny, and we had a friendship built on basketball. Eventually we would play so many hours of basketball on his warped, pockmarked old driveway that we were able to anticipate every eccentric carom and skid the ball might take, and use our secret knowledge to hustle tens of dollars out of our friends in pick-up, two-on-two games.

We had an all-day basketball marathon that Saturday, during which I noticed that when Josh dribbled the ball he bounced up and down along with it. His feet left the ground as the ball came up, and came back down when the ball came down, and none of it disturbed the permanent look of squinty concentration on his face. At some point during the game I laughed so hard I couldn't move my legs, and he *boing-boing*ed right by me to the hoop.

Linus and Leslie Adler were the only adults I had never seen unhappy. Leslie could get frustrated for a minute about an unraked lawn, or Dr. Adler might be "very concerned" about the lack of progress Josh was making on a book report, but they never seemed thrown by anything, or like they would rather be anywhere else.

A few months before I spent the weekend with them, back when I was reading *Death Be Not Proud*, the book by the father of a nine-year-old boy who dies of a brain tumor, Dr. Adler took my call at his office and listened patiently to a detailed description of my many symptoms of brain cancer. When I insisted on coming in that day for an exam, he cleared a spot on his schedule and spent ten or fifteen minutes taking a close look at my tumor, which was already so pronounced it was protruding sharply from the back of my head, just above the neck. When he was done, and without the slightest hint of a smile, he brought out a model of a human head and showed me the little bump that some people, like me, have at the base of their skull. He said it was called "the Occipital Bun," and that it was a prehistoric evolutionary adaptation to help balance the head. Then he patiently answered all the questions I asked about bones and cancer and running from dinosaurs, and complimented me on my careful attention to serious health issues, then walked me out the door to the lobby. And he never told my parents.

Dr. Adler sort of reminded me of Papa, even though he was almost as short and thin as Josh (whom he called "Joshy"). He was unfailingly polite, even sweet, to everyone, but you couldn't push him over in a hurricane. I sat with the Adlers at their breakfast table that Sunday; Josh, his older brother Seth, and the parents, eating Leslie's famous matzo brie, talking about books and music and tennis, and feeling like a piece of matzo myself, soaking up all the good, fortifying Adler-ness around me.

I complimented Leslie on the matzo brie, telling her it was my second favorite ever after my Mom's (which I had never tasted because it didn't exist), and I turned to Josh and said, "You should stay over next weekend and have some, it's really good." The conversation eventually turned to how the Adlers' rabbi had reacted to the first draft of the speech that Seth was preparing for his bar mitzvah. Everyone at the table had a different, but equally smart take on what the strengths and weaknesses of the speech were, and lots of ideas about how to fix it. I gleaned enough to offer a few tentative thoughts of my own, in the very Adler-esque, slightly over-dentalized speech pattern I adopted at their house, and Leslie liked whatever I said. Josh asked me what my mom put in her matzo brie, and with a knowing smile I said, "Oh, you'll find out." And then Dr. Adler put his hands together and said, "You know, Peter, to be honest we're not really comfortable with Josh staying in a house where there are guns."

I stopped breathing. I kept a smile on my face, but I could feel my face get hot. There it was, I thought; it was real. Everyone knew who I was, who we were, and it wasn't good. We made people uncomfortable. It was official now. It had been spoken out loud, by the most normal, comfortable guy in town. But I kept my cool. I nodded, ever so slightly, in sympathy with Dr. Adler. I knew of what he spoke, I said with my nod. I hear ya, Dr. Adler—don't even get me started about the guns. And I respect your decision. It's for people like us— you and me, all of us here at this table, really; the good, peace-loving, gun-not-having people of Glen Cove—to decide how to deal with the gun-havers out there, and to respect the choice that each one of us makes. Far be it from me to tell another gun-not-liking person what that choice should be.

"Oh, sure, yeah, I understand," I said, nodding, and Leslie, God bless and keep her, jumped right back into the bar mitzvah discussion, asking me something that I answered with a story about my grandmother, who still kept kosher and lit the Sabbath candles, and I went on for quite a while, going off on tangents about Uncle Abe and the United Nations and Uncle Dave's poetry, and then at some point I heard myself saying something about when I would be starting Hebrew school and how my Mom was really looking forward to it and how much fun it was going to be for Josh and me to study for our bar mitzvahs together. Leslie looked very happy and relieved, like it was the best news she'd gotten all year, and I tried to be glad about that but I felt sick and tired and awful. Lying to the Adlers wasn't any fun at all.

6

Elaine, you're not doing it right!" Elaine nodded and I looked around. Everyone was staring at me. A couple of people—Tracey, who played my mom, and Aioki, who played the "houseboy"— had their mouths open. Elaine Stritch was a very big deal in their world. Mom had told me that Elaine was a star on Broadway, that she had just won some big awards and *everyone* knew who she was, but I'd never seen her on television or in a movie or anything and when I met her she didn't seem very famous to me. Mom had said the same things about the show we were doing, *Mame*, that it was so popular and so this and so that, but no one I knew had ever heard of it.

And anyway, what was so strange about having a catch with someone? Elaine was the one who suggested it, even. I was just throwing against the side of the little white dressing room barn, killing time until I had to get into costume. Elaine was standing there watching me for a while, and I told her she should help me practice concentrating, and in that broken-throated voice of hers she said, "Oh, darlin', I would *love* to. Throw me the ball." She said it in that way that she said everything, like little bombs were going off inside her, like she was going to take a big, juicy bite out of the world's ass right *now*. And so I said okay, you be the catcher, but also you should yell stuff at me like the other team will if I'm really pitching, so she did. So that's why she was shouting, "We want a pitcher, not a belly itcher!" and "We want a pitcher, not a glass of water!" Except she wasn't saying it right, she was saying, "We want the pitcher! And get a glass of water!" and all kinds of other stupid mistakes like that, so it was really annoying and I asked her to please do it right. So what's wrong with that?

Elaine said, "Oh, sweetheart, I *know*! I just can't seem to remember *anything* these days. Tell me one more time." I walked her through it again, slowly, and this time she nailed it. "We want a pitcher!" And she did a little hop like she was really happy she'd done it right. She was more fun than any of the other grown-ups I knew. Everyone in the cast was fun. They were always playing jokes on each other, or singing, or telling stories with surprise endings. I knew we would all be friends forever, and I was already sad about having to say good-bye to them after all the time we'd spent together. After four weeks of rehearsing and performing we knew each other so well I could barely remember life before them, and couldn't imagine it without them. We were like a family.

Mom said I would also make friends with the cast of *The Sound of Music* and that I would enjoy doing that show even more because there would be lots of other kids in it, but I was pretty sure I would hate them all, and I would never have as much fun with anyone as I was having with Elaine and Doug and Jenny and Xander and Susanna. It had been hard leaving all my friends at home, and I really didn't want to go through that again. But there was a lot more leaving to come. First the end of *Mame* and then, after *Sound of Music* we were heading off to Sussex, England, for the rest of the year. England, for crying out loud. The thought of making and leaving at least two more sets of friends was too much for me to wrap my head around. I was not at all sure I was looking forward to the future.

But I only had a small part in *Mame*. I played Peter, the son of the grown Patrick Dennis, who comes in at the very end and cracks a few jokes with Mame. I would have a much bigger part in *The Sound of Music*. I would get to sing, which I was excited about, even if the songs in the show were incredibly dorky. I was good at acting—everyone in *Mame* said so; they said I was "like an old pro," and stuff like that, which Mom said I "shouldn't let go to my head," but I could tell they really meant it. To tell the truth, acting didn't seem very hard to me. In some ways it seemed easier than not acting. I mean, easier than talking to people and doing things with them in real life. It was just a matter of meaning what I said, of "believing it was really happening, even though it was not" as the director had said to me, and I was definitely an old pro at that. Acting was new and improved truth. When I sat in the audience and watched other actors do it, acting seemed like a miracle. Watching people who were in the same room with me, yet walking and talking and breathing in a whole other room that was just as real almost made the top of my head fly off. And then when I got to step into that other world, I felt the way I did when I ran around in my cape at home, like Superman making the Earth spin backwards and changing reality. Eventually I started feeling like I would be able to put my talents to good use in England, too. Like I could handle it. I was good at adapting. I would be fine. Bring on the new stuff.

Now that we'd all done the show so many times, I couldn't believe I'd ever been nervous about auditioning for it. It seemed like a million years ago that I had gone into the city with Dad and waited with all the other kids in the hallway, outside the big room with the piano in it, and the people behind the table watching you to see if you were the right one to play Peter in *Mame* and Friedrich in *The Sound of Music*. I'd stopped being nervous as soon as I started singing, exactly like Mom had told me I would. I sang "My Favorite Things" and "Do-Re-Mi," and that was okay, but I really liked doing the talking scenes from the shows, reading from the script—*with expression*—and believing they were real.

The only time I got nervous again was after that, when one of the people watching said, "That was wonderful. Can you do something else? Do you know something by heart?" I got tingly all over and couldn't feel my hands, so I thought I might be dying, but then I came up with something and I forced myself to not be afraid and just do it. I tilted my head down a bit and pushed my lips together in a serious, frowny way, and in a slow, thick Texas accent I said, "I shall not seek, and I will not accept, the nomination of my party for another term as your president." And everyone laughed, really hard, which kind of shocked me because I thought everyone would say, "Wow, that sounds just like him!" But instead they all laughed, and then I did, too, because I could all of a sudden see how it might be funny. I felt like I had probably gotten the job right there.

Rudy, the stage manager, came out of his office and yelled, "Half hour, people! This is your half hour call!" And everyone broke off into little groups of two and three and began heading back in. Elaine walked over to me in her way, all elbows and complaints, and handed me the ball. She had her funny frown on, which was almost the same as her angry frown, but very, very different.

Mom had said something about Elaine at dinner that I didn't understand. I was telling her how good Elaine was at "quick changes," how after an exit she picked up speed as she ran up the aisle and into her quick-change booth outside the tent, and how two costume people helped her, but still she had to take off a whole bunch of clothes and put on another in just a few seconds and she never, ever messed up. I said, "That's why she's so thirsty all the time," and Mom said, "What do you mean?" I said, "She has a Thermos—just like mine, only bigger—and she keeps it in the quick-change booth, and every time she makes a change, she takes a big sip from her Thermos cup." Mom said, "A Thermos?" like there was something weird about that. And then after a few seconds she said, "Honey, be careful around Elaine. I mean, I don't want you to bother her too much, she works very hard and she's probably very tired and needs as much peace and quiet as she can get, okay?" Huh? Had she ever even met Elaine? She was the most un-tired person in the world.

But when Elaine brought back the ball and handed it to me, she said, "Pitcher itcher," and her eyes were watery. Not in a crying way, but in an unfocused way, like my dad's eyes got sometimes. And I could smell the liquor on her breath.

When I made my entrance that night, two bad things happened right away. Number one, I banged the top of my foot hard against the little ramp leading up to the stage, and broke a bunch of little bones in it. It hurt like hell. And number two, Elaine tried to say her first line three times but never got it right, because she wasn't even saying words. She sounded like a person pretending to be drunk, that's how drunk she was. But for some reason I didn't panic. Or, well, actually I did panic, but with a purpose. It was like I took all the adrenaline in my body and steered it directly to my brain's Improvisational Comedy Lobe. Everything came into sudden, sharp relief, and it was incredibly exhilarating to walk around the stage on my broken foot, making up lines and blocking and putting a patch on the hole in the scene. It seemed like the audience didn't even know what had happened and that we just hopped right back on track.

It was easy as pie, and incredibly fun, more fun than any of the other performances had been. It felt more real than real life. Most days I spent a lot of time walking around in a fog that would occasionally clear, like I was stepping in and out of lots of different vague, soft pencil drawings. But the show that night when everything went wrong was a bright, clear thing. I had super vision and super hearing. I'd always imagined that when actors were acting they felt like their characters, but I'd felt more like myself than I ever had.

It revved me up to be asked to do something difficult and to succeed, to know I was capable of making everything work out. Everybody called me a "little trouper" and an "old pro" again and said Mom and Dad should be very proud of me. I was giving serious consideration to letting it all go to my head. Mom did seem proud, and so did Dad, although he seemed prouder right after the show than when we got home later. Then he started looking at me the way he looked at Rich when he was being funny.

He and Mom sat with me while I had my special late-night supper, one of my favorite things about being an actor, and Mom talked a lot about my foot and how brave I was, but Dad was pretty quiet. After I had finished my pizza bagel, as Dad was wiping the table and Mom was putting dishes in the sink, she turned to him and said the Meeds were going up to Cape Cod soon—they were sailing their boat all the way up from Long Island—and that they'd invited the two of them out for a weekend sail, a little vacation for the grown-ups. She was thinking they could ask one of the apprentices from the theater to babysit.

I said, "*Ohhh!* I wanna go! That would be so great! Why can't *we* go?"

Dad threw the dish towel really hard against the wall. His eyes were black and burning. "You fuck. You ungrateful little fuck. You *fucking* ingrate. " His face was shaking. "You're out on those boats every goddamn week. We've never gone. That's why you can't go, okay? You fucking little prick."

He blew out of the kitchen and into the living room, where I heard him sit hard on the couch and rustle for a cigar.

I just sat there frozen. I had a strange, sickly feeling, like I had been poisoned. I could feel a little bit of a tear forming in my eye and another one in my throat, but I pushed them back down, just as I had when my foot broke. I looked at Mom, trying to keep a steady expression on my face. She was frozen, too, standing by the sink, a rag in her hands. She looked at me in a funny way, like she was angry and sad at the same time, but I couldn't tell which person she was mad at. She let out a little breath. We were both trying to stay quiet and let the dust settle. She looked down, then up again, and closed her mouth tight, and I decided she must be mad at me for ruining their plans, and that Dad was right—I really was an ingrate. It was true. I was spoiled. Look at me; I'm complaining about not getting to go out on a boat?! Thinking I'm a big shot and not even remembering that ninety-nine-point-nine percent of the people on Earth will never get to live the way we do, not even for one day. Dad had always taught me these things, and I loved him for it, and now I was acting like an asshole. I'd really let him down, pretty much just spit in the face of everything he'd been trying to help me understand.

I knew what I had to do. I was shaking a little bit, so I forced my hips to move, made them get out of the chair, then my knees, then my feet, and I started to walk into the living room. Mom's eyes opened wide, and I still couldn't really tell what she was thinking, but I could tell that she loved me a lot, and that helped me keep walking.

I stepped across the threshold to the living room. Dad was sitting on the couch at the other side of the room, directly ahead, with his arms crossed, and he watched me. I had to tell my feet to take each step and tell my lungs to take each breath. I kept my head up. I finally got there, and I looked at my father and said, "Dad, I'm so sorry. I didn't mean to say that. It was really, really stupid. I'm really sorry," and he looked up at me slowly, frowning, his eyes still oily dark, and in a full, strong voice he said, "*Fuck you.*"

I cried hard into my pillow for a long time afterwards. Full-body, lose-your-breath crying. I wrote a long, angry letter to Dad that I never gave him, telling him why I was running away, which I never did. I looked at the picture from The Before Times again, of Mom sitting with David and me, and I tried to forget about everything that had happened and fall asleep. But it didn't help. What was it about that picture?

As soon as I asked myself, I saw it. In the picture, Mom's nose is a prow, a gorgeous, rounded, Russian shtetl nose, just like her mother's and her grandmother's. Almost a schnoz. In every photograph after that she has the nose we all think of as hers, perfectly straight and nothing at all like the ones on the rest of the family's faces. And Mom was very much not a "nose job" person. So I knew. And knowing made things feel different.

I didn't officially know until much later, when I was in my twenties and finally asked her about it, but her answer was merely a confirmation. "You were both asleep. David was an infant, and you were about two years old. Dad got very, very angry and he punched me. Simple as that. There was a lot of blood, and I knew from the pain and the blood that it was broken. We went to the emergency room at Maimonides Hospital, and he told me to tell the doctors and nurses that I had been bending over him as he was kneeling to pick something up, and that he stood up unexpectedly and his head hit my nose. I did as I was told, and by the look on the doctor's face, and the way he treated Dad, I knew he didn't believe the story. I knew he knew I had been hit, but I didn't dare say anything. I went to a plastic surgeon, who set the bone in my nose. It healed with a big bump of scar tissue, and months later, Grandma, who had completely bought the story about Dad bumping his head into me, offered to pay for an operation to remove the bump."

During the performance on the second-to-last night of the show, Elaine, drunk again, fell from a big, crescent moon hanging ten feet above the stage and broke her arm. She literally bounced right back up and completed the rest of the show, but nobody called her a little trouper afterwards. At a cast barbecue on the beach on the last day of the show, she handed me a Bloody Mary and said, "Here, kid, try this," so I took a sip, and I thought it tasted like spoiled food.

Two weeks after that, and nearing the end of my career as a child actor, I, like so many others before me, sadly became a parody of my former self, delivering a series of progressively overwrought performances each night as Friedrich Von Trapp to Jane Powell's Maria in *The Sound of Music*. Friedrich had not historically been a role known for its scenery-chewing opportunities, but I was determined to change all that. I accepted the fact that audiences came to the show to see Jane Powell,

another apparent star whose fame was lost on me, but I was determined that they would leave with the realization that Friedrich was
the unsung hero of the story. Instead of just "believing the show was
real," I deployed a whole arsenal of acting tricks I'd developed while
plying my humble trade for the better part of a month, and turned
each performance into a face-making contest between me and the
other child actors, my devoted protégées.

It wasn't enough to merely *be* sad when we fled the Nazis, I had
to make sure every member of the audience could *see—really see—*
how *very* sad I was, and how many *different kinds of sadness* I experienced—*really experienced—*as events unfolded. The younger Von
Trapp children dutifully followed my lead—after all, I was the veteran
of our merry little troupe—and we ended up looking like a bunch
of epileptics in sailor suits. When the Meeds came to the show we all
went out to dinner afterwards and Cammie said, "Hey, wow, Pete,
boy, kiddo . . . I've never seen an actor work as hard as you." I was over
the moon.

And, as if Cammie's comments weren't enough, I also seemed to
be earning the appreciation of another attractive older woman, Jane
Powell's daughter, Lindsay, who was fifteen and a fellow cast member. Lindsay was strangely resistant to my acting advice, but did seem
to like sitting with me on the bench outside the dressing rooms and
sharing a box of Sno-Caps. We were always the first to arrive at the
theater—Lindsay because Jane liked to get there early and "warm up
them old bones," as she would say, and me because I'd probably been
at the tent most of the day anyway, wandering in and out of Dad's
office to ask permission to borrow a plastic sword from the scene shop,
or bug him for snack money. Sometimes I'd hang out with the college-
age apprentices in their cabin, lounging on a beat-up old sofa while
they smoked pot and listened to *The Best of Bread*. But the late afternoon was all about waiting for Lindsay to show up.

I knew that if Josh or Ben had somehow managed to sneak up to
Cape Cod and see me collaborating with the cootified they would

have punched my left arm to a pulp, right after blowing my cover with Lindsay by telling her I wasn't technically thirteen. But that knowledge only made our secret seem even more deliciously forbidden. Lindsay was just like her mom, shy and soft-spoken. She asked me lots of questions about my life back home, and sometimes when something reminded her of a song, she would just start singing it, also softly, looking off into the trees and losing herself for a minute or two. Jane was the den mother to everyone in the show, giving everyone else the kind of attention that Elaine had gotten from the cast of *Mame,* and Lindsay was cut from the same cloth, often bringing baskets full of treats for the cast, or volunteering to babysit staff members' kids.

When Lindsay got to the theater in the afternoons, I'd run from wherever I was towards the dressing rooms, then suddenly slow to a casual saunter as I got there. Then I'd start throwing against the wall, or doing some of the stretching exercises I'd seen the other actors do, or pretend to be going over my lines, and wait for her to notice me, which she always did.

Despite all the running and sauntering around, and despite the concerted efforts of my mom and the Glen Cove public school system during the previous year to prepare me for all the hormonal changes heading my way and keep me on twenty-four-hour puberty alert, I was pretty clueless about what exactly was happening to my body and my brain that summer.

And I don't know if it was because of what was going on with me or what was going on with Dad, but since I was entering a hairier stage of my life and he was entering the fatherless phase of his, probably both were responsible for the fact that I started noticing lots of pornography around our house. I don't mean *Playboy*s in the closet, but stronger stuff, in more accessible places. Graphic, hard-core mags under the bathroom sink, or in the trunk of the car. Of course I was happy to find them, but there was no missing Dad's aggression in leaving them around. Mom and Dad's fights seemed to be happening later at night, and Mom was spending a lot more time at the beach than she had in previous summers.

On a Sunday afternoon just before we left for England I was killing time inside the tent, and I saw them standing very close to each other, just outside one of the entrances, speaking very softly. I was surprised at how noticeable my relief was—I could feel my shoulders and jaw unclench, my breathing deepen and slow. I started towards the entrance, following the curve of the tent on the aisle that circled just inside it, so I was blocked from view. I stopped when I got within earshot and heard my dad saying, very quietly, matter-of-factly, "There is something wrong with you. Something wrong. You are repressed. You are a cold, repressed person." Mom said, "No. No, I'm not. I enjoy sex as much as anyone but . . ." And I didn't hear anything after that because I started backing away.

The picture they made—the two of them, standing in the sun on deep green grass outside a big orange tent surrounded by little white clapboard barns—made Dad's words especially harsh and incongruous. When I saw it I had my first real sense, on some subterranean level, that we had started to lose our father when he lost his. There was no doubt now that there had been a real break in something, and that the relative peace of the previous couple of years was gone. And England was the last place on Earth it would ever come back.

We lived in a four-hundred-year-old house in the English countryside for the rest of the year and the whole time it felt like *Beowulf*. It was hard enough hitting puberty, but I really could have done without the castles and the fog and the crooked teeth everywhere. And all the Jesus. Jesus was *everywhere*. Not like in the States, where he was like The Captain of the Other Team, but as part of the landscape. Jesus was a given, like the rain. There were rolling hills and pubs and Jesus. And I got with the program right away, like I had the year before when

I insisted on going to Hebrew school with my friends on Long Island. I was going to get with the program at any cost, whether I had to wear a blazer with shorts, or puka shells with a yarmulke to do it.

My brothers and I attended a drafty little old school in a little town in Sussex and we wore knee socks and sang hymns every morning. "Onward Christian Soldiers." "All Things Bright and Beautiful." All Things Grim and Grimmer. A dull curtain of gray clouds surrounded the town for a month. The kids at school didn't smile much. My teacher had a rubbery pink and brown scar over half his face where he had been burned by a German firebomb in North Africa, and he dragged himself around on big steel polio crutches that squeaked under his weight. There were thousand-year-old churches on the corners, and pieces of Spitfires and Messerschmitts poking up from cow pastures, and it seemed like every single thing was old and misshapen.

Including our house. A lot of the houses had names in England, even the little ones, and ours was called Cold Harbor, satisfying the English penchants for gloominess and irony in one fell swoop. Its stones had been settling into the clumpy old earth for such a long time that the house had become indistinguishable from it, and Cold Harbor lived up to its name by being dark and dank but cozy. And very, very noisy. The shutters banged and the plumbing knocked and sometimes the whole place groaned like a big old dog. It provided shelter from the English storms, but not the kind of climate-controlled, sheetrocked American comfort that made you forget a storm was even happening. There was never any doubt that you were still a part of nature in that house.

Dad had taken his sabbatical from Brooklyn College, and he was going to write a book—he just hadn't decided exactly what it was going to be about yet. But while he may not have had a clear idea about what he was going to do in England, he had meticulously planned our trip there. We sailed from New York to Southampton on the *Queen Elizabeth II*. Kids in one cabin, parents in another. Swimming pools, tennis courts, lobster forks, and lots and lots of boring rich people, for six days. Because, I guess, how else is a family with four young kids supposed to travel?

One day Richard and Alison were in the ship's nursery, a sort of playroom with nannies, as Dad was taking Mom, David, and me up to the bridge to get a guided tour from the captain. We were just stepping into an elevator when we heard a woman's frantic voice from the other end of the corridor yelling, "Mrs. Birkenhead! Mrs. Birkenhead! Please wait!" Dad stopped the automatic door with his hand and Mom stepped out. The woman approached, out of breath, walking quickly, waving her hand. We were all stepping out of the elevator when she said, "I'm afraid your son Richard is missing. He doesn't seem to be in the nursery and we've not been able to find him anywhere else." We all froze, except for Mom, who was already moving quickly back towards the nursery before the woman had finished. Dad put his hand on my shoulder and said, "It'll be okay, we'll find him. Let's go look."

When we got to the nursery a crowd of people seemed to appear from out of nowhere, and were quickly mobilized as a search party by one of the stewards. Dad was very focused and calm. He kept his hand on Mom's upper arm, very gently, as they listened to the steward give instructions. Mom was white, but concentrating hard. A sizable group—the four of us, the woman from the nursery, and three other, older adults who I think just tagged along—headed up the nearest stairway assuming that Richard was more likely to have not been seen if he had taken the stairs instead of the elevator. We climbed the stairs in a clump, Dad's hand on Mom's back, her hand in mine, everyone talking about splitting up and looking in different places once we got to the top. We stumbled out onto the upper deck and into a brilliantly bright, sunny day in the middle of the North Atlantic. The salt smell was almost overwhelming. Mom's eyes went directly to the guardrails, and so everyone else's did, too, and we all could see there were gaps in the rail where the round lifesavers hung, spaces where a small child could easily slip through.

Mom opened her mouth. Her lips were pale and flaking a little. Some well-meaning woman in the group said, "Oh dear, I hope he hasn't gone over the side," and Mom looked like she was about to pass out. Her eyelids drooped, her arms went limp, and Dad took her elbow again. We all just stood there, rubber-legged and paralyzed on the deck, the wind blowing in our hair, the calm and infinite ocean all around us, nobody saying anything. No one knew what to do.

Dad said, "Okay," but didn't continue. I started scanning the ocean, moving my eyes back and forth across the water systematically, checking every cresting wave for blond hair.

And then, after what seemed like an eternity, a short, male crew-member came rushing up the deck, his hat somehow staying perfectly in place despite the wind, and Richard's jumpy hand in his. Rich looked like he was having the time of his life, blithely beaming from the excitement and the sunshine and the chance to run on the deck with an actual crewmember. He had left the nursery and gone back to the cabin by himself to get one of his Hot Wheels to show some other little boy. Dad and Mom showered him with kisses, and neither managed to keep a faint note of admiration and amusement out of their voices as they scolded him.

After we landed at Southampton we waited for three hours on the dock for a car that Dad had bought to be delivered to us. It finally arrived, and as we got in I was reasonably confident that, while we would never absolutely know for sure, we were probably the world's first family of six to ever step off the *QE2* and directly into an Austin Mini.

We began a very long drive to Ticehurst. It was hot and humid and stuffy in the car, and there were four of us in the miniscule back seat, squirming all over each other like puppies. The windows were open because there was no air conditioning, and at some point a wasp flew into the car and down Richard's shirt, stinging him badly. He screamed like, well, like a five-year-old who's been stung by a wasp while riding in a Hot Wheels from Hell. Mom held him on her lap for the rest of the trip, but it barely calmed him. It was an absolute nightmare from one broiling end of England to the other. We got to Ticehurst in the middle of the night, exhausted, but not so tired that we couldn't spare a little energy to be afraid of our new house.

I spent most of my time in England hiding in the loo, simultaneously wanking like mad and praying to English Jesus to forgive me, while outside the stained-glass windows, werewolves and dead druids howled in the wind, almost drowning out the shouts of my parents downstairs by the coal fire. I felt like there were whole armies marching and clanking through my blood, infidels everywhere inside me, and scary Saxon ghosts all over the place.

I developed a chronic stiff neck after about a month. I was convinced it was punishment from English Jesus—not just for wanking, but for wanking to the mental image of Joy Dubois, the prettiest girl at school. The pain was excruciating, but I couldn't stop, and I started to become a little misshapen myself. It would take me half an hour to uncurl myself from the Quasimodo clench I woke up in every morning at five. As I limped down the steep old stairway, I would try not to look at the front door at the bottom of the stairs. It was one of those doors with glass in it. Very old beveled glass, and I was so spooked by the way the cuts in the glass made the darkness outside look even darker that I decided I had to hold my breath for the entire descent, or something awful would come out of the darkness and get me. Every trip down the stairs, every day, I never took a breath.

Dad bought a tweed sports jacket with leather elbow patches and grew a mustache. He became a regular at the pub on the corner, heading over there every day around five. If he was home when we got back from school he would spend some time with us, but most of the time he wasn't. David and I played one-on-one soccer in the backyard, and eventually got good enough to play with the kids at school. We were getting along well and not fighting very much.

We were out back when Dad came home one afternoon from the pub, just as it was getting dark. He came into the yard and watched us silently for a while. He was reeking of beer. David and I kept playing, and I kept a peripheral eye on Dad. He didn't join in (we would have dropped dead from surprise if he had) and it started to feel a little awkward having him just standing there, not saying anything.

"What's your problem?" I said, in my best fake tough-guy voice, hoping to get a laugh. And I sort of did. He said, "No problem," in a way that was one-third sarcastic, one-third menacing, and one-third Please Can I Play With You Guys. He said, "You still think you can escape the Death Grip?" I was dribbling the soccer ball, David covering me, and I tried to keep up my rhythm. I kept my head down, feet moving, my eyes on the ball, and said, "Heh." David stole the ball and shot right by me and scored.

Dad said, "I'll take you both on. C'mon." He waddled over and grabbed me from behind in a full nelson, and I said, "Okay, but I don't want to hurt you—you're getting pretty old, you know," and easily wriggled out of his grasp.

The Death Grip was Dad's name for another wrestling hold he liked to use. He would grab us around the chest with his legs, lock his ankles together, and squeeze. His legs were incredibly strong, and we were never able to escape, although it was sort of fun to try for the first minute or so. But it almost always went beyond that, and a couple of times I felt like I was going to pass out from the pressure around my diaphragm. When Mom was around she'd try to stop him, but that usually earned her an earful of accusations about being uptight, and I almost preferred it when she didn't say anything so I could just wait for it to be over on my own. Anything to avoid having to listen to another fight.

Dad got me around the midsection with his legs, and the breath shot out of my lungs at the familiar first clamp of pressure. I was mad at myself for making a grunting sound, so I tried hard not to squirm like I usually would. I was almost completely still, and I kept up a steady pressure with my elbow against one small spot on his leg. After a minute or two I could sense that it was actually working, just a little. And it was really getting dark now. We were on the grass and David was standing off to the side, holding the soccer ball and watching. There was give in the Death Grip. I was astonished.

I hadn't heard Mom come out of the house, so I was startled when her voice jumped from the dark just a few feet away, saying, "Please, okay, enough." And even more surprised when Dad released his legs and said, "Okay, I am going to spare you. This one time. You have been given a reprieve. But be on guard." All of it in the same trying-to-be-playful voice from before, only with less breath. We all made our way inside for dinner, and nobody said another word until we were at the table. Dinner was tense. Mom was very watchful and tough with Richard and Alison, obviously trying to pre-empt any trouble.

The fights between Mom and Dad were becoming more frequent, quiet, and intense. Dad brought new friends home once in a while but they seemed uncomfortable when they were there. Otherwise he didn't seem to do much of anything, and I think Mom couldn't bear the thought that being in England brought him so little pleasure. It didn't bode well for anyone. And she was at a loss without her friends and her piano. She read to Alison a lot, took long walks, and I often heard her crying in the bathroom. I never got used to that. Not ever. Each time I heard her I stopped in my tracks and stood still, debating whether or not to say something. I think I called out, "Mom, are you okay?" once or twice over the years, but that was all. She said, "I'm fine honey, everything's okay."

So I just went ahead and said it, right there at the dinner table, right to her, with everyone there. It felt foreign, unusual. I was often angry at Mom back then, far more than at Dad. Not for anything in particular. Just because I felt so mad all the time, and I was much too afraid of my father to let myself be mad at him. I said, "Mom, are you okay?" and her face brightened and came into focus. "I am, sweetie.

I'm okay, thank you for asking. Do I not seem okay?" She had her hand on mine. "No, you seem fine. I'm just wondering."

I was changing, a little. I was getting some fleeting sense now of how things weren't right in our family, one that came with a sense of how I was morphing. Whenever I caught my reflection in a mirror I was stunned. Who was this gorilla looking back at me, and where had he put my head? There were sheep roaming around our backyard all the time, and one day when I was out there I crouched down to call one over but when I said, "Here, sheepy," it came out in the voice of Johnny Cash. What the hell? And the sheep didn't even move.

I asked Dad to spend time with us, take us places, and he usually obliged. We visited a local castle and went to London a few times, where he liked to visit the War Museum. A couple of months went by and I realized that Dad still hadn't started writing yet, so I asked him about it during a train ride to London. "Don't be a smart-ass," he said, which for the life of me I couldn't figure out. Then he said he wouldn't be able to do much in the next couple of weeks anyway because Nana was coming to visit, that she was still very sad, still in mourning, deep mourning, which didn't sound very good to me.

She ended up staying for six weeks, which drove Mom right to the edge of her wits. One day very early, just after dawn, I looked out my window and saw Dad and Nana holding hands and walking out into the backyard, parting a group of sheep and stepping over a very old, low stone wall. Dad was holding something metal in his other hand that I later learned from Mom was called an urn. And they sprinkled what was left of Grandpa somewhere out there. I was glad they put him there, in such a beautiful place, and I realized it *was* beautiful, in addition to being scary and haunted. The air was full of moisture and you could see yellow or purple beams of light just floating in front of your face once in a while, or lick fresh water off a stone. The smell of thick grass was a constant, and you never went a day without seeing a horse or a cow or a lamb.

Which was exactly the problem for Mom, I think. She had full-fledged cottage fever by that point, getting frustrated more quickly and staying depressed longer. The house was small and there was only a little bit of a "town" to visit, anyway, and we were all antsy. Richard's troubles didn't stop. Then again, they weren't exactly troubles, either. At school he was already known as "Chatterbox" and one day he challenged a teacher's use of the Bible to explain where the first people on Earth came from, and the headmaster punished him by making him stand on a desk and sing, the way one might punish a gambler by forcing him to, say, gamble. A punishment which, come to think of it, explains not only a lot about where the adult Richard comes from, but where Harold Pinter, Parliamentary sex scandals, The Sex Pistols, Fleet Street, Eddie Izzard, Prince Harry, "Big Brother," the Tate, Martin Amis, the London Eye, mango chutney, and head-butting come from.

Our school experience, though, in contrast to the environmental and familial gloom, was mostly a happy one. We were like visitors from another world, and David and I were popular among our new classmates. But being fish out of water also meant we sometimes felt lost. We were only allowed to bring one record each to England so I brought *Abbey Road* and listened to it every day. Every evening in the shower I sang "Polythene Pam," or "Oh yeah! Alright! Are you gonna be in my dreams, tonight?" And then I'd do Ringo's drum solo with the soap. My performing career had been cruelly stopped in its tracks by our move to England, and I was full of very dramatic impulses and stage-worthy energy that had nowhere to go. So I felt especially lucky when Joy eventually helped me out with that.

I kissed Joy Dubois for the first time in an almond grove in Sussex with three people watching. We had just walked back to our neighborhood from a soccer match against another school. I had managed to get a spot on the team as a goalie, because I was in the middle of the only growth spurt I would ever have and was actually the biggest kid in school. My size and my foreignness combined to also make me the coolest kid in school, which was unbelievably disorienting. I wanted to pull someone aside and say, "Listen, there's been a terrible mistake. You guys are treating me like I'm a killer whale, but I'm plankton. We need to get the food chain back in order or life as we know it might cease to exist." But I didn't do that. I resisted the temptation to let them know who I really was, and I let them go on treating me like somebody else, and pretty soon I started to believe I was who they thought I was: a big, brash, rich kid who probably lived in a big skyscraper on a big ranch in Texas. A rumor started going around that I was distantly related to Elvis Presley, and I did nothing to discourage it. Everything I said sounded like a movie to them. They really loved baseball terminology or anything that sounded like New York–speak. The more I talked about chasing down fly balls or taking the A train, the more the boys wanted to be my friends and the girls wanted to be my girl. The only holdout was Joy Dubois.

Joy wasn't like the other kids. Her father was in the foreign service and her mother was a successful travel writer, and their shambling old house was filled with mysterious objects from everywhere. The Duboises were friends of friends of my parents, and we all had tea at their place once a month. I'd sit in a wing chair and pull at my scratchy sweater and try to think of something smart to say to Mr. Dubois. Joy always came in late, with mud on her riding pants, and she'd plop down on a big, frayed, canary-yellow chair, grab a biscuit, and jump right into the conversation, always managing to get in a graceful dig at one of the adults without getting caught at it. She was living the kind of life I had only seen in the movies, and as far as I could tell she deserved every bit of it. Her dad insisted she attend public school—he was one of those bootstrap rich guys who wouldn't give his kids a penny.

She'd already been to America a couple of times, and Iceland and Peru, and she saw right through me. Yet somehow, some way, she decided that I deserved the first kiss she was ever known to bestow on anyone.

We had just crossed a cow field, and I was winding up a story about standing at the edge of the Grand Canyon—a place I had never been—and as we took our first step out of the sun and into the green light of the orchard, she grabbed my arm, spun me around, and planted a soft kiss on my lips just as I was about to say the word "mesa."

She held the kiss for a beat, and I opened my eyes and saw the blurred image of crossed eyes as seen by crossed eyes for the first time, and then she pulled away, and I got to see the blurred image of a girl who had just kissed me for the first time.

And then she made a little noise. A little "mmm" noise. I wanted to make an "mmm" noise, too, but instead I said the word "mesa."

That's when I got to see the smirk of a girl thinking, "You're pathetic," for the first time. But I didn't care. I knew I was pathetic, and that was fine with me, because I also knew I had been kissed and that it happened in front of witnesses. At school the next day everyone treated me not like a possible distant relative of Elvis, but like Elvis. And I never felt less like Elvis in my life. I felt like a bowl of the warm custard we would eat every day after lunch. Gooey and quivering.

When I came home from the kissing, I burst through the door like a guy in a musical. I started singing, "Joy to the world! I kissed Joy the girl, now . . ." and I spun myself down to the floor, still singing. My parents were stunned and a lot quieter than I thought they'd be. My mom gave me a kind of sweet, crooked smile and said, "Well, sweetie, that's wonderful." And my dad said, "Okay, okay. That's nice. As long as you didn't hurt anyone." And the music stopped. I was suddenly conscious of how tired my face muscles were from smiling.

Hurt anyone? Whom would I hurt? How would I hurt them? What did hurting have to do with kissing, or Joy? My father's voice was careful and compassionate, and I wanted to appreciate it, but I could feel the pudding inside me moving in waves. I didn't say anything. On some level I got that he was somehow talking about himself, and warning me, and feeling some kind of dark regret, but mostly I felt like the faint pencil drawing I had begun to make of myself in the last few days had gotten blown off the page.

I couldn't sleep that night, but I had nightmares anyway. I just lay there in bed watching a movie that my brain projected on the ceiling. I was kissing Joy again, over and over, but each time I did, something terrible happened. The roots of an almond tree would wrap around her legs and pull her under the mud. Or an arrow would cut through my neck and into hers, killing us both. I kept going back to the scene because I wanted the happy memory of it to get me out of the nightmare, but then it would become the nightmare, and I couldn't stop the cycle. But I didn't want to give up, so I stayed awake, trying to kiss her and see her blurry eyes again. All night.

At 4:45 I decided to get out of bed and get the kettle on and maybe have some tea before David got up. I'll let the kiss come back to me at the kitchen table, I thought. I realized as I stood up that there were no druid winds, no shutters or house groans. And that was almost the last lucid moment of that day for me. When I look back on that morning now, I realize that on some level I knew I was headed for a fall, that I even wanted to fall, and so I did. Just as I thought, *It's never been this quiet,* the dark sky outside growled like an enormous empty stomach.

I took a deep breath, and I was comforted by the sound of my lungs working. I took another and it calmed me even more. I kept up the breathing as I put on my robe and made my way down to the kitchen, and I got into a rhythm. Breathe. Quiet. Breathe.

God, even the stairs are quiet, I thought.

Breathe.

Oh God, the stairs.

And at the bottom of them, the window in the door with all that blackness on the other side. I tipped back, away from the window in the door. I wanted to close my eyes to whatever was coming, but they opened wider and looked right into the darkness through the glass, and then a sharp bleach of white light rolled up from the bottom of the window and seemed to fill the house, and I thought, "This is really happening, really," and I heard a sound like old chains clanking, and then a noise, a scream that couldn't possibly be coming from only me but was, stretching my mouth wide, and then, just as suddenly as it came, the light disappeared and I lay splayed on my back on the stairs. I watched my fingers twitching against the cold wood and tried to stop them, like the second hand on my clock. And then a hand closed tight around them and there was flannel in my mouth. My mother was wrapping herself around me and I was pressed against her nightgown and I could feel my toes again and a few seconds later I was able to move my arms. I couldn't speak for ten minutes. When I did, I didn't say much at all. I had no words. I had nothing.

None of us did, back then. No one in the family ever spoke about anything that happened to us, or between us, not until many years later. Once we did, I finally realized that what happened on the stairs that day was a fear attack. Fear of Dad, of what was happening to me, fear of the future. This was when I first wondered, "Am I like him? Will I become my father?" It was a fear so tightly wrapped in a double helix with the hope that I *would* be like him they might as well have been one thing. I started noticing that my mouth was cut like his, especially when I was angry. I was even starting to sound like him.

But I hardly ever let myself think of Dad as a bad guy, because when I did I imagined living without him, and when I imagined living without him I imagined not living at all. History unhappening and me unexisting.

Often throughout my childhood, at night I'd try to imagine unbeing so I could somehow accept it, but I only succeeded in scaring myself even more. When I was younger I would call out for Dad, but now he scared me almost as much as unbeing did, and besides, he hadn't figured out how not to be afraid either, so he wasn't going to be able to help me with that.

By the time I reached the stairs that day, I was filled to the breaking point with fear and I finally broke. Anything would have done it. Even a milkman. Which was in fact all it was. A neighborhood milkman in a cap, the very image of domestic tranquility, a civil servant making his early morning rounds, the beam of his flashlight momentarily hitting our front door window. When he heard my screams, he ran away.

Dad never started his book, and we left England after nine months— three months before we had planned to.

PART TWO

7

We were giants, and we roamed the earth from the cafeteria to the Upper Fields. We had shoulders and braces and pimples. We rolled our eyes and spat through our teeth and sat on walls and affected a world-weary comatosity. We were watched and whispered about and feared. We went to concerts and rode ten-speed bikes and chose our own clothes. Some of us even smoked. We were eighth graders, and we bestrode the known world like colossal doinks.

Soon after we returned to the States my sheen of English coolness, slight to begin with, had been punched to a dull gray finish by my friends, starting with a ramrod to the upper arm from Josh after I took a bite of a hot dog and pronounced it "horrid." Ben called me "Gov'ner" for three weeks after I proclaimed the Rolling Stones' album *Sticky Fingers* to be "fan-bloody-tastic."

But we were junior high kings and queens, determined to take full advantage of our prerogatives before starting at the bottom of another totem pole the following year. Chief among those fringe benefits was the right to make out, and we had parties every weekend devoted to standing in dark corners of backyards, pressing our perfectly still bodies together and stroking the rubber bands of each other's braces with our tongues. I didn't have the faintest idea why. It was like some giant six-year-old picked me up off the floor with one hand, Sharon Klein with the other, pressed our heads together, and made kissing sounds.

When we all paired off at a party, it felt almost exactly like when we separated into volcano-building teams in science class. And I guess we were doing some kind of science. We were engaged in a methodical, year-long study, moving from one partner to the next, testing breath-mint effectiveness, height differential, and susceptibility to Cat Stevens. We might as well have been foraging for mushrooms.

It was also socially acceptable—socially required, really—to talk to girls, openly, in public; a far more treacherous endeavor than kissing them. They squinted at you when you spoke. They didn't even care that you had painstakingly prepared an incontrovertible case for Keith Moon over John Bonham as World's Greatest Drummer. They didn't want to talk about Watergate. They weren't interested in your edict that any heavy metal band that included a keyboard player was by definition *not* a heavy metal band. So what on Earth were you supposed to talk to them about? I felt like someone had changed the rules in the middle of a game I had just been getting the hang of. I'd only recently developed a semblance of an identity that could pass muster with my guy friends, after all, and was just barely keeping that jerry-rigged personality together.

I mean, what the fuck? For years the road to social acceptance runs past comic book stores and ball fields and record shops, and then all of a sudden you hear a voice coming from far, far off the path, a female voice, way out in the woods somewhere, saying, "Hey, you, bozo, we're over here, waiting for you," and you inexplicably find yourself following that voice through a forest where nothing is familiar and from which you might not ever return. And of course it's the most fun you've ever had for exactly the same reasons.

We were pretty cocky—the boys, I mean—but the girls were indisputably in charge. It was like they were sent by the future to teach us what we would need to know there. We were aware that we'd have this one, and only one, year with them, during which they would introduce us to the concept of human interaction without props, and then they would be gone, abandoning us forever for guys with learners' permits and deodorant. So we wanted to make the most of it.

It wasn't as though anyone was going to fall in love, or go on an actual date with whomever a spinning bottle pointed at, and certainly no one was going to have sex. But we were rehearsing rituals, learning how to woo and be wooed, how to break up and be broken up with. There wasn't much in the way of what happened with Joy in England, not much sudden spontaneity, no surprises in orchards yet.

Things mattered, though, in a way they hadn't before. Everybody seemed very serious about everything, and the day's dramas didn't disappear into thin air the way they used to. Our parents were "concerned" all the time. The girls "had talks" with us, talks they then talked about in talks with other people, and you felt like it was all being written down somewhere, or recorded on tape like in the White House, and that it would be read aloud at congressional hearings. Everything had weight to it.

So I figured I should start making plans for college, what with high school graduation being less than five years away, and at breakfast one morning I asked Mom and Dad where they thought I should go. In his slow, rich Professor's voice, Dad said that Brooklyn College, "believe it or not," was now in a league with Harvard and Yale, and Mom put the palms of her hands against the edge of the table and calmly said, "I think that's a bit of a stretch, don't you?"

Dad straightened his neck. I could have sworn there were tiny insects in his eyes.

"Brooklyn College was just rated number two in the *country* for . . ." He started dropping his words on the table like weights on a scale. The bugs in his eyes got buggier, Mom's eyes went cloudy, and we all let him go on for a while.

"Mom, I've actually heard that, too," I said. "It's a very well-respected place now."

"*Now?* It was back then, when we went there," said Dad.

"That's true, that's true," I corrected myself, and nodded. I made a mental note to look up as much as I could about Brooklyn College and find out if Dad was right.

Mom said wearily, "Well, that sounds wonderful—we should look into that."

The doorbell rang and I went to answer it. I opened the door to a girl about my age, with copper brown hair and big green eyes, wearing a gauzy white shirt and a leather string around her neck. She was holding a guitar, but she didn't say, "Hello, young lad, I've come to sing you a tale of woe." She said, "Hi, Susan," to my mother, who had silently snuck up behind me.

"Thank you so much for letting me borrow your guitar. It's really great."

She looked at me.

"Oh, you're welcome, sweetie. I hope it wasn't too out of tune. Gosh, I haven't played it in years."

They were talking over my shoulder, but the girl kept shooting looks at me.

"No, my teacher said it was surprisingly in tune. She really liked it. She said Martins are the best guitars."

"They're wonderful. I love this one. I've had it since I was a girl."

A horn honked. The car in the driveway. Must be the mom. Same color hair.

"Me, too. Okay, thank you again, Susan. I have to go. 'Bye!!"

"'Bye, sweetie."

Mom closed the door and carried the guitar back into the kitchen. *Sweetie?*

Mom said to Dad, "That was Nelle, returning the guitar. I'm going to head upstairs and get ready. Will you be showering?"

Nelle. Nelle. I'd heard that name recently, a couple of times.

Dad was pouring hot water from a kettle into my cup. We all drank tea and ate scones now, because we were Gov'ners. "No, I'm fine, you go ahead," he said.

Nelle.

Mom said, "Peter, sit down and drink your tea."

Oh, wait. Nelle. Nelle Lyon. Her dad is Lee and her mom is Nancy.

Lee had come over to our house the day before, just dropped by like a character in a soap opera. He'd pulled his brown Mercedes into the driveway and didn't exactly park so much as just stop driving, leaving the car at an angle facing the lawn. He came through the front door without knocking, walked right into the kitchen, opened the fridge, and stood there looking at it, something David and I were always getting in trouble for. I loved it. I had seen people do that at my friends' houses, come in and open cabinets and fridge doors and make themselves at home, because everyone was just one big family, and I had badly wanted us to have friends like that. And now I guess we did.

Lee was the first person other than Dad's childhood friend Alfred—a surly, white-haired, mutton-chopped, motorcycle-riding German who visited twice a year with his silent commandant of a wife, Elsie— whom I ever saw take an active interest in my father's gun collection. There was a cigar in Dad's mouth and chunks of Enfield or Martini all over the kitchen table the Saturday Lee came over, and a gun stock without the barrel attached in Dad's hands. He was "aiming" it at the front door from his chair, to test the site placement, and looked like a guy threatening someone with the bladeless hilt of a knife. Lee came bursting through the front door and our insane little dog, Bonnie, came running from the other room, where she had been barking loudly at an air-conditioning duct. Lee rasped at Dad, "Hey, don't shoot the messenger," and strode the length of the foyer in three steps. Bonnie stopped in her crazy tracks and watched him warily. He spoke quickly. "We can't make it later. Nancy says she is not feeling well. Doesn't want to take the chance." When he saw the gun parts on the kitchen table he didn't flinch the way other people did, but instead wrapped a cloth around his hand, picked up the oily magazine, and examined it while Dad gave him a comprehensive rundown on the piece's history.

Lee stood looming over Dad, making wisecracks in a sort of

smart, New York-version-of-Burt-Reynolds, out-of-the-corner-of-his-mustachioed-mouth kind of way, and Dad laughed through his cigar. Once Lee entered a room everything stopped and went his way, but he and Dad seemed to be striking up a hugely improbable friendship despite that, and despite all the strikes against Lee: white loafers, season tickets to the Jets, country-club membership, and booming career in advertising.

After a while Lee asked me what was going on, and I mumbled, "Nothing," but he said, "No, really," and I stammered something about my Little League football team, how practice wasn't going all that well, and he asked more questions, almost like a kid who wanted to be my friend. Pretty soon he was showing me how to improve my three-point stance by keeping my back flat, which felt kind of weird in the kitchen with Dad there cleaning his guns and smoking, so we ended up throwing a football around out front while Lee told stories about meeting Muhammad Ali at a "hot new restaurant" in the city, and seeing Joe Namath driving around in a white Rolls-Royce.

"What's he like?"

"Who, Ali?"

"Yeah. I mean, I just think he's amazing for not going into the army and everything. He's a hero, for real."

"He's a great boxer, for sure, but don't be naïve," Lee said as he wound up to throw me the ball. "Muhammad Ali is a mean. Mother. Fucker." *Boom.* He zipped a bullet right into my chest.

He said, "What position are you playing again?" Again?

And I said, "Guard, left guard."

Lee said, "You've got a gun for an arm, perfect spiral—why don't you tell them you want to be the QB?"

Right. I didn't even try to hide my incredulity. But I could see from the look on his face that he was serious, and also that I was about to drop his throw, which I did. "Hands to chest, hands to chest," he said. "Don't catch it with your body, catch it with your hands, and bring it into the chest." Then more work on the three-point stance.

"Explode off the line. Keep the back flat and stay low. You'll get much more leverage. Explode off the line. There you go."

Huh. Nelle.

"Drink. Your tea," said Dad, and I did, too quickly, because I was glancing back at the door. Maybe I had even started to get back up and walk towards it instead of blowing into my cup, and of course the tea was *hot. Zyaa!* And it burned my tongue.

"Jesus fuck!" I kept my fingers on the cup but dropped it to the table and the hot tea sloshed over my hand.

"Zyaaow! Fuck!"

"Watch it, mister."

"It burned my hand!"

"Fine. You don't need to make a big production out of it," Dad said.

"I'm not making a big production. I'm saying, 'Ow' because my goddamn tongue and hand are burned up."

Dad glared at me. "You're getting pretty full of yourself, aren't you," he said, and David, who I didn't even know had come into the room, said, "Now who's a klutz?"

I said, "David, I'll rip your fucking head off, I swear to God."

"All right, take it outside, you two," Dad groused, and, looking at me, David said, "Unless you're too busy crying, you mean?" and we were off at full speed.

I chased him through the den and out the back door to the yard where, even running at top speed and consumed by rage, I almost gagged from the smell of dog crap. Bonnie had hidden a thousand little terrier shit mines all over the yard that no one had ever cleaned up, so instead of the usual leg tackle I grabbed David by the shoulders in hopes of keeping us both upright and shit-free. I turned him around, pushed him up against the fence, and just as I cocked my fist to hit him in the arm, a yellow loogie blinded me in one eye.

I put my hands to my face, and all the breath I had left my lungs. I puked a little as I fell to my knees. David had kicked me in the balls, and I was writhing on the ground. I wiped the spit out of my eye and looked up to see Dad grabbing David by his upper arms, saying, "You wanna fight dirty? Huh? You wanna fight dirty? How's this?" He brought a fist up hard under David's ribs. David retched, fell to his knees to my left, and looked up at me through swimming eyes. He pounded the ground with his fist, trying desperately to get some air, and little clouds of Bonnie's dusty, white caca puffed up from the dirt. Neither of us could breathe, which, given the feces surrounding us, was a mixed curse, but we didn't need air to communicate our agreement that we were just not learning quickly enough. David got his breath back first, stumbled up, and unsteadily quick-walked, hunched over with his hand on his stomach, back inside. Dad paused, then followed slowly while I stayed on the ground until I could breathe again.

About a half hour later, after licking English muffin crumbs off my plate and putting it in the sink, I went upstairs. I heard voices, or one, anyway, and as I got to my door I saw Dad leaving David's room, where I guess he'd just apologized, and I finally got the rest of my breath back. I stood in the middle of my room for about a minute, then sat down on my bed and opened my notebook. It was only then that I noticed Bonnie curled up on a pillow, pressed against the wall. She was chewing furiously on her right leg, where she'd already removed about half an inch of her thick, white hair. I put my hand on her back to help calm her down and spoke softly to her, but she couldn't seem to stop. When I picked my hand up I saw another small patch of exposed, bloody skin next to her tail.

Later we all went over to the high school auditorium to watch a performance of a children's show Mom had written for the local community theater, a musical version of *Rumpelstiltskin* that Dad had produced and that Richard, as far as we were concerned, was starring in as The Page Boy. Nobody mentioned what happened earlier, of course.

It seemed like the second we got back from England Mom had taken a seat at the piano and hadn't gotten up since. I heard her playing something unfamiliar, playing it haltingly, little bit by little bit, and when I asked her what it was she said she was writing something, a show for kids. She ended up writing two of them in just a few months. They were very good, way better than the Disney versions of the same stories, I thought. The scary parts were scarier, I told her, and the funny parts were "weird in a good way," by which I think I meant ironic.

Rumpelstiltskin was played by Barbara Kind, wearing a beard, curly shoes, and a pointy felt hat. She looked a bit like David and I had when we'd played Sleepy and Grumpy in a school production of *Snow White* six years before, establishing permanent family typecasting pigeonholes for ourselves. I thought Barbara was flat-out brilliant. When she threw the big tantrum at the end of the show, the one where Rumplestiltskin stamps his feet so hard he smashes right through the floor, she sounded like Robert Plant singing "Black Dog," and she had real tears in her eyes. All of that was a bit much for Alison, though, who was so shaken by the experience that Mom had to take her by the hand over to the Kinds' to prove that Barbara wasn't actually an angry, dead pixie man.

Over the next few weeks the show crept into our daily lives. As he passed me on the stairs, David would intone, "If, by tomorrow morning early you have not spun this straw into gold, you must die." Even Alison, after a few weeks, was answering my "Hey, what's going on?" with a flip of her hair and, "Alas, I have to spin straw into gold, and I don't know how to do it." She'd come into my room cradling her threadbare, stuffed, orange gorilla saying, "I will give you all the riches of the kingdom if you leave me my child." And I'd stick my elbows out like Barbara Kind and cackle, "No, something alive is dearer to me than all the treasures in the world. I will give you three days, and if by that time you can tell me my name, you may keep your child."

For years, Mom had been not just been reading these stories to us, but performing them, quoting them, comparing different versions. (Rumplestiltskin literally tears himself in two in a German take, but merely cracks a floorboard before flying away on a giant spoon in a drug-drenched, Dutch version.) By the time she'd written her show, she'd braided the stories into our lives, and our lives into the stories. I still can't imagine the miller's daughter at the spinning wheel in anything other than the shape of my mother at the piano. As I sat in the auditorium, watching Rumplestiltskin proffer his bargain—"If you can tell me my name, you can keep your child"—I felt an exhilarating fear, knowing without knowing at all that if Mom could point a finger at some deformed little thing and put a name to it, say, "This is real, this is happening, has been happening; there it is right over there and it's called . . ." that yes, there would be terrible, fearful tantrums but also maybe a quieter future for all of us. I think I even had an inkling, despite being thirteen, or maybe because of it, of how tempting it can be to believe that creativity is a reward for keeping secrets from yourself, that magic trolls will help you as long as you don't name them, never mind that they're denying you things worth more than precious metal.

So there was a palpable, subtle buzz in us kids at the emergence of one of Mom's stories into a small part of the outside world, and seeing the show performed in front of everyone we knew made the high school auditorium feel like our living room on an imaginary, perfect day; like we'd invited the whole town over to hear Mom tell a story. I was relieved that she managed to show people something of herself without being swallowed up by a big hole in the ground, and afterwards we all felt better than we used to. And Mom seemed like the actors on Cape Cod when they stamped out their cigarettes and stepped into the theater tent, transformed and radiant. A couple of times when I came home from school she even looked flushed.

* * *

Josh and I were playing air hockey at the synagogue community center one night, because what did our ancestors suffer and die for if not the right to utter the words "air hockey" and "synagogue" in the same sentence, when Nelle Lyon with her copper brown hair and green eyes came up to the table, looked right at me, smiled a little, and said, "I've got winners," which was more than enough for me to take my eye off the puck, give up an uncontested goal, and make her smile even more.

"I know you," she said. "You're Susan's son. I'm Nelle Lyon."

A whole bunch of words filled my head, but none of them made it to my mouth.

She said, "Hello? Right? You're Susan's son?"

"What? Um, yeah."

"Okay. Well, I've got winners, okay?"

"Yeah."

"Okay."

Josh shot me a look. I pretended I didn't catch it. I looked down at the board and waited for him to hit the puck, which he refused to do until I looked up and acknowledged his infantile eyebrow raising.

"What?"

"Nothing."

Wham. Puck in goal, uncontested.

A couple of weeks later Nelle and I were in the swimming pool at the YMCA just after the last of our friends had left. We must have been there for a couple of hours—I was so pruny from the water I was dry—and I had my hand on the aluminum ladder, ready to pull myself out, when like a bolt Nelle popped up from the deep, laughing and blind from the hair in her eyes. I laughed at her laughing and we treaded water inches apart. There were only a few people in the pool and our voices bounced off the tiled walls right back at us, making us laugh even more. The light was ricocheting off the walls, too, and off the pale blue water and Nelle's eyes and hair. We sounded like we had suddenly become amazingly stupid. Nelle was getting water in her mouth and spitting it out, pulling curtains of wet hair from her eyes, and then suddenly she was gone, dropping straight down like someone had yanked on her feet.

I followed her immediately, pushing my hands palms up and out to the side, sinking straight to where she was floating in an invisible hammock. We hung there, arms out, legs bent, everything in gentle motion, spinning slowly in a robin's egg, the outside world pushed to the brink of silence. An oblong air bubble shot out of my nose. She opened her mouth to laugh and birthed a perfectly round, big sphere of air that hesitated before heading upwards. We followed it and popped back up into the noise, laughing like crazy, coughing out chlorine, and blinking the sting from our eyes.

We got quiet. We spun our arms and Nelle swiped at her hair. And then she zipped back down and I chased her again and we met at our spot, and this time I reached out and put my hand on her arm. Just put the fingers of one hand flat on her upper arm. Totally surprised myself. I didn't move the fingers at all. She didn't move either. There were no bubbles around us.

The next time down she touched my arm and left her hand there, even when she lost her balance and we tilted, floating and tethered to each other, turning slowly. I felt like every cell in my body had moved right to the edge of my skin. When we needed to breathe we popped back up and gulped some air before heading back down. If one of us had touched the other one with our heads above water it would have been scandalous. No one up there knew that we were leading a secret, underwater life. But then we zipped back under and hung there some more. And then we did it again, and again. I don't think we ever said a word.

We didn't even talk about it afterwards. What would we have said? "Hey—great touching you on the arm the other day. We should do that again!" But a couple of days later I was at Nelle's house getting some football tips from Lee out in the backyard, and when we were done and he was getting his car to drive me home, Nelle came out the back door with a couple cans of Fresca. She looked at me strangely and I wondered if she'd heard something about me, about my sleep-walking maybe, or Dad's guns. Maybe she was wondering if I would ever string six consecutive words together in her presence. Maybe she was noticing the snow-capped mountain range of pimples that had sprung up from ear to chin on the right side of my face. Maybe she was mentally comparing my jawline to a topographical map of Chile and wondering if it would be rude to run screaming from me. But she handed me a soda and said, "My mom said to ask you if you want to stay for dinner," and I said something like, "I can't . . . I always . . . It's weird. I think, yes. That would be great."

She let out a little breath, and two pink waves moved from under her ears to her cheeks. I was just telling her a fact, but after I said it I felt like I was floating. Nelle looked at me with eyes so clear they startled me. I realized I might have been a little off on the sleepwalking/pimple/gun worries. I reached out and took her hand, right there in the backyard, out in the open, standing on terra firma. And we went right back to not talking.

My favorite thing about the Lyon house was the quiet. I was a connoisseur of quiet, and at the Lyons' I could hunt for the deep kind, prowl for the hidden spaces and neglected corners that felt like cool spots in a summer pond. I found a new favorite place every week—a narrow back stairway that led from the big kitchen to the third-floor "maid's room"; a flattened foam pillow on a window seat in the half-renovated attic; a jungle of spiderwebs, coffee cans, and moss in the old ramshackle garage; the backseat of Lee's Mercedes. There was a trove of places to hole up in or disappear to, and you didn't even have to be alone to get some silence. A place as big as the Lyons' didn't make them immune from the universal human impulse to collect together in one small room, though—in their case a tiny den at the back of the house—and Nelle and I spent a lot of time sitting quietly with Lee and Nancy in the six-sided, book-lined little hive. There, the three of them seemed like one person to me. I felt like I was dating a family.

On the weekends Lee and I would work on pass blocking or run blocking, and soon I was playing a lot better on game day. Lee even showed up at practice a couple of times, barking out, "Hands in!" or "Stay low!" and pretty soon he was one of the official coaches on the team. I was almost too inspired, and started racking up penalties for jumping offsides before the snap of the ball. In a game near the end of the season I did it three times in a row, moving the team another fifteen yards backwards with each flag. As I joined the huddle after the third one, my coach apparently yelled, "Birkenhead, out!" but I must not have heard him over the noise. My teammates were all staring at me. I turned my head around a couple of times, looked at Larry Grolnick, our quarterback, and said, "What?" and he bellowed like only a thirteen-year-old kid can bellow, *"Birkenhead, out!"* loudly enough to quiet everyone in the bleachers.

I trotted off the field, barely resisting the temptation to run full speed to the nearest bus depot, and heard my coach say, "Idiot," as I got to the bench. I walked slowly with my hands on my hips, around the bleachers to an empty patch of grass where no one could see me, and took off my helmet. I took a deep breath and held it tight, then felt a gentle slap on my shoulder pads. My dad looked at me with a rueful smile, and real affection in his eyes. He said, "You okay, hon?" I had no idea he was even at the game. I narrowed my eyes and tried to say, "Yeah," but it caught in my throat. "It's just a game," he said. "It's just a game. You'll do better next time. It's okay." And I cried. Coach Russo turned around at the sidelines and glared at me while Dad and I walked back and forth behind the bleachers a couple of times. Dad made a joke about the orange bell-bottoms one of the other dads was wearing, and Lee looked over from the sidelines and gave me a thumbs-up and a wink. When the gun went off to end the first half I rejoined the team feeling pretty embarrassed, but no one gave me a hard time or seemed mad at me, and I was penalty free for the rest of the game.

By the end of the fall I was spending almost every weekend at the Lyons'. If our parents were worried about Nelle and me having sex they kept it to themselves, and in any case we never did. We spent a lot of time lying on couches and floors and beds together, though, slowed with wonder, new to everything and sidling up to passion with glassy-eyed trepidation. I was woozy at the almost invisible hairs on her wrist, and the tiny beads of sweat shaking on her belly when she laughed her strong, easy laugh. Eventually we'd fall into a quiet half-sleep and lie there breathing together, until the record needle hit the scratches at the end of an album side and jolted us back to reality. Damn you, vinyl.

Nelle's dog, Ginger, would spring from her napping spot in the corner when I got up for the stereo, and we'd chase each other down the stairs and outside, where we'd hunt through the sloping lawn for grasshoppers. Ginger was the only even-tempered poodle I've ever met, and her curls had a pinkish hue to them, all of which made it impossible for me to not laugh when she bared her drooling teeth and roared at the sight of one of the green bugs, earning me a sputtering, head-turning look of indignation from the proud huntress. I would have to stroke and soothe and apologize for half an hour after one of our safaris before she'd have anything to do with me again.

Later, Lee and I might throw a ball around or shoot hoops for an hour out back before he went off to wherever he was always off to, and then Nancy, Nelle, and I might head over to the indoor pool at the YMCA if it was fall, or the skating rink in Port Washington in winter, or, that next summer, Jones Beach. On weekdays, Nelle and I would head from school to my house, which was just a couple of blocks away, and camp out in my room until just before dinner, at which time I would begin lobbying my parents for permission to eat at the Lyons'.

This was a schedule that, not incidentally, included very little time with my dad, who nonetheless seemed determined to make the most of our few minutes together each day. He had recently been inspired to begin a rigorous exercise program, lifting weights and punching the heavy bag in the basement, and every morning he would do naked sit-ups and ask me to hold his legs down. He'd do them on the carpeted landing at the top of the stairs, right after taking his morning shit and smoking his morning cigar, so for me the experience was like a mega reverse aromatherapy treatment.

And it definitely contributed to my growing up quickly. It's hard to think of yourself as anything but mortal when you're looking at what I had to look at every morning at seven fifteen, and for that I'm actually a little grateful. I'd try to get through my morning Oxy 10 application and hot-combing as quickly as I could, but it was basically impossible for me to get out the front door without hearing the dreaded words: "Can you hold my legs down, hon?" and I'd have to spend the next ten minutes trying and failing to avoid the wrinkled, purple source of my existence. If you're raising a son, and you want to make sure he grows up to be unfailingly polite, nauseous, and often a jerk, I highly recommend a daily dose of naked Daddy sit-ups.

You also might want to consider the use of public humiliation.

I was sitting on the couch in our shag-carpeted little den with some friends on a typical Saturday night. We were watching "The Bob Newhart Show," eating untoasted Pop-Tarts and telling lies about girls. When we finally shut up long enough to hear one of the lovable nut jobs on the show make a joke at poor, put-upon Bob's expense, we fell into one of those big uncontrollable group laughter spasms, spilling frosted crumbs all over ourselves. And I'm here to tell you, as uncontrollable as those laughter spasms can feel, I now know better. I now know that they can be stopped dead, right in their tracks, by at least one thing. At some point I suddenly realized that I was the only one still laughing, and that the silence in the room wasn't just the absence of laughter, but the presence of something else. Something big. Something tumescent.

My oblivious father was crossing the kitchen, right in our field of vision, just above the television screen in the den, and he wasn't merely naked, he was postcoitally naked. Flying at half-staff naked. Not yet toweled-off naked.

He walked slowly to the refrigerator; he opened it; he took out a can of his favorite "no-cal" diet cola; he opened it; he took a long, loud series of *glug-glugs* from it; he sighed a big fat noisy sigh; and he squinted. Then he let out a squeaky, Dizzy Gillespie trumpet blast of no-cal carbonated fart wind, and he closed the refrigerator door. And against all hopes, his naked and now steaming member was still there, finally shrinking in the refrigerator cold.

I was almost as stunned by that vision as I was frozen with dread at what the next several hundred lunch hours would be like for me.

I could at least be thankful, though, that the only thing he was looking to kill that night was a can of soda. Dad's specialty was being violent and nude at the same time, and just a few days after his performance for my friends, I heard him on the phone with one of his, and he was growling in the way he would only when he was really mad and really naked. As best as I could make out, this friend had, according to Dad, insulted my mother in some way, and Dad was deeply enraged. I was upstairs in my room staring at my clock with only one thought in my head: "Please don't let him be naked." I was asking for so little. But when I heard the screen door slam open, I looked out the window and there was my dad, antique sword on his shoulder, cigar in his mouth, johnson in the breeze, striding purposefully out the door to our quiet, tree-lined street. And then Mom, grabbing him hard by the arm and bringing him back inside.

There was actually an eventual upside to these sorts of incidents. They acted as a kind of *Clockwork Orange*–type aversion therapy thing for me when it came to alcohol, tobacco, and firearms. I can tell you, for instance, that there are few things in life that disgust me more than cigars; for me, the smell of a cigar will always be the smell of existential panic in the morning. But whenever someone lights one up in my presence, I slow my heart rate down and stay calm, I quietly leave the room, and I try to keep in mind what Freud left pointedly unsaid: sometimes a cigar is just your father's penis.

The next day was tense, but better than I expected. I thought I'd probably hear Mom crying in the bathroom again but I didn't. Dad seemed to have simmered down and everyone got out of the house without any of the usual morning screaming matches about bathroom time or breakfast. Mom spent the rest of the day at the piano, working on her next two children's musicals—new versions of *Cinderella* and *Beauty and the Beast*. The music had a calming effect on everyone, and as I went in and out through the front door all afternoon a few of the lyrics caught my ear and made me laugh.

But as I was dragging my bike across the front lawn at the end of the day, I passed the living room window and heard the music stop. I looked up to see Mom with her hands on her thighs and her eyes closed, tears streaming down her cheeks. I ducked down under the windowsill where she couldn't see me, and sat there on the lawn for a couple of minutes. Then I got back on my bike, rode over to the Lyons' house, and invited myself in for dinner.

8

I was in the shower, washing my hair one strand at a time and practicing speaking in a lower voice, reciting my favorite words of wisdom in a pathetic approximation of the deep, southern drawl of Tug
McGraw, the relief pitcher for the Mets who had led their surprising
charge for the pennant in 1973 and turned the phrase "You Gotta
Believe!" into our beleaguered tri-state area's unofficial slogan. I was
preparing to attend my first ever World Series game that night, and
had convinced myself that if the baseball gods somehow deemed me
unworthy by dint of dirty hair or dainty voice, for instance, the Mets
would lose and I would have blue and orange blood on my hands for
the rest of my life.

Dad came into the bathroom without knocking and said, "Peter,
that's enough, let's go. Enough with the racket." I stopped in mid-
McGraw and turned off the shower. Dad left the bathroom door open
and I leaned out of the tub with the curtain around me to close it, but
I paused when I heard Mom speaking in a soft but animated voice
about the Lyons. I heard the names Lee and Nancy and Nelle, and
something about—I don't know, I couldn't really tell.

Dad was speaking in an even softer voice than Mom was, but he
was agitated, upset. I kept the door open a crack as I dried off, but still
couldn't make out what they were saying. When I was ready to go it
was Mom who walked with me out to the car, and Dad was nowhere
to be found. Mom seemed distracted during the short drive to Nelle's,

and barely remembered to say good-bye when she dropped me off. I stopped on the front doorstep and watched her turn the car slowly around in the Lyons' big, wide driveway, feeling a tightness in my stomach, and I waved to the car as she drove off. She didn't wave back.

That wasn't entirely surprising. If she had looked in the rearview mirror and seen me waving she might have had a heart attack. As a high school freshman I was now avoiding behavior that might suggest I had parents of any kind. I probably hadn't said hello or good-bye to my mother in months. I was surprised that I felt even more confident, albeit in a desperately insecure sort of way, than I had the year before, but I did, and it was all because of Nelle. And Lee. Nothing at school bothered me very much. What was the occasional "Brokenhead" or "Birkencock" or "Givemehead" when I could spend all my post–three o'clock time with a gorgeous, funny girlfriend and super-cool surrogate dad, who had pumped up my confidence to the point where I was actually playing quarterback for my football team?

I'd been sitting in the den watching the third game of the Series when Lee surprised us with the tickets. Mom called out from upstairs that he was in the driveway, and I was out the door before he beeped the horn to let me know he and Nelle were there. I let out a giant "Yes!" the minute I saw them through the Mercedes' front window—two gleaming white tickets with big blue and orange letters on them spelling out the words WORLD SERIES. Lee was holding them up high in his hand, looking in the rearview mirror at Nelle and saying something. I just about flew into the car and probably didn't stop talking until we got to their place.

I spent the next couple of days shamelessly bragging about the tickets. Josh pogo-ed up and down in front of his locker while Ben said that if I kept score on an official scorecard, sealed it in plastic, and kept it in a drawer, I could probably sell it for three hundred dollars in twenty years. Cal—Calvin Ring, a new friend—said that if I kept score during the game I would be the biggest idiot who ever lived, since being alone with Nelle for three to five hours at Shea Stadium amounted to a once-in-a-lifetime combo sports viewing/make out opportunity, and then placed a perfectly rolled, long, white joint in my hand. I'd never actually touched one before. Or seen one, for that matter. I got a little dizzy just from looking at it and smelling it and knowing it was real.

Calvin Ring had won my admiration on the third day of school by setting off a homemade smoke bomb in the parking lot that yielded a multi-colored mushroom cloud the size of a Dodge Dart. Within days I'd gotten him to divulge his pyrotechnic secrets, and when I leaned over a coffee can full of freshly packed gunpowder and coloring agents in his backyard to drop a match into it—you know, to get a better look at the fireball heading my way—I set my hair on fire. When Cal finally removed the beach towel he'd wrapped around my sizzling head to douse the flames, half my face looked like Wile E. Coyote's after an Acme package explosion: jet black, a little squiggly line of smoke rising from the top, and half my hair singed to an almost respectable length. The other half retained the enormous, spheroid curliness I had been cultivating for months, and I realized right away that the hardest thing to hide from my parents was going to be the stubborn odor of crispy-fried Jewfro I was emitting. Even the third of a bottle of his mom's perfume that Cal doused me with couldn't mask the acrid smell, so it really was a miracle of motherly tact when, after I jumped into Mom's car and stared straight ahead, so as not to reveal my new, way-ahead-of-its-time asymmetrical hairstyle, she waited at least a minute or two before discreetly sniffing the air and asking, "Honey, are you wearing cologne?"

Game Five of the 1973 World Series was a classic. The Mets won a squeaker, the As' Joe Rudi made a spectacular diving catch in left field, and Tug McGraw himself saved the game with a thrilling strike out, pounding his mitt against his leg as he bounded off the mound shouting, "You Gotta Believe!" Nelle and I tried to make out a little, but people kept knocking our elbows off the armrests and spilling drinks on our feet, and a guy right behind me snored through the entire game, so we didn't do much after the first inning. And I forgot to bring the joint. I probably didn't want to bring it, I guess. I probably wanted to smoke my first joint alone, preferably in a controlled hospital setting, with several wires attached to me that kept track of everything happening to my lungs and my brain, and with my mother sitting next to me holding my hand.

But hey—the Mets had barely won more games than they lost that year, and really had no business being in the World Series, yet there they were, leading the series now, one game away from the World Championship, and there we were taking it all in on a beautiful fall night in New York, with leaves swirling all around Queens Boulevard. As I walked with my autumn-haired girl to the train with all the other Believers, I felt a little like a champion myself.

Nelle looked happy, but distracted. She hadn't sung "Take Me Out to the Ball Game" during the seventh-inning stretch the way she had a couple of weeks before when Lee got us tickets to a Yankees game, and she'd only eaten a few bites of her hot dog. I decided to chalk it up to nervousness about the crowd, which was pretty damn loud and nerve-racking even for a couple of no-curfew sophisticates like us.

I put my arm around her and asked if she wanted to come with me the next day to hang out at Josh's place. She was a big fan of his, and vice versa. Just the week before we'd been sitting with him in the middle of the baseball field at school, Nelle pulling grass up by the roots, and when Josh said, "I wish I wasn't short," Nelle sprinkled his hair with a handful of it and admonished him, "Don't you say that— you're not short. You're shortish. This school is full of Elephant People," instantly winning Josh's everlasting, hyperkinetic love. But she said no, she couldn't make it and that I should go without her. I didn't ask her why.

* * *

Dad had gotten into the habit of turning the vacuum cleaner on as soon as he got up at six a.m. every day, and barging into our rooms with it revving at full speed. The first thing I heard most mornings was the Hoover blaring back and forth across the floor, mere inches from my formerly sleeping head. It was like waking up on a runway at JFK. I'd open my eyes to see Dad's bikini-clad crotch, then look up to see him grimacing like he was looking at fresh dog shit, slinging his arm forward and back, muttering about how David or Richard or I should have done this the night before, or earlier that morning, or while we were sleeping. Once every two weeks or so I'd get up the courage to complain, and he'd shark-eye me back into silent seething, then ask me to hold his legs down for his sit-ups.

One morning I opened my eyes and ears to an empty, quiet room for the first time in weeks, and was so startled by the change in routine I couldn't even take advantage of it and go back to sleep. I tried, but every time I closed my eyes I remembered the knifelike jolt from the night before, when out of a dead, sleeping silence Dad's voice filled the house with, "Stop torturing me!!"

The dead silence became a live one. I could feel everyone wake up and freeze. This was new. We'd heard the sadness in Dad before, and the anger, but never the agony. He'd never pulled the cover off like that. And as frightening and disturbing as it was, it cleared the air like a wind. I almost didn't care what had caused it. Somewhere way down in the basement of Dad a rusty gear had turned with a screech. I felt a fleeting pang of sympathy, like I wanted to run downstairs and hold him as tight as I could and rock him to sleep, and then, quickly, the opposite, like I wanted to fly to Pluto and never see him again. It was the word "torture" that did it, I think. I felt a deep repulsion, a sickening pity in my gut, for days afterwards.

I was just barely able to make out Mom's tightly wound, clipped words in response to Dad's plea. She went on for a while and then some, without Dad making a sound, and I don't think I'd ever heard that before, either. I desperately wanted to know what they were talking about, what had made Dad feel that he was being tortured, but there wasn't another audible word from either of them and the tremors from the outburst slowly faded.

Now I'd awakened to vacuum-free, morning silence. I got up and went downstairs to find no one in the kitchen. Through the ceiling I heard Alison and Richard jumping out of bed and kicking toys across the floor, David walking to the bathroom. Then I heard Mom's voice coming from outside somewhere, sounding strange, almost amplified. I opened the front door and took a step back from the cold blast of air that greeted me, and when I stepped towards the doorway again I realized Mom's voice was coming from the open garage, echoing into the street and back into the house.

Dad answered whatever she had said, sharply. Looking out at the empty, dawn-lit street, yet hearing him as if he was right next to me in the hallway, I had the odd sensation that I was watching a movie with a voice-over narration. At the far end of our street a paper boy teetered on his bike as Dad said, "I'll find you. I will find you wherever you go, and you know that. I will find you." With a sudden, bracing clarity I was transported back to a moment years before in Brooklyn, in the middle of the night, when I heard him say the same kind of thing. I had been in bare feet and a diaper, standing completely still in the doorway to my parents' bedroom, sucking hard on my thumb, sending my tongue back and forth against my knuckle, nail, and cuticle, my other hand bending my left ear over and into itself.

Back then Dad said, "I will kill you. If you take my children away from me I will find you and I will kill you. There's nowhere for you to hide. No way for you to support yourself and the kids. And wherever you go, *wherever* you go, I will hunt you down."

Now I was standing in our front doorway in my underwear, my skin bumping up from the late October chill, listening again to my invisible father whispering threats into my mother's ear. I bounded up the stairs two at a time to my room, threw on a pair of jeans and a sweater, ran back downstairs and out the door, slamming it to let them know I'd heard them.

When I got to school Nelle and Cal were just emerging from their bus. "Nice sweater," Nelle said, with a scrunched-up nose. "Does it come in right-side out?"

Oh, crap. I looked down at my arm and saw big fat seams.

As we started walking together I said, "Yeah, but that's what everybody wears. I'm not some sheep, you know."

"You look like you slept in your clothes, man," said Calvin.

I artfully changed the subject. "Hey, did you tell Cal about that guy at the game? There was this guy at Shea who actually slept, like, the whole time, right behind us. Even when everybody was yelling and screaming at the end, he was out like a light."

"It was a great game, huh?" he said.

"Uh, yeah, you could say that. It was unbelievably great. Seriously, like the best game I've ever seen in my entire life. I can't believe Lee got us those tickets. It was so amazingly cool of him to do that."

Nelle was sort of looking off to the side.

"Yeah, except he didn't," said Calvin.

I looked over at Nelle again. Still nothing.

"Wha-, what do you mean?"

"He didn't give *you* anything. You invited yourself. Those tickets were for him and Nelle, not *you* and Nelle. You just started saying, 'Oh thanks, oh my God,' like some giant dork and he just felt sorry for you."

"What? I did not. What are you . . . fuck you, man. Fuck you. Fuck you."

"Oh, okay, Peter. Okay. Ouch. Wow, fuck me. Well put. You spend all night working on that one?"

Nelle laughed. I felt a vein in my neck throb.

I said to her, "Hey, look, wait, I'm sorry—is that, is it true? I thought— I didn't mean to invite myself. That's so, I mean, I would feel really bad if I did that. I really didn't mean to do that. Oh God. Look, I really feel bad that I did that."

She said, "Okay, whatever, it's ok*ay*. It's no big deal. Don't . . . make such a big deal."

"I'm . . . *not*. I'm just . . . okay, I'm sorry. Okay. Whatever."

For days I tried to make it up to Nelle, but everything I did made me seem even more like the guy who invites himself everywhere. I tugged at her sleeves, carried her books, and said, "No, that's cool," several times a day. But she still asked me over every weekend, until the Lyons took a mini-vacation to visit Nancy's father, and that Saturday morning I realized it had been so long since I'd spent a weekend at home that I hadn't noticed the changes Mom had been making all over the house.

There was a new painting in the hallway, new wallpaper in the kitchen, and Dad's ornate, antique Scottish shield had been moved to a less conspicuous spot on the wall in the den and replaced by a muted, abstract print in a simple frame. I spent most of the weekend in the new, cream-colored reading chair, ignoring Mom's admonishments about how I was sitting and dangling my legs over the side, listening to her put the finishing touches on *Beauty and the Beast*.

Mom had recently met a writer of children's musicals for television who ten minutes later was pitching her ideas for the TV version of *Rumplestiltskin* he wanted to write with her. Dad insisted Mom needed an agent——he was right——and took her to meet a guy who helped negotiate the contract.

My brothers and sister and I appointed ourselves unofficial story consultants for the TV show, as well as for *Beauty and the Beast*, which was just going into rehearsals at the community theater.

Richard, who had gotten a couple of introductory banjo and guitar lessons from Mom's brother, Steve, was already playing by ear the way Mom did, and was especially enthusiastic about sharing his vision of a bluegrass/hillbilly take on *Rumplestiltkin* set in Depression-era Appalachia. He was so full of music and ideas that he literally couldn't contain them, and was always getting in trouble for bursting into song at the wrong moment.

He listened to the original cast album of *Hair* over and over, several times a day, and at Grandma and Papa's Passover seder that year, just as Moses was enumerating the many misfortunes that would surely befall Pharaoh's Egypt, Richard launched into a heartfelt, clueless version of his favorite song from the show, crooning over a hard-boiled egg in his boy's soprano, "Sodomy, fellatio, cunnilingus, pederasty . . ." My grandmother instantly dropped an enormous bowl of matzo ball soup to the floor, shattering it to bits and showering everyone's calves in hot chicken fat, making an enormous racket but only quieting Richard a little, as he whisper-sang the climax, "Masturbation can be fun!" and hastened Exodus by six or seven plagues.

It was the kind of thing Dad would usually respond to with anger, but he could barely contain his enjoyment of Richard's accidental subversion of the seder, which Dad referred to every April as the telling of a fairy tale. We all flinched when he said it. We loved Passover, and being with Mom's parents. And we loved stories. They were helping us each make comprehensible, spine-stiffening sense of a goddamn frightening world. Dad loved stories, too, but his were always about politics or war or getting cut off on the highway. And now that Mom was throwing herself deeper into her work, Dad was noticeably drawing back into himself and communicating almost exclusively through lectures on Dunkirk or rants about local restaurants.

I don't think he ever talked to us for more than a few sentences about anything other than his preferred subjects. He'd talk about guns and we'd nod until he was finished, but we never really discussed our lives in any way. I would try all the time. I'd tell him about a new girlfriend, he'd look at me like I was speaking in tongues, and then pick up his end of the non-conversation right where he'd left off.

So politics became code for everything else. Most of the fights in our house that weren't about spilled milk were about politics. Dad compared all of us, at one time or another, to the Nazis, and we did the same to each other. If anyone suggested at the time that we were just finding a way to express things that we had no other language for, I probably would have compared that person to a Nazi. Learning about each other and ourselves was all about deciphering the code. I didn't realize it at the time, of course, but the only way I knew how to say, "Why do you think you broke Mom's nose?" was, "You know, I think Ed Koch might be right about that."

We all tried to do it his way, sometimes tried to deal with the world the way he did. When my ninth-grade English teacher asked me to name my three favorite movies, I included Sergei Eisenstein's *Alexander Nevsky*, a pre-Nonaggression Pact, post-Potemkin, anti-fascist polemic about an eleventh-century Russian victory over marauding Germanic tribes dressed in suspiciously Nazi-looking uniforms, who end up literally falling through thin ice and drowning like Pharaoh's charioteers. It was the second movie I ever saw, after *Zulu*.

We did it his way to discover him, to extrapolate from it and divine him. Through Kremlinology and inference, through the acceptance of almost anything, we would know him. Dad felt compelled to tell me, as I was leaving for a birthday party at a Mexican restaurant, that the right wing in Argentina tortured women by breaking glass vials full of habañero peppers in their genitals. God knows what lesson I was supposed to take with me to The Flying Burrito that night, but I was usually more grateful than appalled by that kind of fright-bomb from Dad. It was contact. Scary, inscrutable contact, but contact just the same, with the only father I had. A verbal Death Grip. It offered revelations about him, glimpses at who he was or wanted to be, at the tragic grandiosity of his aspirations.

Gonville Bromhead, for instance, as played by Michael Cain, is not your typical movie hero. He's the kind of character who these days would end up on the wrong end of a catchphrase. Ten minutes into

Zulu the guy has been endowed with all the qualities that should earn him a belly full of spear: Englishness, smarts, and good grooming.

But then the big battle starts, and Michael Caine, instead of arrogantly sending his men to certain death, or hiding under a horse cart full of burning hay, fights. He fights like an eighties-era Schwarzenegger jacked up on Twinings, mowing down Zulus left and right. And then comes Dad's favorite part of the movie.

The Zulus and the English have exhausted themselves. The natives have retreated from the siege of the English camp, and Michael Caine looks like he's counting the days until he gets to start shooting *Alfie*, but just when he thinks he and the boys may have pulled off a miracle, he hears the sound of lots of spears pounding on lots of shields, and he looks up to see lots of Zulus coming over the hills that circle the camp. Then they stop advancing and he watches as they stand there, banging their shields, and he turns to the crusty old bugger next to him and he says, "Those dirty bastards. They're taunting us!" And the crusty bugger starts cackling like he'll never stop, but he does, and he says, "You fool! They're not taunting you! They're *saluting* you!" And so they are. Michael Caine watches as the Zulus slowly turn, one by one, and disappear down the other side of the hill, until there's just one proud warrior left, standing at the crest, lifting his spear in tribute to his valiant foe. Michael Caine slowly rises to his feet, and brings a bloody hand to his pith helmet in a weary salute, and the Zulu soldier slowly turns and follows his brothers down the other side.

My father really, really loves that salute. He's as big a fan of wartime gallantry as he is of wartime atrocities. He loves to tell stories about navy captains saluting each other stoically as one of them bravely rides his ship to the bottom of the sea. His all-time favorite is of course about the sinking of the HMS *Birkenhead* off the Cape of Good Hope in 1885. Apparently the captain fired a pistol above his head and warned the crew not to get into the lifeboats, shouting: "Stand fast! Women and children first!" which is where that famous phrase comes from. The men obeyed the order without complaint, four hundred and fifty of them were eaten by sharks or drowned after going down with the ship, and ever since then the principle of "women and children first" has been known as "The Birkenhead Drill." My dad was always quoting a line in a Rudyard Kipling poem that went, "To stand and be still to The Birkenhead Drill is a damn tough bullet to chew," proving each time that he wouldn't recognize irony if it was doing naked sit-ups right in front of him, but also pulling the curtain back on the theatrical workings of his mind, which were epic in scale. These were things none of us could see with any sense of perspective or nuance when we were kids, but the vividness of what we saw meant we didn't have much trouble remembering it when we were ready to.

We saw his eyes light up when he imagined a connection between the chivalry of the men who went down with the *Birkenhead* and the name of the ship. Dad was joking when he talked about it, of course, but not entirely. He lit up in the same way when he told us that Frederick Law Olmstead had been inspired to create the Central Park Boat Pond on a visit to Birkenhead Park in England, which the landscape architect described as possessing " . . . more than natural grace, all set in borders of greenest, closest turf, and all kept with consummate neatness." His sense that these attributes were somehow a reflection of him was present in the kind of brothers-under-the-skin connection between himself and Gonville Bromhead's men that Dad liked to spin out of the thin suburban air, and with which he tried to imbue us every day. It made me feel, along with many other emotions, a deep and painful love for him.

I used to think I could pinpoint, in any given incident, the single second when Dad turned the wrong way, the moment when he made an irreparable mental mistake. When I was six I saw him pick up our barbecue grill—for me a secretly prized possession, a symbol of normalcy—and smash it against the cement wall of a tool shed. As he stood looking at it, all the tension in his face disappeared and his skin went pale. His eyes shone. I watched him from our kitchen window, and I thought I could see what he was thinking. I imagined that the sight and sound of the cheap metal crunching against the concrete had given him some satisfaction, but that once he saw the wreckage on the patio he was struck with a deep sadness at the cruel and useless thing he'd done. That he felt sorry for doing it, but then realized he couldn't bring himself to apologize to us, and so, by the time he had crossed the lawn and re-entered the house (and I had scurried away to my room) he'd understood that it wasn't his fault at all, really, but Mom's. If he acted like a crazy person it was because of her, and us, and the world, not him. I'd seen him go through that cycle dozens of times since then, and I wondered what would happen if I caught him at the moment his skin went white and said, "Dad, it's okay, you can say you're sorry. You don't have to be afraid to say it, really. Everything's going to be all right."

On the Saturday morning the Lyons were away, I was sitting at the kitchen table in my football uniform, not eating a soggy bowl of Quisp, and dreading the game we had later that day against a team of future puppy mill owners and slumlords. Dad came up from the basement wearing a big, olive green, broad-brimmed hat with a leather chinstrap, which was part of the uniform of the Ghurkhas, a regiment of Nepalese soldiers who had fought on the side of the British Empire in East Asia. He greeted me with the English salute, palm turned out, and recited the Ghurka regiment's motto: "Better to die than be a coward."

I said, "Which means getting my ass kicked in a football game must be way better. So how come I'd rather jump off a cliff than play these guys?"

Dad said, "After the Nepalese war, the Ghurkha commander said, "These British soldiers are very good warriors. They are nearly as good as us." I just looked at him. "No, really," he said, "he was that confident." He poured water from the kettle into a mug and dunked a tin ball full of tea. "They're probably, all things considered, the toughest fighting force in the world. You know how they do their training? They start the day by running up a hill for an hour, carrying seventy pounds of rocks in a basket on their backs. That's before breakfast."

"So then 'Ghurkha' is Nepalese for 'insane'?" I said.

Dad bristled. "Did you finish the vacuuming? I don't want it left till later."

"I did it."

"Including under the bed?"

"Yes."

He narrowed his eyes. "Why do I not believe you?"

"I did it, I swear."

"Good." He sat down. "And you're okay with holding down the fort on Monday while Mom's in the city for her meeting?"

"Yeah."

"We'll see if this guy is all he's cracked up to be. Frankly I have my doubts. I talked to Stan Lutz, from the Melody Tent, and he recommended an agent he's known for years, someone who's really considered the top person in musical theater. But I understand why Mom wants to talk to this guy first. She should go. Just as long as he's not one of these charlatans who promise the world."

"He sounds good to me. Mom said something about a client of his having a show on Broadway," I said.

"No, that's true. I'm a little suspicious that might be his *only* client, that's all. Anyway, you're okay with making dinner? We'll leave out some Hamburger Helper. Don't forget to pick up some milk on your way home for the following morning. I won't be home until late. And don't let Richard get away with not doing his homework. Make sure he sits down as soon as he gets home."

"Right, okay. I won't. "

I guess it was time for the biannual flurry of interest in our homework.

"And if you and Nelle are going to be having sexual relations you need to use protection. It's important. Now if you're not sure about what to do I can pick them up for you. But you need to make sure you use a prophylactic."

Okay. That just happened. This is happening. He really said that stuff. Okay.

Say something.

"No, oh, wow, no, Dad, I mean, thanks. That. We're not, actually. We're not having sex. We. I mean, thanks, but I don't need to. Thank you."

He looked at me like he was indulging embarrassed fibs. "Okay, well, if you decide you need to get something, let me know and I'll help."

"Thanks. Thank you."

Well. Okay. Fourteen years of conversations about war and presidents, and it was all a setup. Jesus.

The Falcons were as badass as they were rumored to be. Mean, mean people. In the first five minutes of the game, one of their guys followed Tim Greeve, our running back, ten feet out of bounds, picked him up like a sack of potatoes and threw him against a big rusty garbage can. He didn't even complain about the penalty, or get in any kind of trouble from his coach for it. It was worth it to them just to fuck with us. When I helped one of their guys up and said, "Good play," he spit out his mouthpiece and said, "Fuck you, you battery-neck motherfucker."

But by late in the second quarter we were only behind by a touchdown due to the many penalties the Falcons were willing to take in exchange for hearing our cries of pain, and we were starting to see the game as a contest between good and evil, one that we could actually, if somewhat accidentally, win. The few times I had dropped back to pass I'd gotten pretty well creamed, and I decided to try to use the Falcons' bloodlust against them by "rolling out" away from the protective pass pocket formed by my blockers, letting defenders come pouring across the line, and forcing them to chase me as I took the outside route to what I hoped would be pay dirt.

As I headed to my right with the ball, straight toward the sideline, I thought how weird it was to expend all this dusty effort—and I was really, really expending—to go nowhere, just to get to a place where I might possibly be able to turn upfield and only then start heading somewhere. But I liked rolling out. It was a fully approved excuse for running away. The bad guys chased you, and you ran away from them like you'd been dying to do all game and you thought you might just keep going, right off the field and through the parking lot and up to Canada, but you didn't.

I didn't. I made the turn and leaned, just barely out of reach from a Falcon with red eyes and a scar on his forearm, and just like that, I was looking at sixty green yards of open field and glory, plus of course the eleven guys on my left who wanted to kill me. I "turned on the jets," as the sportscasters said, meaning I got very, very afraid of being thrown into a garbage can, and used that fear to run away from Falcons as fast as I possibly could. I was really moving. Oh man, I was going to be mobbed when I got to the end zone. I wish Nelle were here to see this. This is the neatest damn trick in the book, I thought. The more afraid you are, the more credit you get for being brave. The bigger the coward, the bigger the hero. Fine with me. Unbelievable.

I tore up the sideline and started to hear, through the jiggly racket in my helmet, the muted sounds of people cheering. I crossed right in front of our bench and bleachers, and all my teammates were standing up, leaning over the sideline and making big circles in the air with their arms. All the moms and dads were standing up and doing the same thing—mine were up there somewhere—and I could tell by the rising pitch in their voices that I was putting distance between myself and whoever was chasing me. I didn't dare turn my head to look. It would have slowed me down, and scared the shit right out of me.

Which might have been a good thing. I was kicking and pushing, and as I passed the bench I heard everyone screaming and I felt like a god. And then *wham! Kyaa!* Everything went gray and I was flying sideways, my whole body vibrating. Then another *bam!* And my lungs and legs went dead. As did my kidneys and stomach and liver. I had something in my mouth. Dirt. Ugh. Dirt in my mouth. *Ptiuu.* Oh, wow, wow, and a pain, in my upper back and head, so comprehensive it felt like heat.

I opened my eyes and saw my mother, five feet away, down near my feet. I was on my back. On the grass. Lying still. Panting. Huh. And Coach Russo was right in my face, an inch away. Jesus he had a big, big mouth. Huge. Giant yellow teeth, too. Lots of white spittle on his lips. Gross. God, you're an ugly man, Coach. What? How many fingers. Seriously? You're kidding me, right? You're actually asking me that? Okay, Jesus, don't get upset, Two. Two fingers. Right? What, okay, everybody calm down. I'm fayne. I'm fone. I'm line, I'm fline!

On the way home Mom said, "God you scared the hell out of me. I hate this game. Hate it. Don't close your eyes, honey. It makes me nervous. How do you feel?"

"I feel fine. Really. Just a little woozy. I can't believe I didn't see him. God, I thought I was home free."

"You mean Dad?"

"What? No, I mean the guy who whacked me, who sent me flying out of bounds. What do you mean, Dad?"

"I mean when you hit Dad. Do you not remember? Didn't you see him? You went sailing right into him, into his legs, knocking him over."

"Seriously? Dad, is that why you're limping? We should take you to the hospital and get it looked at."

Dad slipped into his movie-Nazi accent. "Hospitals are for ze veak. I'm fine."

Mom said, "You should at least put some ice on it."

"I'm fine. Enough."

I said, "Sorry, Dad. God, I had no idea. I feel bad."

He limped around the house for days after the football game, which made me angry in a way I couldn't understand, before finally giving in to Mom's insistence that he see a doctor, who told him he'd fractured his knee and needed to wear a cast. He seemed deeply embarrassed by it and rarely went out while it was on.

On Sunday I answered the phone and heard someone swallowing on the other end, catching her breath.

"Peter?"

"Hi. Nancy?"

"Sweetie, hi, we came home a few minutes ago and found Ginger on the kitchen floor. She's, well, she's dead. Nelle's very upset and Lee won't be back until late tonight. I hate to ask you this, but do you think you could come over and deal with taking her away, maybe just put her someplace, in the trunk of the car, maybe, so Lee can take her in to the vet tomorrow?"

I stood in the Lyons' kitchen doorway for half a minute before I could bring myself to walk into the room. Ginger was on her side by the sink, near her water bowl. People in the movies always say "she looks like she's asleep," but she didn't look like that at all. She looked dead, unmistakably, like a thing. I walked as quietly as I could over to her, unfolded the old pink beach towel Nancy had handed me when I got there, Nelle hanging on her arm, crying and saying, "Thank you." I laid the towel next to her and crouched down, took a breath, and said, "Okay, Gingy." I put a hand under her head and another under her rump and lifted her onto the towel. The weight and stillness of her caught me completely by surprise. I'd picked her up from naps a dozen times, but she felt twice as heavy now. The tears just popped out as I gently wrapped her up. I said, "Okay, that's a good girl," and I carried her out the back door and to the car.

I didn't see Nelle until late the next morning, at our 11:00 lunch period. We skipped the Salisbury steak and tater tots, went right for the ice cream sandwiches and took them out to the baseball field. It was a blustery gray morning and we sat behind the home bench and watched the wind lap at the edges of the tarpaulin covering the infield, listened to the crispy, curled brown leaves falling from the trees to the stands, heard faraway car horns and seagulls and, once in a while, a wave of girls' voices from the cafeteria.

We silently licked the dripping sandwiches until they started to fall apart, and then watched as they melted into sticky pools on the wooden bleachers. Nelle pulled her hands up inside her sweater sleeves, and hunched her shoulders against her ears. I put my arm around her back and rubber her side.

I said, "I'm so sorry about Gingy," and she said, "I know, me, too. I sort of can't believe it. She was so young. We still don't know why she died. Are you gonna go to the Homecoming thing Friday night?"

"I guess, yeah, maybe, are you? I mean, do you want to? The bonfire should be cool. I don't really know what they do at these things, do you?"

"No. I think there might be a lot of pep involved. And vim. Possibly vigor."

"That's what I'm afraid of. But I kinda want to do all those corny high school things. It makes me feel like Archie and Betty or something. We can always leave if we don't like it. Wouldn't it be great if we could just go to a hotel and spend the whole night together?"

"I guess."

"You guess?"

"No, I mean, yeah, I just like having all my stuff and everything."

I was quiet for a minute. Then I said, "You know, I can't believe I don't even know what color your toothbrush is."

She put the ends of her sleeves together and crawled her hands up her arms and hugged herself. She didn't say anything.

An hour later I was watching the now empty bleachers through the window of my earth science classroom when I felt a sharp pain in the back of my head, right where my former "tumor" had been. The wind was really picking up outside, and big patchwork collages of term papers, student council campaign literature, leaves, and ice cream wrappers were forming against the chain-link fence around the field. I turned to point one out to my lab partner and got hit with a vicious pain spasm. I went downstairs to see our three-hundred-year-old school nurse, but I didn't tell her what had happened at the football game on Saturday because I knew that my mother was at a meeting in the city and my father was at work, and I didn't want her to make a big thing. So I told her she didn't need to bother calling, and that, really, I'd be okay making my way back home on foot, and she said, "All righty—suit yourself, big shot. It's your funeral."

A couple of times during the walk home I thought I might actually take flight. My headache had spread to my neck and was already forcing me to walk slightly sideways, like a dog, and I kept getting nudged to the left by a sudden gust, which would turn the pain up another notch. Then, as I crested the hill that overlooked our block the wind completely stopped, as if it had never been there, and I stopped to appreciate the sudden quiet.

I was looking at our driveway for probably a full minute until it registered. A brown Mercedes. Parked at an angle. Next to Mom's car. It was Lee's car. In the middle of a Monday. It took another couple of minutes for the image to melt and seep into my brain. Mom and Lee. The wind picked up again, but I stayed there at the top of the hill, not moving and watching the Mercedes not move, either. I got progressively more nauseated. Eventually I turned around and headed back to school.

I didn't say anything to Nelle. Or anyone. But boy, I was amazed at how much I could not know when I wanted to not know something. It was suddenly clear to me that something had been going on for months and that until this moment I had successfully ignored it.

It wasn't until I heard the head cheerleader say my name, into a microphone no less, that I realized just how humiliating and not fun at all—not even in the sort of ironic way I hoped for—winning the Homecoming blueberry-pie-eating contest would actually be. What in the name of all that was dignified was I doing there? I guess the decision to enter the contest had something to do with my Archie aspirations. And the half bottle of beer I'd consumed five minutes before. And the lack of sleep I'd had all week. I'd been staying up at night and listening for anything I could glean about Mom and Lee, and Dad and the whole goddamned secret-keeping world.

By the time I got to the bonfire I felt like something was sitting on my chest. And then before I knew it, the cheerleader was holding my hand up in the air like a boxer's, screaming, "Let's hear it for this year's champion"—and here she paused to look down at a slip of paper, a gesture I had long ago gotten used to—"Freshman Peter Brick-in-head?" and she laughed and laughed and laughed while great showers of sparks burst all around us. I wiped some of the gooey, blue sugar paste off my face—we'd had our hands tied behind our backs for the contest—and smiled a please-can-we-never-speak-of-this-again smile at the crowd. I probably won because of my hair. It had acted like a mop and was now full of syrup, blueberries, and crumbly piecrust.

As the pie-eating music faded and the bonfire pep talks began, I searched the crowd for Nelle's face, hoping for a personal pep talk, but I couldn't find her through the flames and banners and blueberry juice. I made a full circuit around the fire, which was much bigger and louder than I had expected—a huge, angry, unruly monster of heat and bangs and crashes, but still couldn't find her. Just as I turned to make another round, I literally bumped into Josh, who had a girl I'd never seen before on his shoulders. She was whooping like she wanted to scalp someone, and I yelled over the yelling and the music, "Hey, where's Nelle?" And Josh said, "What?" and I asked him again, and when he said "What?" a second time I knew there was trouble. So I stopped, and he fixed me with a stare and said, "Man, she went that way—toward the bleachers. With, you know, Cal. Um. They were holding hands, and kissing and stuff."

Cal. My new best friend Cal.

I felt numb all over, but somehow my feet started moving and I marched off into the dark field, which suddenly seemed twice as big and empty as it had before. I headed to the baseball diamond, a hundred and fifty yards away, and I reached it quickly, and there was Cal, all alone, walking slowly towards me and barely illuminated by the distant bonfire light. I ran right up to him and punched him in the stomach. And even though he was wearing a thick down parka he doubled all the way over and made a clipped, little whistley sound.

I said, "Oh God, are you okay?" like someone else had done it, and I bent down and put a hand on his back, and he looked up at me with narrowed eyes and I wish I could remember what he said, because I know I deserved it, and if I had heard it maybe I wouldn't have left him there and gone after Nelle.

I slashed through wet grass with my sneakers, the tops of my toes getting wet, the stickiness on my face hardening to a mask, moving at a steady, thoughtless pace, with a growing taste of tin in my mouth, and I finally found her in the middle of a group of girlfriends, behind a handball wall, giggling. They all were, and the giggling grew bigger and eyebrows shot up under wool hats when they saw me. They backed into each other and kind of all coalesced into a single mass of down-packed nylon as I came at them, and when I got to the circle I pressed myself against whoever was on the outside of it, jumped in the air, and threw my fist into the middle of the pack at Nelle's head—the only one without a hat on it. My punch landed on the side of her face, just below her left ear, and she didn't move. I hit her pretty hard, but it didn't even make her budge.

As the pack of girls collapsed around her and moved her away, I put my hand up to my cheek, imagining what Nelle felt. The blueberry juice on my face felt like plastic.

Josh came barreling into me from the right and grabbed me in a bear hug meant to restrain and comfort, almost knocking me down and jostling a nugget of piecrust out of my ear. I turned the artifact around in my fingers and examined it for clues—to what, I don't know—then I looked up to see Josh, standing in the orange glow of the still-roaring fire. His mouth was hanging open, and his eyes were wide and sad. I felt like someone had touched a match to my blood and all of me had just gone *whoosh, crack, boom*. Up in flames.

9

I ran all the way to the Lyons' house without stopping. I don't know
why I didn't just get on my bike, which had been my sole mode
of transportation for years, and would have gotten me there in ten
minutes. I'd been sitting on the grass at the high school for, I don't
know, an hour or maybe two. I must have been too disoriented and
distracted, or maybe I wanted the trip across town to take a long time
so I could think more and clear my head, or maybe I wanted to sweat
and pant and feel some pain, even if it was just an ache in my foot or
soreness in my ribs. In any case it was late, probably one in the morning by the time I got there, and I stood on the Lyons' front stoop,
my finger poised in front of the doorbell for minutes, thinking, *This
can't be happening, this can't have happened, I couldn't have done this,
I couldn't, but I did, I did though, I did, I did it, oh, my God,* before
finally, shakily pressing the button.

It opened almost right away, and Lee stood there in the full light
of the hallway and the broad upstairs landing above and behind him.
Clearly everyone was up, and very up, lights on and all. Lee was ruddy
and slit-eyed, but fairly calm. I started speaking right away, and I was
surprised at how steady I sounded.

"Lee, I feel so awful," I said, "I don't know how much Nelle has
told you but I did something awful, I hit her tonight, a little while
ago. I don't know, I just, what came over me, I don't know, but I did

it and I'm just really so embarrassed and I just wanted Nelle to know how sorry I am that I hurt her like that. I can't believe I hurt her like that, I'm so sorry."

He looked me in the eye while I was speaking, and I felt afraid, but not too much. I was only afraid of the pain I would feel if he belted me, and I knew that would pass quickly and that I could take it, because it was the least I could do.

"You made a very bad decision tonight," he said, "very bad. You understand that? You're pretty brave to come here, I'll give you that, I really will. Because I can be a mean motherfucker."

From upstairs near the master bedroom Nelle called out, "Dad, don't hurt him!" and my breath caught in my throat.

Lee's eyes flickered, and he said, "I appreciate you coming over here. Now you need to go home. Get some rest. You need to think very seriously about what you did tonight. Okay? Do you understand me?"

"Yes, I do. Yes, I do."

"Good night, Peter." And he closed the door slowly, and I waited for a moment before moving.

Then I walked home. And I was so, so grateful, and deeply, deeply tired.

And yes, I heard him say "motherfucker," and yes, I wanted to kill him.

Mom continued to spend her days at the piano, and it started to pay off in a big way. She landed a job writing songs for the "Captain Kangaroo" television show, and, soon after that, a not-as-well-paying but infinitely more exciting job writing some of the lyrics for a new musical based on Studs Terkel's book *Working*. She'd gotten a call out of the blue from Mary Rodgers, daughter of Richard Rodgers of Rodgers and Hammerstein fame, who was one of the writers on *Working*. Mom's agent had given Mary some of Mom's lyrics to read, she liked them, and called and asked Mom to work with her. Mom was thriled, of course, and brimming with energy.

Dad seemed energized, too, although in an unnerving way. The first thing he did was quit his job. Just like that. When he told us about it he sounded as troubled or excited as someone changing his order at a restaurant. He left his job at Brooklyn College, his tenured, salaried job with benefits, to apprentice in a Broadway producer's office. As important as being a professor had seemed to him, as fundamental a part of his identity, he seemed to disconnect from it the way he would move on after a fit of anger, as if it had never happened. And, as usual, I don't think any of us ever really talked about it at all. We were so used to not talking about big things (or small things, or anything) that we didn't realize how revealing Dad's decision was until many years later.

And then, soon after he quit his job Dad bought a car. A mustard-colored, twelve-cylinder Jaguar sedan that looked like it ran on Dewar's Black Label, the kind of car that would be driven by the Broadway producer he was now determined to be.

I quit my job, too, doing no schoolwork and leaving no pot unsmoked for two years. I stayed up at night, fell asleep at school, and smoked weed wherever and whenever I could. So whenever I passed through a room that Mom or Dad or Alison were in I would hug the farthest wall from them, on the theory that if Thailand was on fire no one would be able to smell it from ten feet away.

One afternoon I was loitering in a fog behind Mom and Alison as they waited by the front door for Dad to come home. Richard was rocking back and forth on his feet in the driveway with a soapy rag in his hands, putting the finishing touches on a wash-down for the Jag. He was eleven years old and acting out in school and getting into trouble on a pretty regular basis (he'd had a radio confiscated by the middle school principal, whom Dad then accused of racism—the principal was black—and whose "fucking head" Dad threatened, to his face and in front of Richard, to "blow the fuck off") and I could feel Rich badly wanting to escape Dad's casting of him as the family Wild Child. Dad's selective obsession with cleanliness had grown even stronger. When he wasn't having a cocktail he was usually vacuuming a floor, washing a car, or cleaning a gun, so as soon as he left to run some errands in Mom's car that morning, Rich grabbed a bucket and a rag and ran out to the driveway to prepare a big surprise gift for him. Like everything else Richard did for the first time, washing a car seemed to come to him naturally, and the Jag looked brand spanking new.

Mom called out for David, again, to come up from the basement and share in Richie's triumph, but he was working out to the rebel yells of Lynyrd Skynyrd and couldn't hear anything happening above ground. He'd recently announced at the dinner table, in a calm voice, that John Wayne was his favorite movie star and that he was thinking of joining the marines after graduating from high school. He withstood the inevitable shit storm from Dad with defiant serenity, and a few days later hung a Confederate flag on his bedroom wall.

Alison was holding Mom's hand and wearing the unflinching, wait-and-see expression that had settled on her face a while back, her early shyness turning out to be, like that of a lot of kids, probably as much a refusal to be cowed into acquiescent small talk as a fear of speaking up. A few months before, I was in my room reading when I heard her run downstairs to the kitchen and greet Dad, who was just getting home and fumbling audibly with his car keys. She said hello, and he mumbled something that made Ali laugh and say, "Dad, you're drunk!" and there was a frozen pause. As quietly as I could, I lifted my head just a bit from the pillow. Dad took a loud breath and in a voice as black as petroleum said, "Fuck. You." There was another pause, and then the sound of Ali's feet pounding the carpeted stairs quickly upstairs to Mom, where she inhaled with a squeak and opened the floodgates.

The same unblinking openness that made Alison more forthright than the rest of us made her more vulnerable, and I felt proud when I heard her stand her ground by crying loudly, in stark contrast to her brothers, who ran from frightening encounters with Dad to heavy bags, notebooks, and rationalizations. For a couple of weeks after that she looked like something had chased her up a tree, and now, standing in the front door, she was still wary but keeping her shoulders square. She was nine and just starting to see what was what, but she wouldn't bother with the phase Richard was in (and that David and I were just moving out of), the one full of car washing and joke telling. Ali would find her own variations on smoking pot and lifting weights soon enough.

I started backing up as soon as I heard Mom's car scrape the concrete lip of the driveway. I could tell from the higher-than-usual pitch of the sound that Dad had touched the accelerator rather than the brake, a first sign of his imminent attack. Richard must have known, too, but I don't think he moved. I watched Alison's back as the door to Mom's car made the kind of sharp, wrenching noise it only did when Dad opened it in anger, and my eyes locked onto the end of her ponytail, where a small curl was framing a smiling yellow moon near the zipper on her dress. Dad slammed the door and approached Richie. He said something like, "What the fuck have you done, dildo?" and Rich offered a meek protest of some kind, and Dad said, "You fucking scratched it. Look at this—look! You fucking scratched the finish, you moron. I told you to never touch my car, didn't I? Didn't I?" Alison's ponytail shook and rose slowly, half an inch up her back, eclipsing the moon as she fought the impulse to curl into a ball. She held tight to Mom's hand as Mom stepped towards the driveway, and just as Ali tugged her momentarily back into place, I heard the punch. To the gut, as usual. It made a creaky *whoof!* sound, and Rich let out an animal noise, a strangled howl that died as soon as he made it. Dad spat out, "Huh? Huh? You fucking moron!" And Mom grabbed Ali around the waist and picked her up, sort of putting her behind her hip as she walked towards Dad and said, "Get away from him! Get away!" Dad came banging hard through the door. His whole body glowed with rage as he barreled at me. I clenched with woozy readiness, but he marched right by me like I wasn't even there, clearly not seeing me at all. I ran outside and took Ali's hand as Mom helped Richard to his feet and put her arms around him. He didn't cry until a few minutes had passed, and when he did it wasn't for very long.

I think of that day as the moment when the wind that had been swirling around our house for years finally picked us up off the ground and started throwing us in circles. The long pauses between brief storms became shorter reprieves from a permanent, slow-moving tornado.

About two years later, when I was sixteen, our living room was filled with eleven-year-olds in brand-new polyester shirts and rope bracelets, boys with hands on girls' waists, girls' hands on boys' shoulders, all of them avoiding eye contact and listing from side to side like they were dancing on the subway. Alison's first party, and the only one ever thrown by one of us kids. Also probably the only middle school party ever thrown in a living room, as our basement was still a cement dungeon furnished with Dad's and David's barbells.

Alison had been nervous about the party for weeks, going back and forth with Mom about the proper ratio of Tab to Coke, pretzels to chips, and slow songs to fast. She was tall now, possessed of a quick smile, and a sly, punky wit. She was ready to party. Just before her guests arrived, I watched her from the dining room table where I was setting down the ice bucket as she unscrewed the lightbulb in the tall, standing lamp behind the couch, then kept her head down and her lips pursed in concentration as she moved quickly to the stereo, blushing just a little and praying with all her might that no one had noticed the lightbulb move.

The kids all came pouring in at once, and the noise was like nothing I'd ever heard in our house. Because they weren't sequestered in a finished basement, the kids could be heard by me and Rich, just a few feet away in the den, and Mom and Dad, up in their room. I couldn't resist getting up from the couch a couple of times to get glasses of water I didn't need, just to steal glimpses of my sister holding a red paper cup in her hand, nodding with great interest at the monologue of an eleven-year-old Romeo with a concave chest, both thumbs in his dress pants pockets and a very serious look on his face. His lips were moving at a furious pace. After about an hour I noticed that I had cramps near my ears from smiling so much.

I went ahead and turned up the volume on the TV in the den, and Rich got up to steal us a couple of Cokes and some soggy popcorn. Bonnie was huddled at my feet, chewing at the remaining hair on her belly. She was more bald than not now, with little white tufts on her paws and a narrow strip on her back the only places still covered. The rest of her was skin, scratched and puckered, covered with new small cuts every day. Mom and Dad had tried all kinds of drugs, even changed the carpet, but nothing had worked. She was very unhappy.

While I was stroking Bonnie's head I realized I'd heard Alison say, "No!" so I walked into the living room. She was pleading, "Richie, stop! Stop it!" Rich was standing on the couch, a couple of pretzel rods up his nose and his butt sticking way out behind him, rocking back and forth to The Captain and Tenille's "Love Will Keep Us Together." I crunched my lips to keep from laughing as I walked over to him, took him by the arm, and hauled him off to big-brother prison. He kept up a seated version of the butt dance in the den and it was all I could do to pretend to ignore him and pay attention to "Welcome Back, Kotter."

The next thing I remember is the sound of Alison's feet pounding up the stairway just over my head. I slowly lifted myself up from the couch as she yelled, "Mom, Richie's ruining my party! He won't stop it no matter how many times I tell him!" And then came the padded booms of Dad's heavy, quick descent down the stairs.

He didn't even pause at the bottom, but barged into the living room at full speed, walked straight over to Rich, and slammed a fist into his chest. Rich must have somehow managed to keep his feet, because I heard him immediately tear up the stairs in a panic, and as I entered the foyer I saw him, eight or nine stairs up, trying desperately to evade Dad's grasp, almost making it but catching a toe and tripping, falling forward and leaving his back exposed to a rain of punches. Dad's hair was flopping over his brow, his mouth pulled back like a dog's, and he went at Rich with a palpable sense of release. Rich was silent. The first two blows landed flush on his back and didn't seem to hurt him very much, but then a third bounced off his ribs as he squirmed and he finally yelped loudly in pain. He twisted to his right and tried to stand up, but pushed too hard and fell backwards, down the stairs. He grabbed at the rail but missed it and skidded along the edges of the steps, bouncing hard a couple of times before finally landing on the tiled floor of the foyer, in front of Alison's friends, who stood frozen with their eyes opened wide. Olivia Newton-John warbled on the stereo as Richie stood up and brushed his pants leg. He was red and bruised and ashamed, and he walked quickly, with his head bowed, out the front door.

Alison looked stricken, and most of her friends were staring blankly at nothing. I attempted some distracting cleanup, and probably some lame, quiet humor, but of course everyone quickly lined up at the phone, and soon after that were safe in their parents' cars.

Rich started spending lots of time at friends' houses, just as David and I had, and lots of hours in his room with his guitar.

Alison did plenty of visiting, too, but mostly she retreated into books. I'd often take a break from a reading jag to walk into her room (which she had started decorating in a kind of late-nineteenth-century, Secret Garden-ish style,) where I'd find her on a jag of her own, sitting up in bed with her legs bent into an easel for Judy Blume or Lewis Carroll.

She had almost no contact with Dad after the incident with Richard, and I think that might have been as much his doing as hers. Alison seemed to make Dad nervous and he kept every kind of distance he could from her. She and I were often the only ones home in the afternoons, or the only ones willing to come out of our lairs, and we became good friends. I was constantly amazed by her ability to say, "That is one big, pink elephant over there, huh?" At how she would just go ahead and feel whatever she was feeling. Her casual, emotional honesty nudged me towards the knowledge that vulnerability and confidence were two sides of the same coin, and that it was the coin of the realm.

David started disappearing for long stretches, staying out late at night with a group of friends none of us knew much about. The kids I hung out with were all connected to Mom and Dad's friends, but David was asserting himself on every front and spending most of his time with the younger brothers of guys who had been stealing lunch money from me and my friends for years. He was getting into bars without any problem because he had literally become the biggest, strongest guy in school—probably in town—and looked like he could break your arm just by thinking about it.

Whatever meager, older-brother leverage I still had somehow survived the first few months of David's new massiveness, probably because Mom left me in charge of the kids while she and Dad, who was now a full-fledged manager at the same Broadway production company, were at work every day. Not that David, Richard, or Alison had any interest in submitting to my erratic whims, but they had to be at least a little bit cooperative if they wanted me to make them dinner every night. And a little pretend deference was a small price to pay for the opportunities my toothless leadership afforded.

David was still a year away from getting his driver's license when he started taking the Jaguar out for joy rides on days when Dad took the train to work. I yelled, "Do not fucking take the car," and "Do your homework!" at him until the veins in my neck bulged. I said it matter-of-factly from behind biology textbooks, and I whispered it through clenched teeth, Dirty Harry style, yet I was somehow never able to persuade David to pass up leather seats, surround sound stereo, and 175 horsepower in favor of the Pythagorean theorem or the Louisiana Purchase. Things between him and me were pretty quickly set on a high burner, and we veered between all-out rock-throwing, album-vandalizing warfare, and mere under-the-breath insults as we passed each other in the kitchen.

If I'd been smart I would have used that time to butter him up and ask him to lobby his friends on my behalf. Some of their older associates had approached me in the school parking lot one day as Josh and I sat on a bench eating a couple of cheeseburgers. The ringleader, Anthony DeCello, who could have easily gotten work as a stand-in for the actor John Cazale from *The Godfather* and *Dog Day Afternoon*, with his massive upper cranium and a hairline that was already fleeing from it at high speed, tapped me on the shoulder and said, "You say somethin' about Catholics?"

He was referring, I quickly surmised, to a cartoon strip I wrote for the school newspaper called "A View from the Top" in which God and the Angel Gabriel were rendered as a clueless bigot and smart-ass coronet player, respectively, and in which I had satirized, for that month's issue, the rampant commercialization of Christmas. It was, I thought, a brave, subtle, take-no-prisoners attack on bourgeois society's alienation from its own rotting soul, but apparently it had been misinterpreted—isn't that always the way—by the poor benighted lunch thieves of Glen Cove High. Well, I thought, that's all right. One was to expect such misunderstandings, and I assured Mr. DeCello—Anthony, I called him—that I had not, in fact, said anything about Catholics, unless by "somethin'" he meant the observation that the original meaning of Christmas, a holiday enjoyed by Catholics among many others, had been warped by—and, well, that's pretty much where I let my thoughts trail off, as Anthony had quite rudely interrupted me with a jab to the diaphragm, causing me to double over in pain and drop my cheeseburger to the pavement. His friends joined in the fun and pummeled my back until I was reunited with my former lunch, then subsequently separated from the portion of it I had already consumed. I was incredibly proud.

This kind of thing happened a lot at Glen Cove High School. The lunchrooms were always boiling over with old grudges and vendettas, sometimes to the point of cops and ambulances arriving. During one especially horrific brawl, I saw a former student spear a senior in the neck with a metal chair leg, piercing an artery and creating a terrible, bloody panic that verged on a riot.

Stories like that were a kind of familiar music to Dad's ears, and he never failed to fan the flames of whatever dramas we'd gotten ourselves involved in. When I was in elementary school and complained about a bully, he told me not to come home unless I'd hit my young tormenter over the head with a chair. He gave the same advice to Richard a few years later. (Both of us ignored it, and both of us told Dad we'd followed it.)

David, Richard, and I became habituated to bringing the anger we were steeped in at school back home with us, and in turn bringing our homemade rage to school, mostly in the form of "funny" name-calling and smart-ass comments. Richard and I both developed reputations as guys who were quick with a quip and, having kept it up into adulthood, were often shocked years later when girlfriends and colleagues didn't seem to get the joke.

Our after-school schedule went like this: At 3:30 every day I told the kids, "Do your homework"; at 3:40 I screamed it repeatedly; and at 6:00 we threw forks at each other and kicked holes in locked bathroom doors.

Mom would get home before Dad most nights, coming through the door in a crouch position to pick up remnants of noodles, notebooks, and *White Albums*. She'd endure wave after wave of complaints and grievances, then proceed to conduct investigations, perform triage, pronounce sentence, and administer comfort, all before sitting down to re-re-heated, leftover eggplant parmesan.

She looked preoccupied, but not checked out, and once we got through the crime and punishment portion of the evening she'd tell us about a new song she'd written for Captain Kangaroo, or what Mr. Green Jeans was like in real life.

The theatrical adaptation of *Working* was more exciting for her, of course. It would take the book's collection of interviews with nurses, masons, and cops, and turn them into encounters between those characters and a fictionalized, suburban family of five. Mom and Mary Rodgers were writing all the songs for the family, in addition to one for an aging schoolteacher character. We loved hearing the stories about writing sessions with Mary and all the rumors about who might be in the cast. We all had plenty of our own personal teen and pre-teen drama going on, not to mention our daily performance of *If You Don't Give Me Back My Notebook I'm Gonna Wipe the Dog's Ass with Your Shirt*, but nothing could compete with the drama of real, professional Drama and the effect it was having on Mom.

Every time she crouched through the door she looked a little different than she had the night before. Her clothes got softer and darker, her hair progressively looser and curlier, her eyes more receptive and alive. As tired as she was, she was showing more of an interest in our schoolwork and personal lives than she had before (not that we were any more inclined to share) and she was taking a noticeably less-indulgent tone with Dad.

Sometimes when he would start the wheels of confrontation turning she would stop him short with "I'm not going to talk about that," or "I'm sorry, I need to finish this now." And it often worked. She was more deft at steering conversations toward non-inflammatory subjects, but also braver about going right at the inflammatory ones with a crisp, confident style that pre-empted attacks.

I no longer spent my weekends at the Lyons', of course, and Nelle and Cal were now a long-established couple, but miraculously they were still my friends, sort of. They probably just didn't know how *not* to be my friends. But I walked around with a physical sense of poison in my blood, consciously angry, finally convinced that I was a younger version of my father, for good or for ill—the two poles that I vacillated between almost hourly as I tried to decide how to regard myself. Righteous rage was intoxicating, a release from inhibition and ambiguity, a surrender that felt like a triumph because you were so right about . . . everything, that you were permitted to—no, you were *obligated to*—do whatever was necessary to make others see things your way. And of course, as good as it felt, nothing felt worse. The sickening sense of displacement, the bone-eating guilt, the crushing knowledge of someone else's pain, of Nelle's pain. And those *were* the sensations, for me. I was so steeped in melodrama, so swollen with grandiosity and convinced of my own inadequacy that nothing felt manageably small scale. These experiences were still, thankfully, more powerful and longer lasting than the fleeting thrills of indignation. They at least kept my rage in check, to some extent.

Every night I'd lie awake thinking about Nelle and what she must have felt when I hit her. I replayed the night over and over, almost hyp-notically, trying to spot my own irreparable moment, wishing again that I could spin the world backwards. And if David and I had had a door-kicking fight that afternoon I'd analyze that, too, and promise myself I'd stay calm the next day. I had only some luck with that, but not much. I wished I understood myself more.

I wasn't doing much of trying to understand Dad anymore, though, and wouldn't return to that project for another ten years or so. He hit Mom again about a month after I hit Nelle, lashing out suddenly in the middle of a whispered argument in the kitchen that I suspected was about Lee. Mom was holding a set of keys and that's what I remem-ber most—their incongruous jingling when he hit her, and the unex-pected sound they made when they hit the kitchen floor, not a clatter, but a sickening, dead splash. I only saw the edges of their bodies from my perch in the den, Dad's leg stepping to the side for leverage, Mom's sweatered arm suddenly jerking up to protect her face. I ran away. I threw the garage door open and got on my bike and rode forever, cry-ing furiously with fear and anger, peddling up and down hills, all the way to the beach, but getting no distance from myself at all.

* * *

I was never sure when Mom's affair with Lee ended, but eventually I noticed that it must have, that there were simply no more calls or visits from the Lyons, or even mentions of them. There was no acknowledgment that an affair had happened, of course. I had no idea if the other kids knew about it, or if Mom knew I knew, and I didn't want to know myself, so I put it out of my mind. Or tried to.

I ran into Nancy one day at a bookstore, and she asked about Mom and Dad. I told her that just a week before they had hosted their annual Christmas party, the one Nancy and Lee had attended several times over the years along with all of Glen Cove's other Jews, and she said, "Was it happy?" I was stunned by the well-meaning sincerity with which she asked it, and the different kinds of knowledge it implied, whether it was specifically about Mom and Lee or just about Dad, and us, in general. I felt a little like I had the night Dr. Adler told me he wasn't comfortable with the idea of Josh sleeping at our house. I didn't speak for a second or two. Then I said, "Yeah, yes. Everyone had a good time," which wasn't really true but was all I could manage.

I was there with my new girlfriend, Martina. She was searching for a gift for her father, who had just come through very dicey open-heart surgery, and I was looking for a book on Che Guevara, the subject of my worrisome world history term paper. Martina walked a couple of steps ahead of me, her long coat and long hair swaying to the beat of long strides; she looked like a woman in a shampoo commercial. I don't think she had any interest at all in being seventeen. Nancy kept sneaking appraising glances at Martina, and smiling, but I felt like whispering, "Yeah, I know, she's stunning. So how come I feel so tired when I'm with her?"

A week earlier, under the Caterpillar's Mushroom at the boat pond on New Year's Eve, I'd taken a long draw from an unlabeled bottle of homemade apricot brandy and passed it to Martina Kluhm. I shivered one of those little shimmy-shivers you get from stuff like homemade apricot brandy, and right after putting my drinking hand in my coat pocket I pulled it back out again, grabbed the bottle from Martina, and bestowed a kiss on her sticky, syrupy lips.

The Kluhms had moved to the States from Salzburg only a few years before and had brought their brandy recipe with them, but spoke without a trace of an accent. They lived in Glenwood Landing, one town over, but were frequent patrons of the community theater in Glen Cove and big fans of my mother's shows. Despite their hot cocoa and Linzer torte homey-ness, Martina could be cold and very quiet. Where Nelle was all soulfulness and laughter, Martina was, well, not. Our parents had been friends for a year, and we'd been in the same room a half dozen times, but never shared more than a few words. Yet now she had sort of become my girlfriend. Kind of. Actually, I'm pretty sure that if someone had asked her if she was my girlfriend, they wouldn't have gotten to the word "girlfriend" before she said "no," but we spent a lot of time together. We smoked pot, which made her very funny and sweet, and we tried to figure out what *The Battle of Evermore* was about, and once in a while she'd let me kiss her. But that's as far as it would ever go. I wouldn't have kept trying except for the fact that she seemed to want me to. She would tell me stories about being with other guys, guys from Switzerland and Austria who were on their national ski teams, and she strongly implied that she had gone all the way with them, and that she had because *they* knew how to get a girl to go all the way. She never missed an opportunity to make fun of my clothes, or my jokes or my hair. Or the things I said. I wasn't very good at talking to people, but I talked a lot, so that was a problem.

"I think it's the best movie of the year. When he throws that beer can at her head? I mean that's where that fucking win-at-all-costs bullshit takes you. It's . . . look where it's taken this country. I mean, I think it's *really* about that, about where that stuff has taken us, you know? About how America has just sold its fucking soul to the devil."

"*The Bad News Bears?*"

"Yes, *The Bad News Bears*. What, because it's a comedy it can't be serious? I mean, what do you think *Sleeper* is about?"

"The future."

"Is it? Yeah, sure, it's set in the future, but I don't know—it sure seems to be about a lot of stuff we're dealing with today, doesn't it?"

"Dealing with? Oh my God, it's a fucking movie."

"Oh, okay. Right, fine. And I guess *Mein Kampf* was just a book. Okay, then."

"What?! What the fuck are you talking about? Why do you do that?"

I don't really have any memories of her saying anything that *didn't* begin with "Why do you . . . ?"

And that's what she said after I kissed her under the mushroom.

"Why do you do that?"

"Do what?"

"Shake like that every time you take a drink. It's like you've never had a drink before or something. And why are you wearing that stupid hat?"

I said exactly nothing in response. I was still hoping that the Polaroid picture she had given me when we got to the mushroom, the one of her sitting on her bed, cross-legged, all bundled up in a big old man's sport coat, the picture I had felt the edges of in my pocket when I stuffed my drinking hand in there and that gave me the courage to take my hand back out, that that was an invitation, or confirmation of something. So I decided that the best thing to do was to kiss her again. To show her what she obviously didn't realize—that my disguise was just a cover for the Alps-climbing, brandy-drinking, ravenously manly real me. And I didn't just kiss her, I put the move on her, the one where you put your hand on Jill St. John's neck and pull her towards you because you're James Bond and her mouth might be saying "no," but her eyes are saying, "Shake me and stir me."

Martina pulled away, smiled a dazzling smile, and said, "Is that all we're ever gonna do? Jesus." She was out of the mushroom before I could answer.

I made my way back to the Bethesda Fountain, where Martina's parents and the rest of our friends were, along with hundreds of people holding hands, dancing around the statue with giant gargoyle puppets on long poles, and ringing in 1976. It was the best place in the world to be on New Year's Eve, the opposite of Times Square. It was homey like the Kluhms, and the kind of people who made their own apricot brandy and knew how to drink it were there. I sat on the stone steps leading down to the fountain and watched the crowd move like a flock of birds, a huge, V-shaped progression, sub-patterns opening within it, a dozen diamonds expanding and collapsing in time to the music. Kids on fathers' shoulders, walls of teenagers linked arm over shoulder, a pair of gray-haired women waltzing in floor-length gowns, kicking up spray from the pavement.

Something pulled at my wrist and I was standing up before I realized it was the hand of a girl, maybe a year younger than me, her bright red curls peeking out from a hat. "No sitting!" she shouted, and we were swept into the tide, circling within circles, moving in every direction at once. It was delirious. We did that spinning-while-holding-both-hands thing that people do in the movies and it looked just like it did in the movies. We danced on the edge of the fountain and got hit with snowballs. I kissed her. She said, "Oh, my goodness." Another girl jumped on my back and covered my eyes with her hands. I spun around until we fell, and someone's mother offered a hand to each of us and pulled us up. A cop in uniform holding a joint asked me if I had a match. By the time midnight struck I'd probably kissed twenty people. The secret to successful socializing was clearly doing it with strangers, and keeping my mouth shut.

A couple of months later Martina and I were doing the subway dance in the Glen Cove High School gym, which had been decorated in jet black construction paper and gray yarn to reflect the theme of that year's prom, Pink Floyd's *The Dark Side of the Moon*, to a song so long we danced to it twice before it was over. We were of course dancing at probably the least danceable moment in human history. The song list for the prom was dominated by flute-laden, dirge-rock, but we did our best to smile through the endless drum solos. As we tripped the heavy fantastic a second time, Martina actually initiated a conversation. She said, "Your father really appreciates food, doesn't he?"

I sneezed.

"Wow, bless you," she said.

Dad had used the traditional pre-prom-picture-taking time at the house to give us a bean-by-bean account of a meal he'd had the day before at his favorite "truly authentic" Cuban-Chinese restaurant in Spanish Harlem. I came downstairs to find him in mid-monologue and Martina in full thrall as he went on about how the waiters spoke Spanish and "they used only authentic ingredients—none of this tepid American crap." He said, "I told the guy who ran the place that I wanted the spicy pork the way he and his friends ate it, the genuine dish, not the Americanized nonsense, and he said, Oh, no, you no, you no rike, it not for Amelican parette, it a tase a too hot for you, I sink. So I said, okay, fine. Bring me that. Bring it to me, and I want it as hot as you can make it. I want it the way they eat it in China. So they brought it out, and the whole restaurant stopped eating. I'm not exaggerating. Every waiter in the place stood in the kitchen doorway and watched, whispering to each other, oh no, he not gonna able to do it. And not only did I do it, I did all of it, the whole thing in one sitting, which the chef came out of the kitchen and told me no one had ever done before. No American. And I said I'm only technically an American, old boy. My grandparents used to run your country. He said, Oh! You Eengrish, I rove dee Engrish so much. Much to give China. It a shame you leff, I sink. And he pulled out his secret stash of twelve-year-old Scotch and we talked all night about how he's gotta serve all that Americanized crap to fat midwesterners every day. He said he was thinking of just retiring rather than keep going. I don't blame him. What's the point if you can't be authentic?" And Martina said, "Absolutely."

"Yeah, he does," I said, "He loves food." *Aahfluuuhh!!*" I sneezed hard, over her shoulder.

She said, "Does he cook a lot for you four?"

"Yes, he does," I said, "His specialty is shrimp in lobster sauce. That and roast beef with Yorkshire pudding. He stands outside to make it. With a bowl. He whips up the mixture in a bowl with a spoon, in the backyard, because the fresh air makes it puff up more, makes it airy."

As we slowly shuffled in place I noticed that lots of people were sneezing. In a misguided attempt at verisimilitude the prom committee had covered the gym floor with what looked like the emptied contents of three thousand vacuum cleaner bags, and we were all kicking up a lunar dust storm.

"Oh, how wonderful," Martina said, "that is so wonderful. Attention to detail like that. Do you realize how lucky you are?"

"I do. Yes, I do. *Oblaaaa!*"

She said, "Oh my God, this song is so *grim*. Can we sit down? My feet are killing me."

I was trying hard to remember what had sparked a laughing fit for Martina the last time I saw her before the prom. We were walking in the woods and she got a case of the giggles so strong it literally brought her to her knees. Afterwards we sat on the spongy dirt for half an hour while she told me about the trees that grow in the Austrian Alps. She was glowing with nostalgia, and she grabbed my hand every time she remembered a new detail.

We sat down at our table, and Josh and his girlfriend took turns shooting me looks that said, "Hey, what a pretty, forty-year-old date you have there!"

Ben was moving toothpicks around the table, doing one of those brainteaser things and smiling to himself as everyone tried to figure it out. I hesitated for a moment, and then leaned in with my buddies to solve the problem, which Martina responded to by turning from the table to watch the dance floor with her chin in her hand. She didn't turn back until Ben's date, Rebecca, said, "Oh man, I can't think! I'm totally light-headed. I had too much champagne!" Martina offered over her shoulder, "It wasn't Champagne." Everyone looked at her. "It was sparkling wine but it wasn't Champagne. Champagne is a region, not a grape." Rebecca took two toothpicks from the table, arranged them in her mouth like fangs, and snarled at Martina's back like a werewolf. I smiled and thought about how just the day before, when Dad had found Richard and David fighting and accused David of fighting dirty yet again, he'd grabbed him in a viselike grip from behind and told Richard to "Kick him in the grapes. C'mon, kick him in the goddamn grapes!" I wanted to tell everyone that story, and laugh about it all night, but I didn't have the slightest idea how.

So instead I told everyone about how I'd gotten an F on my Che Guevara paper—the first one I'd ever gotten—because the teacher thought I had plagiarized the material. Never one to shy away from an opportunity for a dramatic gesture, and inflamed with the passion of a momentarily reformed bullshitter accused of bullshitting, I'd responded by dumping all the encyclopedias and biographies I'd used onto his desk and protesting, "Mr. Bremmer, if you can find one word from my paper in any of these books . . . then . . . well . . . you should . . . please let me know."

When I got home I told Mom all about it and she made me feel like I was César Chávez on a hunger strike, like a hero for the ages. I knew Dad would eat it up, and as he came through the door I went to greet him and give him the rundown, but before I could get a word out he said, "Come see my new toy." I stepped outside into the early evening light and almost had to rub my eyes. Sitting in front of our modest suburban tract home, on a driveway the length of the car itself, stood a mint-condition, chocolate brown and tan, 1957 Bentley S1 with red piping, whitewall tires, and running boards. A bunch of kids who had been playing touch football were walking slowly towards it. One neighbor stopped mowing his lawn, and another one was calling to his wife with a smile on his face to "Come out here and get a load of this."

I didn't tell my friends at the prom table about the Bentley, of course. They all "congratulated" me on my F, and laughed and told some stories about Mr. Bremmer, but I couldn't let it go and ended up going on at way too great length about Communism. Specifically, Latin American interpretations of Marxism, and Che's role in the development of guerilla warfare, and the history of the despicable United Fruit Company. The ears of my friends glazed over, and over and over, but I couldn't stop, and after a while everyone got up and danced as best they could to the grinding sludge of Jethro Tull's *Aqualung*.

Ben was our chauffeur for the night. He had a license, a VW Rabbit, and an old black fisherman's hat, which he finally took off when we got to Martina's house at two o'clock in the morning. Martina whispered to me, "Come in and we'll go up to my room," and Ben and Rebecca caught my eye in the rearview. I kissed Martina and said, "Really?" She said, "Really," and I said, "It's a long way home. I don't think Ben and Rebecca would want to just hang out here." She said, "They should go. Tell them they can head home. This was so nice of them to do this." I kissed her again and said, "Really?" and she said, "Really," and opened the car door. She lifted an eyebrow and stepped out.

After an hour of face-turning, hand-redirecting, mouth-closing, and shoulder-scrunching from Martina, I called home and woke my parents. I asked Dad if he wouldn't mind picking me up. It was pretty mortifying, but he was great about it, unfazed, and he got there pretty quickly. He pulled up in the Jag just before four and let it idle at the curb, his head facing forward, the muffled, urgent sound of WINS News Radio leaking from an unclosed window, the tailpipe billowing clouds of steam into the quiet night.

10

I t wasn't like the Bentley was the first statement of its kind on the block, of course. Just a few doors down a couple of white plaster lions stood sentry over a four-step, marble walkway to a gigantic Greek Revival front door framed by thirty-feet-high, faux marble Doric columns, lit day and night by spotlights shining through large, rotating color wheels. It was the Disco of Parnassus, and it was one of the Three Wonders of the Neighborhood, along with The Garage Mahal and The Shire. And now for all I knew we probably lived in Fuckingham Palace or Flaunticello, although the truth was that even though Dad thought a Bentley in the driveway was just the tweedy thing for a guy like him, the effect was far less Country Squire than First Round Draft Pick.

We encouraged him to drive it as much as possible, just to keep it out of the driveway, and in David's case, to free up the Jaguar for well-appointed beer runs. He went out for what was supposed to be a quick one soon after Dad bought the Bentley, on a Friday afternoon around 2:30, but an hour later he still wasn't home and Dad was due back at six. I tried to read, watch TV, eat, but I was too nervous to do anything except pace back and forth in the street and watch for the Jag to come up over the small hill two blocks away. I tapped the front of my foot against one curb, crossed the street and tapped the other, over and over, as a giant rubber band inside me twisted tighter and tighter, until finally I caught sight of the Jag. At first I thought I was hallucinating from staring at the horizon for so long. It was moving very slowly, listing to one side like a boat taking on water, and as it got closer I could hear that it was making a nausea-inducing *clunkey-clunkey-clunk* sound.

I immediately ran back inside and up to my room, hauled a chair over to my closet, and reached up to grab an old shoe box where I kept my cash. I had been working as a dishwasher at a local restaurant that specialized in French onion soup, which meant that I carried small amounts of very smelly, rotting cheese with me everywhere I went. But there was simply no question about giving up the money, along with anything else that wasn't nailed down, in order to avert the disaster that would ensue if Dad came home to a dented Jag. Yes, it would be worse for David, but that was like making a distinction between the passengers on the *Hindenburg* and the people standing below it.

I ran downstairs holding four hundred dollars in my stinky hand and found David just inside the front door, white as a ghost. We hadn't shared two civil words in months, but he had a look on his face that I imagined only people on their death beds got, one of sober, all-inclusive forgiveness and apology, and it served as an instant, permanent peace treaty. "Pete, I fucked up," he said. "I don't know what to do. I got a flat tire on the Jag, and there's no spare in the trunk. Plus, there's kind of a nick next to the wheel. More of a dent, really. I'm kinda freaking out." His voice was constricted, like he'd gone into anaphylactic shock.

We walked out to the driveway. The dent wasn't too bad. He'd driven into a sunken sewer grate on a corner and dinged the wheel well against the curb. A protruding bar on the grate had punctured the Dunlop tire. But the dent was a clean little thing, and the tire could of course be replaced. The whole job could probably be done in an hour, which left us half an hour to get the car to and from a garage where a mechanic would have to do the job immediately. Which meant our only hope was that someone was filming us for an episode of a TV show that we would all laugh about in ten years. But I called a tow truck anyway and the driver said he knew a guy who would do it and David went with him and I went back to my widow's walk.

I thought about how David and I had gone at each other with such a bottomless tenacity for so long—pinning each other down, letting each other up, getting pinned, crossing fingers, crying uncle, getting up, pausing, punching, letting up, and on and on until, I guess, right about now, on a Friday in 1977 with finally enough bruises between us for a truce.

David pulled the Jaguar into our driveway very slowly and very carefully, as if the car had a pyramid of champagne glasses on the roof. The twisted rubber band in my gut turned another notch when I realized that I should have gone with him and driven the car back myself, since I had a license and he didn't. If Dad came back now we'd be in so many different kinds of trouble we'd never escape them. And of course he did come back now. The very moment David closed the door of the Jaguar behind him, Dad pulled his Bentley into the driveway.

There was no way of telling if he'd seen David get out of the Jag. I was sitting on the front stoop, elbows on my knees, looking at David and quietly hyperventilating as Dad stepped out of the Bentley with a big smile and a hearty "Hello there." David and I locked eyes, running super-fast inner examinations of Dad's words and tone of voice, trying to determine whether they were sincere or sarcastic. Dad came up behind David, dropped his chin, narrowed his eyes, and slapped his hand, hard, against David's right shoulder. David kept his eyes on me. This was going to be bad. But I was not going to freeze. I stood up. My legs were shaking so hard I thought I could hear my joints rattle. My mouth was bone dry. Dad gripped David's shoulder and in a low voice he rumbled, "How much are you benching these days?"

There was a small pause, and then, as I let out a breath I saw in my brother's eyes that we were both experiencing the same instant flood of endorphins or dopamine or whatever it is that makes you feel so high after the kind of good, extended scare we'd just miraculously lived through.

We'd also gotten a good healthy dose of recognition from each other, an acknowledgment that we hadn't cared about Lucky Charms in a while and that it might be time for something new between us. I realized that I secretly admired David for taking the damn car, getting into bars, for making choices and taking risks. He was cool. I liked him, and I kind of wanted to be a little bit more like him. A couple of days later, when we caught sight of each other in the school cafeteria we nodded hello, almost imperceptibly, but for the first time that I could remember.

We probably would have done some palling around for the first time in a while, too, if I wasn't working most days and too tired to do anything but read when I wasn't. I was saving up for a car of my own and eventually left the soup bowls behind for a job as a driver for a large drug store/surgical supply outlet, delivering hospital beds, oxygen tanks, and commodes, which meant that every day my partner Ted and I visited homes where someone had just died or gotten the news that they were dying.

We were the first people called after diagnosis and the second people called after death. At first I dreaded every little red PICK UP notice on our schedule board. Once or twice a month we would go on a run that would leave us speechless for the rest of the day. I once walked into a master bedroom holding a large portable commode to find the man for whom it was intended, emaciated and lying in a fetal position on a sheet-less mattress, tears falling off his nose. He looked at me and said, "No. No. No."

Then there were visits that were speech robbing in a different way. We would be greeted at the door by a woman—almost always a woman—who had just lost her husband, sometimes an hour before, and because we were strangers she'd want to know about "the outside world" and because we were young she'd want us to know about her husband. Sometimes she'd offer us orange juice or homemade iced tea, and show us wedding photos or war medals. One woman took us on a tour of her husband's sculptures, scattered through two acres of birch wood behind their house. She showed them to us in chronological order, as signposts in the story of his life, and the sudden swerves and switchbacks of our improvised path created a physical sense of vicissitude, an almost satirical re-enactment of one particular, pinballing life's journey. There were dozens of pieces arranged in groups, each series progressively simpler and more abstract, except for the last, a collection of small clay turtles with broken shells.

The woman never cried. In fact, she seemed absolutely buoyed by the tour, energized with pride. She watched us load the bed and the tanks and the tubes, all the detritus of her husband's last stand, into our van, with a look of someone standing on the deck of a ship leaving port. I wondered the whole way home if I'd ever know anything about living like that.

Sometime later that month I was driving the van through a slashing rain, back from a nursing home where Ted and I had just delivered a few dozen gallons of cough syrup and laxatives. It was getting dark, and porch lights were starting to come on, each one distracting me for a moment and illuminating slick spots on the road.

A wet lawn full of gnomes appeared in a swell of amber light just ahead of us and to the right. I was momentarily transfixed by the chipped plaster dwarves, hay wagons, and woodpiles, a small thatch-roofed hut, a plastic chimney with plastic smoke coming out of it. The house behind them looked neglected and was dark inside except for the faint blue glow of a television in the front room. Ted's hands suddenly hit the dash and I quickly turned my head to see that we were about to slam into the back of an idling motorcycle. I hit the brakes, harder than I wanted to, and we fishtailed to the right. I took my foot off the pedal and steered into the turn just like they taught us in driver's ed and touched the brakes again, and this time it stopped us cold. We bounced off of our seat backs and for a few seconds just sat there, hunched over and breathing hard.

We hadn't hit the bike, but the van was at a right angle to the road, the back end facing the gnomes, the windshield looking at a house across the street. An old man in an old, plaid wool coat had just emerged from its side door and picked up an overflowing trash can, and was now carrying it carefully down the driveway to the curb. A page of newspaper was ripped out of it by the wind. Cars were backing up in the lane our van blocked. I put the van in gear, eased my foot onto the gas, and a horn tooted impatiently a few cars back as our rear wheels spun a bit and tried to get some traction. It felt like we might have slipped into a shallow rut or a pothole.

I looked over at Ted, then up again through the windshield at the man across the street, struggling with his trash can, trying to secure the lid. He backed off the curb, first one foot and then the other, into a mini-river of gurgling rainwater, oblivious to it and to the oncoming traffic, then threw up his hands in exasperation and took another couple of steps backwards. Ted groaned with worry, but the cars on the old man's side of the road immediately slowed down and started easing their way around him, the *shunk-shunk* of their wipers a cautionary rebuke. I was relieved, but I should have known better. The drivers of the cars I'd been blocking were all pent up, and one of them, a guy in a dirty white Camaro with a missing hubcap on the front right wheel, reared out of the line like a bull from a pen and zoomed by us, right at the old man, then swerved hard and roared away, splashing the man with a wave of cold, oily water.

The man bent forward in shock from the noise and the chill and the wave, and froze for a moment. Then he tipped forward, his bend accelerating, and he slammed hard against the sidewalk, his forehead making an audible slap on the wet concrete.

I immediately shot the van straight across the street and bouncing up over the curb onto the old man's lawn. Ted and I flung our doors open and almost dove across the grass to where he was lying facedown. We picked his head up gently and revealed a small, thick pool of blood on the sidewalk, breaking up under needles of rain. As we turned him over slowly, I expected to see a nasty wound on his forehead, which I did, but far more shocking was what was happening to his face. It was turning a pale, glowing, light blue, everywhere. Then blueish red, then purple, and now gray. As gray as spent charcoal. It was horrible, like he was becoming something other than a human being, right in front of us, right now, with the force of a runaway train. "Heart," Ted said. "Heart attack," I said. "Yeah. Go call," and Ted ran to the house next door.

I took off my jacket and bundled it and put it under the man's head, and I leaned over his face to try and block the rain. I was close to him now. His eyes were open and covered with a milky-gray film. He moved his lips but I couldn't tell if he was trying to speak, or breathe, or if he was even conscious. I had my hands on the wet plaid wool of his shoulders but I didn't know what to do with them. I knew I should say something. I didn't know what to say. I said, "Okay. Okay, okay. No. It's all right. It's all right. We're gonna help you. We're calling help. You're gonna be okay. You're okay."

He was looking at me. His lower jaw was moving, straight up and down, open and shut, open and shut, like a marionette's. He wasn't breathing.

Just as that realization straightened my back, Ted showed up with first one, and then quickly half a dozen people, adults, and they swarmed around the old man with quick and deliberate movements. They took over.

Ted and I backed away, onto the lawn, and watched a circle of raincoats close over the man and block him from our view. We heard a siren in the distance. We got back into the van and slowly backed off the lawn into the street, and as we bumped hard over the curb we heard the sound of three big oxygen tanks clanking against the floor and into each other in the back. Oxygen tanks. And first aid kits and stethoscopes. Ted and I turned to each other with open mouths but didn't say a word. We pulled away and I took one last look out the window. The garbage can lid was still loose.

* * *

"You have to call them, you have to call the hospital." Richard's eyes were full and locked right on me.

"I know, I did, I did. They won't tell me anything. I don't even know his name and they won't give me any information because I'm not a family member."

"But do you think he's dead, did he die? How did he look when you left?"

"Um, I don't know, not great, but the ambulance got there really fast. I just hope he's okay."

Rich inhaled. "Holy *shit*."

"I know."

I had already told him this story three times over the last couple of days. But each time he reacted like he'd never heard it before. He looked like this a lot lately. Like an archeologist lifting the lid of a coffin in a mummy movie. Head pushed forward, jaw clenched, eyes big with curiosity. He was twelve now, and he'd been reading Edgar Allen Poe, teaching himself to cook, practicing his guitar for hours, disappearing with my records for days, staying up to watch movies at night. He asked me questions about every goddamn thing I said and did and thought. We enabled each other's obsessions, poring over newspapers and liner notes, picking up record needles and putting them down again all afternoon, isolating strange chords and tape splices. He'd come into my room with his hands in his pockets and his chin up, pronouncing his latest find, issuing challenges and verdicts, asking questions and eating up answers like a shark. He leaned forward when he watched movies, like me, and memorized lines after hearing them just once, like me. It was the most fun, annoying thing you could imagine. He was absolutely insufferable and my new favorite person.

But I didn't want to tell him the story of the old man's heart attack again. I wanted to tell him that, first thing that morning, I'd gotten the very good news of a "grade readjustment" for my Che Guevara paper. Mr. Bremmer had handed it to me without comment, a fresh, blue A at the top of the page, and in return I graciously refrained from tap dancing on his desk. When I sat down in my American lit class the following period I received big congratulations from friends and felt relaxed for the first time in weeks. Then Mr. Francis started handing out graded papers from the week before and when he gave me mine he looked like he was handling medical waste. There was a C on the front page. I looked over at Ben's paper, the one I'd helped him with and that wasn't any better than mine, and saw an A at the top. I mumbled, "What the fuck?" and Mr. Francis wheeled, as if he'd been waiting for me to say something. He shot out, "Not happy? What are you gonna do, Peter, get your father to come in here and threaten another teacher into changing your grade?"

I felt a sudden sting in my chest. My father? He threatened Bremmer? Oh God. My classmates were all looking at me. Everything started cramping up. I pictured Dad putting his nose right up to Mr. Bremmer's face and telling him that he would blow his fucking head off if he didn't change the grade. And then Bremmer telling Francis, and then all the faculty in the teachers' lounge, all of them getting a good laugh and chiming in with their own crazy Birkenhead stories, and then all the other students in the classroom telling everyone they knew, their friends and their parents and their parents' friends, and then everyone looking at me, everywhere I went, tomorrow and the next day, and I picked up my chair and I said, "Yeah, well, my dad's a better fucking guy then you'll ever be, you fucking asshole," and I sent it skidding hard across the floor into a wall, and quickly walked out the door.

That's the story I wanted to tell Rich, instead of telling about the old man's heart attack again, but I didn't get around to it until eleven years later.

Just as I finished the heart attack story, Dad came into the den and said to me, "Can you come with me for a minute?" I followed him upstairs to his bedroom, and after he closed the door he looked into the middle distance and said that Bonnie was in a lot of pain. His voice cracked a little, and he went on to say she'd chewed almost all the remaining hair from her body and wasn't able to fight off the infections on her skin. She was so weak she couldn't walk, and we had to take her into the vet to be put down. He never actually asked me to come with him but I understood that that was what he wanted. I picked old Bonnie up very slowly from her favorite spot on the floor next to the fireplace bellows. The first dozen times we'd used it, back when she was a pup, she'd barked like mad at the strange, breathing, wheezing creature in our hands. After a few years, though, she pretty much adopted the thing and had since stood guard over it with a maternal ferocity, not letting anyone get near it for a very long time. I picked up the bellows with my free hand and held it close to her on my lap in the car.

When we pulled into the parking at the vet's, Dad left the engine running and very carefully reached over and lifted Bonnie off my lap. You could see in her eyes that she was grateful, and so tired, and a little embarrassed. Dad spoke to her for a minute, called her a "sweet lady," and took her inside, telling me to wait in the car. I said okay, and Bonnie blinked at me. I blinked back and they got out of the car.

Dad came back out about ten minutes later, held the front door open for a woman with two cats in separate carriers, and then strode quickly to the car. When he sat down I saw that his eyes were wet. He put a hand on the wheel and another on the shift but we didn't move, and when he finally let himself breathe, a very teary cough escaped. He held on to the wheel and just let the crying come, softly and steadily, and I turned my head forwards to watch a big, scraggly mutt pull a young couple across the parking lot by his leash. I wondered where Bonnie was, what would be done with her body, and I wondered why we never had a funeral for Grandpa. I rested my hand stiffly on Dad's back and felt his lungs filling and pushing, like the leather bellows in my lap, which my own tears were now falling on in thick drops. Dad said, "Oh. Hoh boy, hoh boy," and wiped his eyes with his hands, and we sat for another minute or so, sniffing occasionally, not talking, and rocking gently with the engine.

* * *

Working opened at the 46th Street Theater on May 15, 1978. Mom had been in Chicago for several weeks during its out-of-town tryout, and had come home exhausted and a little down. Stephen Schwartz, the director, had decided against using the device of a traveling family to connect the show's vignettes, so only one of the songs that Mom and Mary had written would be included for the New York run. But there were several other terrific songwriters on the team (most of whom also contributed one or two songs), and Mom was thrilled to be working with them, to have her name on a billboard over Times Square and a whole new life in front of her.

As for us kids, all we knew was that our mother was about to have a show open on Broadway. There was going to be a big opening night party at a restaurant, and afterwards we would spend the night in a room Dad had booked for us at the Plaza Hotel. We maintained our cultivatedly glum exteriors, but we were beside ourselves.

Yet my memories of that night are the opposite of what I thought they'd be. I thought I'd remember watching Mom walk into the theater, surrounded by famous people and flashbulbs. I thought I'd remember the curtain going up, a big splashy musical number, a joke that brought down the house. Congratulations afterwards, the lifting of glasses and the reading of reviews. I don't remember any of that, or anything else that happened in front of my eyes, except for the show itself. What I remember is the private experience of listening to my mother's song, and the slowly accruing effect of the story it told.

The song was sung that night, with beautiful indignation, by an actress named Bobo Lewis. She played a schoolteacher named Rose who has found herself living in a future that infuriates and frightens her. The lyrics progress from nostalgia to complaint to bitterness, and then to a chilling coda, yet they manage the compassionate trick of revealing the character's humanity even as she's moving away from it. It's like its own little play.

My classroom was always a showcase
In those days we did it ourselves
With colorful pictures and charts on the wall
A snowman in winter, a pumpkin in fall
And all my supplies were in neat little piles
On the shelves

My children were always examples
When the principal came, they would rise
If I had to leave for a minute or two
They always found something "constructive" to do
And everyone sat in their places according to size

But kids don't know how to behave anymore!
Ask them to rise and they'll ask you: "What for?"
They write on the walls and they sit on the floor
It's called "informality" now
They want me to teach in a classroom like that
But nobody tells me how

I made a big thing about spelling
But they learned by the time I got through
They copied the words till they knew them by heart
Ten times for the dumb ones, and twice for the smart
And gold stars were given to those
Who made sentences too

But nobody teaches them spelling today
Who has the time between weaving and clay?
The words they can write I'm embarrassed to say
They're free to "express" themselves now!
The way I've been teaching for forty-one years
Is no longer "effective" or so it appears

Well, damn it!
It worked for me then, so what's wrong with it now?
They say I'm supposed to "keep up with the times"
But nobody ever tells me how . . .
(spoken)
There is one little girl who stands out in my mind in all
    my years of teaching . . . my favorite . . . Pam.
She was special . . .
She wasn't very bright, but she was never any trouble.
I see her every once in a while.
She's a checker at the Treasure Island supermarket.
She gives no trouble today either.
She has the same smile for everyone.

The hairs on my arms stood up, each one for a different reason, when the orchestra played the chord under that last line. The song was a revelation, not just of the character's inner life, but of Mom's, of how closely observant, clear-eyed, and humane she was. And how alive.

Why did this feel like a surprise? Yet also a confirmation? How could I know someone so well, and not at all, yet deeply recognize her either way? And what was this sense of "opening" in myself I was hit by, of clear skies, recognition, permission, and possibility? I couldn't have articulated any of these questions, of course. I was just barely beginning to pay some small attention to the unseen, to not put all my trust in what could be talked about, but I knew I wanted more of whatever this feeling was.

And I wanted to know this new Mom. I had been listening to a lot of songwriters who favored unreliable or unlovable or morally ambiguous narrators and characters, and as I watched Mom's song being performed that night, I realized that this schoolteacher of hers would fit in pretty well with Warren Zevon's Thompson Gunners or Elvis Costello's detectives. I couldn't believe it. I was ready to enjoy

Mom's succeeding on her own terms, sure, but who knew that she'd be cool?

Her coolness would come at a price, though—I was sure of that. The contrast between my parents' worldviews was another of that night's revelations, and it now couldn't have been clearer. As I watched the show I kept an eye on Dad and tried to gauge his reaction to the all-too-human schoolteacher, and to the particular kind of success Mom was enjoying that night. Her song would have been the star of the show for our family no matter what, of course; she could have set the phone book to music and I would have thought it was the greatest thing ever written. But its startling fullness made it one of the emotional highlights of the evening for a lot of people, and I could feel that her achievement was of a deeper kind than Dad might have been expecting, and that the implications of it, of Mom's fiercely living consciousness, had shaken him up a bit.

Alison had a headache. She asked for an aspirin a couple of times after we got back to the hotel, but Mom and Dad were distracted by phone calls, so Rich dug a couple of pills out of Mom's purse for her as she tried to curl up with a book on the big foldout bed in the "living room," where the four of us would be sleeping. She was at the end of six full hours of concentrated brother-and-father time, never an easy thing for her.

David and Rich were having some kind of low-grade, running argument about who was going to sleep where, and each time it rose to audible levels Dad wearily announced, "Enough!" and they continued the argument via bird flipping and crotch grabbing.

The whole family probably hadn't been in the same room together in years, and it had been even longer since we'd been on any kind of group outing. Alison was eleven, Richard twelve, David seventeen, and I was eighteen, and we had all sort of shuffled and shambled through the events of the night, sitting in the wrong seats, laughing at the wrong times, being too quiet or too loud, while Mom and Dad were doing their own careful dance with each other, trying to find some kind of solid footing on shifting ground.

Dad had given Mom a big, smiling kiss as the curtain went down, and for a while afterwards he was beaming and talkative. But he'd watched the show in a constant state of motion, flaring his elbows, scooting his feet, folding and refolding his hands. He frequently dropped his chin and leered at the stage with what looked like a combination of menace, lust, and critical judgment, and just as often tilted his head back with a huge, eye-crinkling grin on his face, letting out a high-pitched "Hee hee," or a sudden bark of "Ha!"

He became tense at the hotel, coiled and wary, clenching his teeth. I realized that the hotel was *his* thing, his contribution to the night, and that it was a very big deal to him. He had really enjoyed telling everyone at the party that we were staying there—but there must have been two dozen far less expensive, much nicer hotels closer to the theater. In 1978 the Plaza still had tiny, turn-of-the-century-size rooms that hadn't been renovated in decades, and the place was barely getting by on its crumpety charms. Our suite was . . . well, if Dad's old Mini and his new Bentley had a baby, it would be this hotel room. Too much and not enough. It was a perfect place for a second honeymoon, but not so good for putting up a cranky family of six.

All I knew that night was that something about it made me uncomfortable, and being uncomfortable made me feel guilty. Why couldn't I just enjoy this generous thing Dad had done for us?

The stuffy closeness of the room felt especially constricting after the wild blue yonder of the opening. We wanted to be striding across pretend stages and booming out reenactments, or packing into the car and huddling together in pride and falling asleep watching the city speed by, not tiptoeing around a museum, not listening to Dad talk about the Plaza and its history. We wanted to talk about Mom and the show and the future.

Dad asked us to get ready for bed. David and Richard were

wrestling on the floor, and when David banged into a lamp, almost knocking it over, Dad fumed, "Goddamn it," and moved it to the side with a dull clang. "Cut the crap," Dad said, "and decide where you're sleeping. There's a cot here somewhere for one of you." Mom was looking into the middle distance the way she had years before on Cape Cod.

A chorus of "I'm not," "Not me," "No way" greeted Dad and his jaw tightened. He flung open the door of a closet and said, "Peter, you will sleep on the cot. You can sleep on a cot for one goddamn night." I said sure, fine, of course, and Richard and David made funny faces at me while Alison tried to shrink into the corner of her bed and Mom started back into the bedroom. The cot was nowhere to be found. Dad let out a grumble as he slammed the door shut on another closet, and Mom turned around and asked, "What's wrong?"

He spat out, "Nothing! Nothing is goddamn wrong. Can we just have some fun? Or is that not allowed?"

"Don't you dare speak to me that way," Mom said, containing her obvious anger as Dad stormed over to a desk by the window overlooking Fifty-eighth Street and grabbed the phone. He didn't say, "Hello," or "This is room 812," he said, "I asked for a cot. I spoke to the manager a week ago and asked for a goddamn cot to be put in room 812. It's eleven thirty at night and I've got four kids in this room and not enough beds. Bring a goddamn cot up here, immediately," and hung up.

Mom and Dad disappeared into the other room. David and Richard got undressed, I brushed my teeth, Alison closed her eyes, and we all tried to ignore the muffled racket coming through the wall. It got very quiet after a few minutes, then started up again, then quieted one more time. Finally, Dad came charging through the door in his underwear and a T-shirt and grabbed at the phone.

"Where's the bloody cot? . . . The cot, the fucking cot! . . . Oh, yeah, you think so? You know what? You don't want to mess with me. Because I'm a crazy, crazy fucker . . . Yeah? Come on up, then. Come on up so I can throw you out the fucking window. I'm gonna throw you right through this fucking window and end your fucking life." Mom was standing in the doorway to the bedroom trying to wipe some cream from her face and her hand stopped. She had a look of blazing disgust in her eyes.

We kids got very quiet and tried to disappear. We barely breathed for five or ten minutes. Finally a knock on the door came, and when Dad threw it open there was a folded cot standing there, but no one with it, so he stepped out into the hallway in his underwear and yelled with increasing volume, "Where are ya? Where are ya? Where are ya?!!"

Alison put a hand up against her face and looked like she wanted to die. David and Richard kept scuffling under the radar, and with each carpeted *thwump* and upholstered *foonk* you could feel a little more air go out of Mom. Dave twisted one of Richard's fingers; Rich fought the impulse to scream but his face got red and tears formed in his eyes. I could see he wouldn't give in. Dave's jaw was set with rage. He leaned into the twist and Richard bucked as Mom examined the cotton ball in her hand. I grabbed David by the arm and got kicked in the leg in return, as David rumbled, "Get off!" I pulled harder and finally freed Rich, and he wheeled a kick at David's leg but hit mine, right in the same place David's kick had landed. I muffled a shout and hopped around the room as Rich punched away at David's arm, growling under his breath, "Fat. Fat. Fucking. Cunt." Ali lifted the old frayed bedspread all the way up over her head and buried herself under it.

I was booked on a flight to West Palm Beach the following weekend. Mom's parents had moved there a few years before and had a little house where they welcomed a seemingly endless procession of friends, each one armed with news of the latest accomplishments of their progeny. The perpetually opening and closing screen door at their place was like a swinging saloon door in a Clint Eastwood movie, and each day brought a different gunslinger. Visitors would stand in the foyer, silhouetted against the sunlight streaming through the doorway. My grandmother would slowly stand to greet them as spaghetti western music whistled in the background, and then, after a brief pause, they'd each fire in quick succession: "This is my grandson, Peter. He's starting at NYU in the fall." "That's nice. Ray got into Yale." *Boom. Splat.* Just like that, it was over. And the townspeople would slowly emerge to collect the bodies.

I was openly idealizing Grandma and Papa at that point. How could I not? They were the ideal corrective for adolescent self-pity, and living proof that I might not be genetically doomed.

A trip to Florida was something to be jealous of, and David was decidedly not interested in my preparations the morning of my flight. He groused from under his pillow when Dad came into his room at 6:30 to pull a suitcase down from the closet for me, and again when Dad shook him and reminded him he was supposed to take me to the airport. The night before, David had insisted on driving, since he'd just gotten his license and was looking for any excuse to legally have the car for an hour or two. But by the time I'd made myself breakfast and finished packing he still hadn't pulled himself out of bed, and Dad was starting to boil, so I headed off disaster by cranking up David's bedside radio and putting it out of his reach, figuring I'd make it up to him with a doughnut on the way to JFK.

I shoved half an English muffin in my mouth and stood up from the table as David came groggily and shirtless into the kitchen. He groaned and plaintively asked Dad, "What—what time does he have to be there?"

The air filled with combustible silence. David was at least a head taller than Dad at this point, and much bigger. They shared the weights and workout equipment in the basement but David was obviously getting much more out of them, a fact that Dad reacted to by habitually calling David "fat." He used the same inside-out logic to describe him as "lazy," which particularly stung David because of the trouble he'd been having paying attention in school. The thick filter he created over the years to block Dad's words kept a lot of others out as well, and we could all feel how desperately he wanted to grab hold of information as it came flying at him, and how afraid he was to admit that, or to speak up about anything, really. Each of us had borders we were afraid to cross, and for David it was the one between silence and speech.

So when Dad set the air on fire with, "You lazy fuck," David didn't say a word. He didn't answer when Dad spat out, "Fine, forget it. I'll take him. No wonder you're so fucking fat," or when he said, "Just go back up to bed, fatso." But when I complained, "Dad," David started for the stairs to get dressed and very evenly said to Dad, "It's okay, I'll drive him. I never said I wouldn't. I was just bitching about it being early. I'm a teenager."

Dad kept at him, though. "Don't bother. Really. I've had it. I should've known better. You're a lazy goddamn fuck."

David turned on the bottom stair and faced him. "Don't say that to me."

"Why not, you're a lazy fuck," said Dad.

The muscles in David's back were clenching. If he threw a punch at Dad he could kill him. "Don't talk to me that way. Don't."

"Why? Come on, I want to fight you. Come on. Right now."

"Dad, Jesus, c'mon," I said, and David stepped down to meet him.

"You kidding? Are you kidding? I could kill you. Don't talk to me that way. That's it. Don't talk to me that way." He waited a beat then turned slowly and walked up the stairs, leaving Dad stuck in place, fuming and sputtering.

We didn't even turn on the radio in the car. We just rode silently for five minutes. I had no idea what to do with the flood of love and admiration I was feeling. David turned to look at me, something neither of us did very much, but he didn't say anything, he just cried. I grabbed his arm and said, "He's an asshole. Don't let any of that shit he said get to you. It's bullshit and you don't deserve one fucking word of it. You're amazing. Seriously, you are. To not sink to his level like that? I don't know how you did that. But you know what—you showed him, you showed him how a real person behaves. Really. I'm so fucking proud of you, man."

"Thanks," he said, "thanks. I didn't want you to think I didn't want to drive you. I just, I don't . . . God, why does he talk to me like that?"

"I don't know," I said. "I really don't know."

He said, "You probably don't remember this, but one time, when you and me were fighting, and he punched me in the stomach . . ."

"Yeah," I said, "he thought you were fighting dirty or something,"

"Right. Well he came up to my room after, like a while after, and I figured okay, at least he's gonna apologize, but when he came in he looked at me and said, 'I don't love you and you're not my son.'"

I couldn't speak for a minute. And then I just said, "God. Dave, I'm so sorry. He's just a fuck. I can't believe it."

We rode the rest of the way without saying much, but thinking a lot. In another three months I would be at NYU and Dave would be spending most of his time with his new girlfriend Kathy, whom he would go on to marry six years later. We would only live in the same house a little while longer, and it would be many years until we spent any real time together again. But at least on that day, in the car, for the first time ever, after almost eighteen silent years in the trenches, we had finally talked about Dad.

PART THREE

11

The sidewalk on Nineteenth Street was full of people who had clearly been paid to fuck with me. There were a large number of well-trained, fuckhead stunt walkers who had been paid to ruin my day, all of whom were masters of the ancient Chinese art of veering into your path at the very last second so that you actually ended up— I swear, I don't know how they did this but I swear—you ended up *farther back* than you were before.

I didn't let them get to me, though.

I hated auditions. And I was on my way to one. I was twenty-nine and I had no skills besides acting. What else could I do?

You know what? I thought. *In France, they don't ask you what you do for a living when they meet you. You're not what you do for them. You're who you are. I am who I am, that's what I think,* I thought.

There were probably four or five different plays and television shows holding auditions at the casting office that morning and the hallway was teeming with people behaving in ways that would've gotten them taken to a shelter anywhere else: pointing invisible guns at invisible perps, silently mouthing off to potted plants, flirting with their knees. Most were subtly davenning over scripts, mumbling and repeating lines in between frozen moments of self-scrutiny and not-so-furtive glances at the more famous, better clothed, and much better prepared sitting across from them.

My guys were in a big, dark bunch, a gaggle of prospective Osvalds and Reginas, there to audition for Ibsen's *Ghosts*. A guy I had a few sandwiches with when we did a play in Brooklyn; a girl I'd done a reading with and who caught me staring at the downy, blond treasure trail on her belly, but who talked to me anyway. There was Crane, a great guy, chronic perspirer, his hand against the wall, legs crossed at the ankles, looking like a big, sweaty Cary Grant. But before I could talk to any of them, the casting director's assistant came out of the office and said loudly, "Mr. Birkenhead!" doing her best to sound exactly as friendly as she had for the guy before me, and I thought, this is just the most pathetic way for a grown man to make a living, ever. This is like lining up in kindergarten to do somersaults one at a time. This is ridiculous. But God I want to do this play. I love this play. I really do. Shit.

And so I went in to the audition full of road rage and ambivalence, but I got the part anyway. Or maybe because.

In keeping with the family tradition, I'd come to acting—or come *back* to acting—fairly late. Later than many actors I knew, anyway. I started taking some classes at twenty-three, after snapping out of a three-year sleepwalking spell that began the day I walked out of a senior-year lecture on the Soviet Politburo and never returned to NYU again. (It would be many years before I realized that I had left school right around the time my parents' marriage was breaking up.) I spent many, many days wandering, literally wandering around the city, nursing a knish or a falafel, circling within neighborhoods, stopping to watch street fights and photo shoots, dogs being fed and sofas being hoisted through windows.

One Sunday morning, while waiting at the Port Authority subway station for the 7 train to Flushing, I noticed that the post I was leaning against—one of the dozens of blue pillars in the station, like in every station in New York—had the word "PRAY" scratched into it.

This would have seemed totally unremarkable in the graffiti-plagued New York of the early eighties, except for the fact that I'd noticed it before, on other pillars in other stations, enough of them to make me suddenly realize that I was witnessing a feat of breathtaking insanity.

I started checking the other pillars on the platform, and every single one of them had PRAY carved into the side, vertically, at eye level. Over the next few days, and then weeks, and then months, I made a habit of checking all the pillars I leaned against or walked past, and on every one of them, in every station, in Manhattan, Brooklyn, Queens, and the Bronx, I spotted the word.

By the time I came to a pillar at the far end of a station in Far Rockaway, a platform I'd just checked from one end to the other, I finally understood that I was looking at someone's Sistine Chapel or Hoover Dam, a masterpiece of applied schizophrenia, and that the only person in the world who might be crazier than the artist himself would be a devoted admirer. I forced myself to stop reading pillars. But it was hard to lose the sense of a deep stream of desperation coursing under the city, as constant as the Hudson and easier to fall into.

I'd started at NYU as a political science major, but ended up studying almost exclusively with one teacher, a brilliant religious studies professor who offered two or three new courses every semester with names like "Atheism, Theism, and Existentialism" and "The Perfect Society." I hadn't finished my degree. I was as employable as a felon.

I worked as a waiter, a movie theater manager, a telemarketer, a waiter again, a shoe salesman, an answering service operator, a house painter, a chauffeur, a temp, a waiter again, and an actor. My social life consisted almost entirely of meeting friends at revival houses for double features, then a scotch or three at the Cedar Tavern or some other past-its-prime, formerly legendary place where we would bitch over boilermakers and pretend to be dissolute geniuses.

I also took a bunch of not-for-credit classes, and a classmate in a writing seminar suggested taking an improv class to help with character development and dialogue. That led to a proper "scene study" class taught by the character actor William Hickey, who had a head of hair like an old paintbrush and a voice like a goose but who turned my life around one night when I was declaiming a speech with my back turned oh-so-dramatically to my scene partner, by suddenly slamming a hand on his desk and honking, *"Stop acting!"* After Bill I studied with Geraldine Page, then Uta Hagen for three years, and finally I started getting work in small theaters, for no money but lots of dates with actresses.

I spent whole weeks in the Fifty-eighth Street branch of the New York Public Library, reading until my eyes were raw. I moved nine times. I started getting paying work, and began to understand that being a "New York actor" often meant being a Philadelphia actor. Every couple of months I'd tell some friend who was doing a play that I was thinking of getting out of the business, that I just couldn't take one more minute of wondering if I'd ever work again, one more restaurant manager tirade, or dead houseplant, or unemployment form, or bruise from a loft ladder, or non-ringing phone, and then the next month I'd listen to the same friend tell me the same things, while I reassured him that he'd be back on his feet like me in no time.

I'd pretty much lost touch with friends from home. Josh came to see me in a play once, and I'd met him at his office uptown for lunch soon after, but we hadn't talked since then. Nancy Lyon had stopped in to a little theater I was working at downtown and we caught up a bit. She'd been divorced from Lee for a while and looked great. I told her about Mom remarrying in 1984, and how much we all liked Jere, her new husband. I told her about David becoming a cop and getting married and having kids. I told her that Richard and Alison were out on their own now, living in the city, but that none of us saw each other very often. Nancy told me that Nelle had married and asked me when I was going to "settle down." She told me that she was a little surprised to hear I'd become an actor because she always thought of me as one of those people who was an extrovert when he's one-on-one, but an introvert in big groups.

I said, yeah, that sounded about right, and that I knew it might be hard to believe, but a lot of the actors I knew were painfully shy, attention-averse loners with huge record collections and probably several dead bodies in the closet, and I related to them a lot better than I did to the party-people kind, and that's when she said, okay, I gotta go. A lot of my conversations went like this these days. I had no "off" switch, no brakes.

Osvald Alving in *Ghosts* is a classic prodigal, an impulsive young painter who has just returned from his bohemian life in Italy to his mother's home in Norway suffering from an unnamed disease that a doctor has "diagnosed" only cryptically, telling him, "The sins of the father visit the son." Osvald has ostensibly come home to spend the winter with his mother, but in reality he's there to ask her help in ending his life when the disease, almost certainly syphilis, inevitably progresses to the point of dementia.

He's at a loss to explain the doctor's words because he still believes in a threadbare family mythology that casts his now dead father as a devoted husband and upstanding member of the community. When Osvald first appears he's proudly smoking his father's pipe, and is pleased when another character is startled by the similarity between the cut of his mouth and that of the late Captain Alving's.

Osvald remembers getting sick when he smoked the pipe once before—as a small child, at his father's urging—and is clueless enough to consider that memory a happy one, and to rant about the soul-crushing gloom that hangs over his provincial hometown and its hypocritical residents. By the end of the play he's learned the truth about his father's neglect and philandering, and resigned himself as best he can to the end of his own life.

Two pages after I read the line about the shape of Osvald's mouth I realized that my jaw was clenched so tight it hurt, and that I was in equal parts excited and repulsed by the idea of playing the part. By this point, in 1989, almost ten years since my parents' divorce, my father and I had settled into a wary routine of lunch visits every couple of months (always me visiting him), phone calls every six weeks or so, and dinner once or twice a year. My brothers and sister had the same sort of relationship with him, and while we often felt our jaws clench when we were with him, we also noticed that Dad apparently hadn't been violent, at least as far as we knew, since the marriage ended, and that after a while there was a noticeable ebb in his anger, and even an improvement in his wardrobe.

It was clear he was trying to stick to the rules of the unspoken probation he was on with us, and maybe even earn his way back to something more. Sometimes it seemed like he could hear our conversations about him from thirty blocks away and make adjustments accordingly. Just a couple of days after my audition for *Ghosts* I asked Rich why he thought our father still, after ten years, didn't have a pillow on his bed. (He reminded me that Dad used to say, "They didn't have pillows at Stalingrad."). But by the time I visited Dad one morning a few days later, his big, old gray and orange cat, Miss Marple, was happily ensconced on one. He didn't acknowledge it, of course, but he did take me into the bedroom and show me an antique Scottish saber he had just hung over his bed, right below a Ghurkha machete, and it was obvious that he wanted me to see the pillow, too.

I looked around the tiny room and was struck by the other small improvements he'd made. There was a small scratching post for Miss Marple. The bed itself, while still only a full-size model, was a real bed with a new, polished wood frame, a significant improvement over his old, purely functional, black steel cot. His cigar humidor and pipe rack, full of cleaned and polished Briars and Meerschaums, were both proudly displayed on his dresser, right next to his Brooklyn College "Teacher of the Year" award from 1972. I picked up the pipe at the end of the rack, a very dark, curved-stem Briar I remembered him buying when we lived in England, and the smell of it put a shot of that old medieval fear in my blood.

Instead of curtains Dad had hung flags in front of his windows:

the cross of St. George and the cross of St. Andrew. They're the flags of England and Scotland, and when you put them together with the cross of St. Patrick, they make the Union Jack. Weird touch, I thought, but still, a touch.

I asked him if he was still smoking Bances, the cigars he'd sent me to the store for every weekend when I was a kid, and he said no, he was trying to give them up. He even looked like he'd finally lost all the weight he'd gained right after the divorce.

As Dad cooked us some breakfast, I tried clumsily to tell him about *Ghosts* a few times and didn't get anything more than an "Okay," or "That's nice," in response, but I had learned not to expect too much in the way of acknowledgment for my work, and anyway he'd recently given me more than I'd ever hoped for. I'd heard from other people that he'd bragged about a couple of things he'd seen me do, but he'd never shared that with me until just a few months before, when he came backstage to see me after a performance of Neil Simon's autobiographical play *Broadway Bound* at the Broadhurst Theatre on Broadway.

I'd played Stanley, the older of two brothers who are trying to break into show business as a writing team, and my big moment came in the second act when, after listening to a radio show we'd written, our father accuses us of humiliating him and the rest of the family by using his personal stories as material. He goes off on a long, paranoid jag about our betrayal, at the end of which he admits to cheating on our mother, and that's when I go off on a jag of my own, angrily calling him on his hypocrisy and selfishness, blasting him for his treatment of Mom and telling him to go to hell.

I wasn't surprised at how fired up I was during the monologue the night Dad came to see the show, but it was still an intense enough experience to leave me wondering, "What just happened?" afterwards. I thought I might have hit it out of the park, but I also thought I might have completely embarrassed myself. The actor playing my father and I had previously played father and son, although in much more idealized form, in *Brighton Beach Memoirs,* the "prequel" to *Broadway Bound,* a couple of years before. He had always been completely honest and constructively critical with me and I thought of him as a mentor, so I was beside myself when he put his hand on my shoulder as the curtain came down and said "Way to go, champ." I took a relieved breath and was about to leave the stage when I saw my Dad coming out of the wings and onto the set.

Usually we would meet visitors in our dressing rooms, after we'd had enough time to change and they'd been able to make their way backstage, so when I saw Dad the first thing that hit me was how quickly he'd gotten to the stage. The next thing that hit me was that Dad was crying, which stunned me, and very quickly after that, the realization that I was having this big, meaningful moment standing next to Joan Rivers.

She was playing Kate Jerome, the mother of Stanley and Eugene, and had surprised all of us with how hard she worked at making her theatrical debut a success. Dad was able to take advantage of meeting Joan to get himself together, and she was able to quickly pick up on the feeling in the air and make a jokey, hasty exit, glancing back supportively at me as she stepped into the wings.

Dad and I were standing in the "living room" of the set, a re-creation of an early fifties, working-class home in Brighton Beach, a stone's throw away from where we'd actually lived in Sheepshead Bay, in the building where I'd flown down the stairs. I was right in front of the couch, and he was standing by an old wing chair—the precise positions in which my stage father and I had been an hour before for our big confrontation. It was very quiet now that everyone had gone, but we could feel the reverberations of the show, of the past, all around us. After a pause, Dad said, "That was great, hon. Really wonderful." And that was all he said, but it was plenty. He still had tears in his eyes, and I was sure he'd "gotten" the scene the way I'd hoped he would, that he had appreciated it in some way, in addition to the pain and embarrassment he must have felt. And in case there was any doubt, a familiar voice barked from somewhere in the wings behind me at full "Can-we-talk" strength, rich with plotzy farklemptness, as Joan made her way to her dressing room, "Uch, your father loves you!" And I had to agree.

So as I sat on the couch in his apartment months later and watched him making breakfast I thought that his "okay" and "that's nice" would do for now. The moment after the show from a couple of months before never came up. He talked for a while longer about his new sword, said he'd driven all the way down to a big gun show in Baltimore to buy it, and that he'd been waiting for months to make the trip. He said in a suddenly wistful tone that he'd left at five in the morning, and that the drive reminded him of the ones we used to make to Hyannis every summer. I scanned my memories for a moment from one of those trips when Dad wasn't threatening to pull the car over and make us walk to Cape Cod or engaging in a high-speed chase with a fascist, and I couldn't find one.

He toasted thick pumpernickel bread to go with the eggs, and I listened to him go on at some length about how cold it was outside, a subject I knew would take him directly to the inadequate boots the Germans wore when they invaded Russia in 1940, so I headed him off by telling him I'd been to a new restaurant the night before that I thought he might like. They had Yorkshire pudding on the menu. He asked, "Which restaurant?" with his eyes narrowed, as if he was asking, "Which bridge did you buy from a stranger?" and I told him about it, and about the sea scallop sandwich with pesto I'd had. He said, "Oh *God,*" like I'd just told him I'd ordered braised money on a bed of stolen baby candy topped with slave sweat. He kept his eyes on the pan as he stirred his eggs. "Oh brother," he sighed. "Nouvelle cuisine, I assume. What did they give you, half a scallop on a slice of organic carrot?" Big breath, big, noisy sigh. The fight against pretentiousness and enjoyment was never-ending, a lifelong struggle, and it was taking its toll. But he'd handled worse before and he could handle this. Somebody had to.

With probably a little too much energy I blurted out that I was seeing someone, that her name was Nora and I'd met her at an audition and she was an actress from outside Savannah and I really liked her. And Dad took a big bite of bread and a slug of tea and said, oh that's great, and God, he knew a guy from Atlanta once, a real prick named Mangold whose family moved to Bed-Stuy in the late thirties, and who led a local group of Nazis in attacks against the neighborhood branch of the Communist Party. Actual Nazis? Oh yeah, in full uniform—brown shirts, swastikas, the whole deal—and they crippled a guy, broke both his knees with a Billy club . . .

Miss Marple tried to claw the toast out of my hands, and when Dad turned his head away I let her get as much of it as she could. When Nora had asked me about Dad that morning I'd given her my usual vague spiel about him being "eccentric" and when I left her apartment I had to fight off the impulse to turn around and tell her the truth.

Dad somehow segued from Mangold the Prick to the internment camps in California for Japanese Americans, and from there to George Bush's record as a bomber pilot in World War II, how he had possibly jumped out of his damaged plane before he was supposed to, and I said, "Really?" and "Huh," and "Wow," and finally he brushed his hands off and headed into the bathroom. I tore off another little piece of my toast for the cat and let her lick it from my hand, and from behind the bathroom door Dad said something, sharply, so I would hear it, but it echoed in the tiny room and was hard for me to make out. I thought he said, "She can't have butter. Do not give her any!" but I wasn't sure, and the sound of it hit me in a strange way, like I'd heard him say it before. It sounded like something, but what? I tried to focus and grab at whatever it was I was remembering, but it slipped away. I thought about how often we had all heard Dad speaking sharply behind closed doors, how many times I'd found myself wondering what I had just heard. Dad peed forever behind the bathroom door, and I got up from the couch to stretch. I put my arms over my head and suddenly felt woozy, and it came back to me: David's room. The day we were fighting in the yard and Dad hit him in the gut. I remembered what David had told me about that day years later. About after, when David thought he was coming to apologize. But instead he said, "I don't love you and you're not my son." That's what he said to him. David was eleven.

I watched a column of winter light break and reassemble, break and reassemble, as one of the flags rose and fell from a window over the steam pipes. I heard Dad finishing up and I got my bearings. I turned and strolled quietly back into the bedroom, Miss Marple following excitedly at my heels. I heard Dad turn on the tap in the little bathroom sink. I stood at the bedroom dresser and put my hand on top of the pipe rack. I lifted the curved-stem Briar from its place, turned it around in my hand and watched a bit of light bounce off the bowl. I brought it to my nose and sniffed again, and as Miss Marple's watchful eyes got very big, I slipped it carefully into my pocket.

"You're going to learn so much!" Nora said, grabbing my arm with real strength. She leaned in and focused her eyes on mine with an almost unsettling intensity. Red haired but dark eyed, a spray of freckles across her long, straight nose, she was especially beautiful in winter.

"I feel like this is going to be a real experience for you, like playing this part is going to make something crack right open. You were meant to play Osvald."

We had stopped moving. She'd stopped me. We were on Cornelia Street in the Village, walking off a couple of bowls of minestrone, ducking our heads from the cold and leaning into each other. She turned to face me, the wind blowing her hair back heroically, a Polish-Jewish, southern Joan of Arc.

"What? Crack open. Okay, I don't know what that means. And what do you mean I was 'meant to play Osvald'?" That's what I said. For years I would think about reversing time and taking it back. Not because it was the worst of the dickish things I said—far from it—but because it was the first one I could remember when I tried to understand how I blew everything up.

Nora knew about my dad, or knew there was a lot to know, anyway. She knew that I mostly brushed the subject off, and I'm sure she could see more clearly than I did that I needed to stop doing that. That I needed to "crack something open." But all I heard when she said those words was, "You're a mental case from a family of mental cases. You're one of those kids from that crazy house with the guns."

"So ask me nicely," she said. "Okay? Ask me what I mean. Or don't, if you don't want to know."

"I do. I want to know. I do. I mean, I really do. Tell me."

I wondered if I was up to this. I wondered if I could keep up. I wondered if there had ever been a dimple like Nora's—not a dimple at all, really, but a crescent carved around her mouth by bemusement and enjoyment and disappointment, already, at twenty-eight.

"You seem ready for this. Like this is the right thing at the right time, that's all. I can tell how excited you are about it. I knew you were going to get it, just from the effect it had on the way you walk. When you left for the callback you were completely in the grip of it, on fire." She stopped in mid-stride. "Oh God, look at this!"

She let go of my arm and put her face against a fortune-teller's window and looked in. Her voice stayed in my ears for a few seconds every time she spoke. It was deep, clear, musical, buttery. She knew it was powerful and she wielded it gently.

I watched the back of her head as she peered into the purple room. I was maybe two feet behind her, and then the next moment I wasn't and my face was in her hair. I leaned into it, got lost. I kissed the back of her head. She turned around and took my face in her hands and I felt light-headed with love. I love you, I said and she said it back.

At that point in my life I had the romantic metabolism of a house-fly. I would buzz around a new girlfriend, noisy but elusive, unreachable and too close at the same time, until finally hurling myself at the invisible barrier between us and ending up flattened and embarrassed on her front stoop. I'd start finding reasons to leave as soon as I was invited to stay. As soon as sisters were invited over for dinner or shirts were given as gifts, I would need to pay more attention to my career and zip off somewhere. Making a relationship real was out of the question.

Reality itself was an outrage, a reminder that I was going to die, and the part of me that still occasionally made plans to manage the Mets and fly the space shuttle and remake *Sullivan's Travels* just wouldn't hear of anything as small-minded as dying at some point, or as limiting as possessing only a single personality. Going out of town every couple of months to do a play and have another desert-island fling with someone new suited me much better, and gave me lots of excuses for "taking it slow," as I very much liked to say.

But I was finally becoming aware of the dangers of isolation, of how hard and important it was to resist the siren call of the dive bar, the unalphabetized collection of John Prine bootlegs, and the life they were a harbinger of. I'd finally started to understand that memorizing Monty Python routines would not, despite the infuriating unfairness of it all, be rewarded with the love of a good woman, and so I was learning to fight my den-ish tendencies, and poke my head into the soft and scary light of restaurants. I'd admitted to myself that I in fact did not want to be Superman, resigned to a life without Lois in the Fortress of Solitude, telling myself isolation was the price of being so super.

And then, at an audition for a play, for the part of a physically imposing, roguishly charming, small-time hit man for the South Bronx mob, a part I considered myself *perfect* for, I found that I could not take my eyes off an actress sitting across from me with a beautiful, crescent-shaped dimple in her left cheek who looked like she was trying to resist the urge to throw herself into the arms of the girl next to her and weep, like she just wanted get this last audition right and maybe never, ever come back. It was only when she took a break to talk to a four-year-old kid sitting across from her that I saw her dimple deepen and realized she had actually been immersed in her preparation and probably wasn't going to leave before auditioning.

They called my name. Someone with a southern accent said, "Wait, are you Peter Birkenhead?" It was the woman with the dimple, talking to me.

"What? Yes, I am, yes."

"Oh. I have a blind date with you later."

"You—You're Nora? Beth's Nora?"

"I am. Yes."

I didn't say anything.

"You should go in now, sugar."

"You know, you're right, I should."

"Good luck."

"Thank you very much. See you in five minutes."

On the way to our chaperoned, blind lunch date I asked her a dozen questions about herself. She was an only child. She'd grown up near Savannah, Georgia, attended the Royal Academy of Dramatic Arts, and had a day job as a vocal coach. She thought Scorsese and Mamet were overrated. Her father died when she was three and she wasn't sure any of her memories of him were real. She thought I asked a lot of questions.

At some point she took my arm, and it felt more easily intimate than it did flirtatious. I liked her very much.

We made a big show of walking into the restaurant arm in arm and it had the intended effect on the jaw of our mutual friend, who indulged our few, half-hearted attempts to include her in the conversation then made an early and satisfied exit.

Three days later, at her place, Nora put a plate of swordfish, baked potato, and spinach in front of me and I didn't take my first bite until three hours later. When she had to fly to Georgia the next weekend she called me from both airports.

I would be leaving for Maine and *Ghosts* in two months, so we tried to pack in as much time together as we could before then. We cooked together, read together. Bought seven different kinds of feta cheese in Astoria. I took her to her first Mets game. We drank hot chocolate with marshmallows for breakfast in bed one morning and talked about Osvald.

I was nervous about playing him. He spends most of the play in self-flagellating regret, believing he's caused his own sickness by living a reckless, bohemian life. In the first act he praises his late father for "having managed to achieve so much in the world, so much that was good and useful," and then when he finally learns the truth about him he seems unfazed, adopting a pose of protective cool and saying, "I don't really see what difference it makes . . . Obviously I'm sorry for him, as I would be for anyone else, but . . . I never knew anything about Father . . . I never knew the man."

This was pretty close to my usual line about my father. I used almost the same words when one afternoon Nora segued from Osvald, to me, to Dad. "I really can't say that I know him very well. I see him every once in a while, but he's a troubled guy. Eccentric. Although he does seem to be doing a little better lately. I don't know. I was lucky. My parents divorced when I was twenty, so it didn't really affect me the way it would if I was younger. Everyone's good now. We've put it all behind us."

I paused, hoping that might be enough, but I knew she was going to ask for more information. This was always a crucial moment for me, the broaching of the topic of my father. I wanted to prepare Nora for her eventual first meeting with him, to make it less likely that she'd be caught off guard in any of the many ways she might be. But I needed to do it without scaring her away.

So when she asked me about him again, I handled it as I often had before with other girlfriends, by enlisting the help of Albert

Finney. Seriously, just bear with me, I said, really, look—he's physically a dead-ringer for my father, and it's like every movie he makes depicts a different side of Dad's personality. For a good example of his table manners, I said, you couldn't do better than the famous eating scene from *Tom Jones*, which in the movie is supposed to be earthy and erotic, but which, when Dad did it in a Chinese restaurant on Ninth Avenue was often the highlight of the trip for stunned tourists at the next table.

I told her that Dad's talent for understatement was best illustrated in Sir Albert's depiction of the delusional Shakespearean actor playing King Lear in *The Dresser*, that his commitment to sobriety is hinted at in *Under the Volcano*, and that the movie that comes closest to a short seminar in Life with My Father was a pretty-much-forgotten film called *Shoot the Moon* in which Finney does his best to push his long-suffering wife, played by Diane Keaton, into the arms of a much younger, less tweedy and drunk guy, so that he has an excuse to throw typewriters through windows and tear up tennis courts in fits of dramatic self-loathing. I told her how much I had looked forward to seeing this movie when it came out, hoping that someone had finally figured out a way to make a film about a family like ours, but that, while for people who have never seen their father's name on a police report it takes things about as far as they can believably go, for my family it was just an example of how much nicer our life together could have been if someone named Gerry Hambling had edited it.

She said, "Okay."

Ouch. The Albert Finney stuff had always worked before, but now I was embarrassed by my glibness. I felt like I'd just answered a serious question by blowing a clown horn.

And Nora had just asked another one. "Police report?"

She really wanted to know the answer. I didn't have much to say, though, because I realized I could barely remember anything about the last months of my parents' marriage. As soon as I told her that, though, I remembered a little more. But not much. Which was fine, she said, you can't grab or grasp at these things, you have to be patient. They come, though, they come.

I knew she was right, of course, and I did want the memories to come, I wanted things to change, but I had no idea how that would happen. I was tired of distracting myself, of pushing uncomfortable thoughts out of my mind, but I was crazed with frustration at not knowing how to do whatever it was I needed to do.

And shit, grasping was what I was good at. My old habits were dying hard. I was still secretly convinced that the universe could be comprehended, even restored to order, if only I *knew enough*. It really is amazing the kind of talents you can develop with a brain that's been playing with itself for years, undistracted by the emotional demands of other people. I had become an insufferable motormouth. I would hold forth on any and all subjects except what I was actually feeling and thinking, blabbing away for hours and hours without any sense of boundaries, subtext, or common courtesy.

Imagine if you will, Nora and me sitting across rapidly chilling plates of pad Thai, a grumpy waiter hovering in the background, and my usual floorshow already in progress:

"Okay, but here's the thing. How far do you take this whole 'recognizing someone's humanity' stuff? I mean, someone kills your wife, say. Do you favor the death penalty? That's the only time it means anything, right, when it's personal? Otherwise it's just an abstraction. But the whole point of the law is to save us from ourselves! That's the point! Of course I'd want the guy to be killed, I'd want to fucking pull the switch myself, and that is precisely why we *shouldn't* kill him. Everyone has a 'good reason' for doing what they do—I mean, the stronger the urge to kill this person—that's what *he* did, the killer, he listened to voices that made this horrible thing seem reasonable. But you know, one man's freedom fighter is another man's—at some point it goes too far. We all know that. We may have a different sense of where the line is drawn, but we know we've crossed it when we have, and then everything just gets turned around, which I guess is what you should expect from crossing a line. But, you know how they say that the water spins in the opposite direction when you cross the equator, like in a toilet? The water spins the other way when you flush, and this is if you walk, like, *six inches* to your left or whatever, you cross the equator and it changes completely. So what do people want? Nobody's allowed to mention Hitler in an argument anymore, right, because that's where we agree that it's maybe not only *inadvisable* to try to understand but immoral. You say, you know, I'm not interested in the Little Corporal or the frustrated art student, that giving in to that curiosity makes you complicit—and that's not entirely off the mark—but the thing to guard against doesn't come with a twirling mustache, it comes with a smile, and yes, sure, the banality of evil, but what about the evil of banality? I mean, call me a heartless bastard, but what *is* it with all these teddy bears and candles that pop up against chain-link fences for whatever fucking tragedy du jour—the resentment or whatever that gets all dressed up like something else, and it just makes me nuts, it makes me nuts! What?"

Osvald in *Ghosts* was part of what turned out to be a long series of sons I would play—sons who had particularly troubled relationships with their fathers. Probably an unavoidable thing for any actor in his twenties, but these were an especially fed-up bunch of long-winded ranters and they ended up doing as much work on me as I did on them.

Playing these characters felt like such a collective experience for me that no matter how hard I try I can't remember one without the others. But I've never had an easy time doing that with anything. Memory doesn't feel like a "lane" to me at all, but more like some ancient and enduring civilization—Egypt, say. Cities buried under cities, layer upon layer, built, reclaimed and built over, tower tops poking through floorboards and mummies falling from ceilings, all of it becoming one thing. If I think about one play I remember ten.

Lines from *Ghosts* mix with lines from *Conversations with My Father*, bits of *Broadway Bound* mingle with words from *The Substance of Fire*, and all those parts become a whole.

> Go to hell. No more Pop, that is *it*. . . . All my life you taught me about things like dignity and principles and I believed them. . . . Everything I wanted to achieve in this world...I don't dare think about it anymore...I *can't*. . . . You're so damn guilty for what you've done, you're accusing everyone else of betraying *you*. . . . It's not my fault that life does seem real to me, and I can make peace with that. . . . Vos *vilst* du? What do you want? That prize you don't know the name of? I won it Pop, *me*, I *did* it. . . . You may have been proud to other people but you never said a word to me. . . . And it's still so dark here. All the times I've been home I can never remember seeing the sun. . . . I do not want to set life back to its beginnings. I do not need to suffer in order to feel alive, Pop, I'm sorry. . . . I work, I work, there's like a fire in me and I don't know where it is so I cannot put it out. And the fire is you. . . . Do whatever you God damn please, but don't blame me for humiliating you when you're the one who's been humiliating us. . . . What do you fucking want? . . . What's this child got to thank his father for? I never knew the man.

Nora was right about playing Osvald, of course. It taught me a lot (including the fact that I don't have a suicidal bone in my body. If you don't kill yourself doing Ibsen in Maine in February you never will) and it felt unavoidably, stingingly real.

On a day off from the show I took a walk on an island in Casco Bay. I'd been struggling with one particular scene where Osvald goes on a drunken rant of regret and mourning for the carefree life he enjoyed so much with his friends in Italy. Each time we rehearsed the scene I would get derailed at the same spot, just before the speech really took off. I was getting more nervous about it every day.

The big questions for an actor are always, "What do I want?" and "How do I get it?" Intention is everything. It launches you into each moment and animates everything you do, just like it does in life. But unlike life, acting requires that you *know* what your intention is. I wasn't sure what Osvald wanted in the scene. I thought his speech was self-pitying and melodramatic, and I was embarrassed by it. So every time I did the speech I came at it sideways, trying out an assortment of vague ideas that all conveniently led to the same sort of detached, ironic take on it. Ibsen is about as subtle as a hammer, and while *Ghosts* has always been considered the first modern play, there's nothing detached or ironic about it. The whole point of the play, in fact, is that we use all kinds of detachment to cut ourselves off from the truth of our lives—that in order to avoid pain, we can end up living out a kind of waking death.

So I decided to get out of my little hotel room, get away from the script and the rest of the cast, and see if some fresh air could help me sort things out. Mackworth Island is just a short drive across a causeway from Portland, but it's a million miles away, completely undeveloped except for a school for the deaf that occupies the center of the island, housed in what used to be the home of Percival Baxter, governor of Maine from 1921 to 1925.

The day I visited the island it was almost empty except for a few strolling families and the occasional seabird. The midday sun bounced off patches of crunchy snow. Stubborn ice chunks clung to the granite jetty at the high tide mark.

Halfway through my walk I veered off the narrow hiking path into the woods and soon found myself in a small clearing, at the center of which was a low stone wall surrounding several large, rough-hewn gravestones. An enormous boulder was inscribed with the words,

"Jerry Roan, a noble horse and kind friend." This was the cemetery where Baxter had buried his pets, including his thirteen Irish setters. I laughed with amazement, and took two or three slow tours of the place, reading the inscriptions and imagining Baxter's life.

I stopped at the largest of the stones, which read, "To my Irish setters, lifelong friends and companions, affectionate, faithful and loyal." And then the names: Skip, Carry, Deke, Mike, Pat, Fanny, Cary, Eirie . . . and Gary Owen, a favorite for whom, upon the dog's death in 1923, Baxter ordered all flags in the state to fly at half mast. I leaned against the stone, put my hands in my pockets, and watched through the trees as an old barge moved slowly through the bay. The gravestones looked handmade. I wondered if Baxter fashioned them himself, how much time he spent here. I couldn't think of a better use of it. Carving this place out of the woods, putting the names on the stones, keeping the weeds away. A good way to go. I thought about the sculptor's widow from years before in Glen Cove. I thought about Irish setters and terriers, and remembered Bonnie leaping onto my stomach in the middle of the night and scaring the hell out of me. I wondered what had happened to the fireplace bellows now that Mom and Dad had each moved into the city. I thought about Dad crying in the car when we put Bonnie down and I realized I was holding his old pipe in my hand. It had been in my coat pocket since I'd stolen it.

I examined it for a long while. The tiny bits of charred tobacco in the bowl, the scratches on one side of the stem, the tooth marks on the mouthpiece. Memories started flooding in, nothing specific, just snippets and shards—Dad smoking, Mom smoking, Mom singing, model boats, pizza bagels, David laughing, Ali reading.

I put the pipe in my mouth and it slipped right out and fell into the snow. I cleaned it off and tried again. How in hell do people hold these things in their mouths? My teeth hurt after five seconds. Tears were coming now, and they felt good. The barge disappeared, a leafless sapling bent in the wind. Good God almighty this thing tasted horrible, even unlit. Like licking an old ashtray. I started walking quickly.

I wanted to get to a phone, to talk to Nora. I was still crying and my cheeks were icy cold. I was sniffing up a gallon of snot every few seconds and was probably going to throw up. But I felt good.

Just before I got to the end of the trail I noticed a house, just off to the side. But this house was very, very small, less than a foot high, maybe two feet long. And it had a "front door" that looked suspiciously like a flattened pinecone. Then ten feet down the path I saw another one, another little house, made from rotted spruce bark and rye bread. I stood over it for a couple of minutes, cocking my head like a dog's and smiling, and then the goddamn pipe fell out of my mouth and caved in the carefully constructed roof. I got down on my knees in the snow, gathered the pieces together with some nearby twigs and tried to rebuild it to its original specifications. And just as I was almost finished with my repair job a very serious little four-year-old boy walked by with his mom and said, "Oh, that one isn't very good."

Around the next bend I saw another house. And then another, and another and another. A perfectly square twig cabin with a crab-shell roof, a little reed hut with a sea-glass skylight, a dark slate castle flying birch-bark flags. I started to wonder if I was going to end up tied to the ground by a hundred tiny lobstermen. Then I noticed a sign that told me I was in the middle of the island's Community Village, where kids from the surrounding area had been coming to build these "fairy houses" for decades. There must have been sixty or seventy of them, maybe more, each one unique, all constructed out of bits and pieces of whatever the kids had handy.

It's not complicated, what Osvald wants. He wants to live. He loves his friends, he loves his work, he loves wine, he loves his life. It's real. It matters. Because it will end. He doesn't want it to end. Who would?

Fresh air really can do the trick sometimes, and quickly. I'd been walking around in such a muddled state of mind for so long that when a little bit of clarity finally came to me, it seemed to come from out of nowhere, all at once. Maybe it had just been lying dormant, waiting for a cold, Maine breeze. I hadn't been embarrassed by Osvald's raw feelings, but my own. I loved my friends and my work and New York and the occasional really expensive, delicious, sea scallop sandwich. I loved Nora and my family and the Great State of Maine. Enjoyment was not phoniness, dreariness did not equal authenticity. Excitement was not pretension.

I still got nervous every night before the show, but actually doing it was like getting as far away from fear as I could imagine, like riding a rocket away from fear and becoming weightless. When I was up there with the other actors it was just us, talking to each other and listening, as privately as in a space capsule. I was able to keep that feeling from the clearing on the island with me without even trying. I was incapable of thinking, or caring what anyone else thought, and when I woke up the next morning I couldn't wait to float around in that stupid delight again. Every night I told a whole bunch of people that I knew I was going to die, and that I deeply loved the people in my life. Doctors order such things. But for two months I got paid to do it.

I sat with Mom in her living room up on Eighty-first Street, a few weeks after returning from Maine, looking at a photo album that her parents had sent. This "not my son" business was nagging at me. Why did he say that to David, why those words, what could he have meant? She said she had no idea, that it was just another one of those things he said, another example of him going as far as he could, all the way to the worst possible thing. I asked her if Rich and David were in fact his kids and she said yes, absolutely, a hundred percent, no doubt, and I would tell you if it weren't true, I promise. And we went back to looking at the pictures.

12

Dad answered the door the moment I knocked on it, his face pink and hands jittery, chuckling a big, singsong "How are yoooo?!" for me, and a "So nice to meet you" for Nora, then nervously ushering us into a noticeably spruced-up place. Miss Marple watched indifferently from her perch on the back of the sofa as we awkwardly stepped around each other into the living room, Nora's eyes landing immediately on a photograph of me at six years old, sitting on a bike and laughing for the camera. "Oh, my gosh, you were such a cutie patootie!" she said. "It's true," Dad chortled, "he used to be a handsome guy—I don't know what happened." Nora shot me a crooked smile, and in time-honored, time-filling fashion we turned to focus our attention on the cat.

While we patted Miss Marple Dad gave us the rundown on a newly purchased, mint-condition Enfield he'd bought from a dealer in New Mexico, still sitting by the couch in its box. After Miss Marple fled our harassment, we watched from the windows as the noontime wave of waiters and tourists rushed and sauntered down Forty-ninth Street, and Dad talked about how the neighborhood had changed over the years, how the diner on the corner was barely hanging on and the bridge and tunnel crowd had taken over. He said he was thinking we'd do Indonesian for lunch, and Nora said with relief that it sounded great and I jumped into the bathroom while Dad got his coat.

Nora must have spotted a poster on the wall from a musical that Dad had been the company manager for, and she asked him if he remembered a friend of hers who had been in the cast. He made some mumbly, "I'm not sure" noises, but then, when Nora said, "Tall, dark hair, Canadian," he pretended to remember and said, "Oh yes yes yes yes yes."

They were quiet for an awkward minute, and then just as my bladder opened, Nora said, "So what are you doing tonight, do you have any plans?" and Dad said, "Yes, my friend Helen is coming over at eight, and we are going to spend the rest of the night making love."

I turned before thinking and my pee streaked across the bottom of a bath towel as I yelled, "Whoa!" and clenched as hard as I could, but I wasn't able to stanch the flow and as I twisted back into position I splashed the walls with even more pee before regaining my shaky aim while cringing over the toilet and listening to Nora stutter, "I, well, congratulations, that, um, that sounds, like, uh, fun."

I'd given her the nudity disclaimer. I covered weapons, alcohol, England, torture. But I forgot about the Sexual Tourette's. It was always something.

I shouldn't have worried, though. We were a couple now, Nora and I, well past the sizing-up period, and when I emerged from the bathroom she was barely suppressing her laughter.

"You must try the Babi Kecap," Dad said to Nora when we sat down at the restaurant, his chin low, his eyes narrowed, his tone menacing. He pronounced "Babi Kecap" the way the guys in *The Deer Hunter* said, "Ditty Mao!" And you could tell he thought he was being an incredibly charming host. The place was awful in every way, as usual. The Babi Kecap, a spicy, roasted pork dish, made Nora's skin go yellow. The rest of the food was overcooked yet somehow sour. There were dirty ashtrays on the table, worn-out carpeting curling up at the corners, and a surly waitstaff who greeted Dad knowingly and put us at a table near the back.

Nora asked Dad about another musical he'd recently worked on.

She said she still played the record all the time just to hear the performance of one of the actresses, and Dad replied, "Well, I'm sorry to say she's an absolute *monster*." The word wore a Halloween mask when he said it, rumbled as darkly for an actress as it would for Eichmann, and Nora smiled with amazement at Dad's near-comic contempt. "No, really," he said. "She's an absolute cokehead. She asked to have her contract renegotiated every month. Literally. All she cared about was money. Frankly, that's all any of them cared about. God save us from *actors*. I mean, this is the show that made her a star, for Chrissake. The absolute nerve. Like the world revolves around her."

Nora finally cut through the long, tense pause that followed and mentioned how excited and moved she had been to see the Berlin Wall come down the week before, and how startling it was to see that East Germany had been frozen in time since the end of the war, that it made her want to book a trip there soon. Dad slipped immediately into his B-movie Nazi voice and said she wouldn't *hoff to leave ze hemisphere to see some old Chermans. Zere are many uv us who are frrroezen in time right here on zees side of ze ocean.*

As he noisily slurped his pork, he gave a dissertation on the highly imaginative methods of torture that former Nazis had supposedly shared over the years with their South American hosts, especially those methods employed on women. He described the insertion of vials full of insects, peppers, and acid. I could feel Nora's breath get shallow. She stopped eating. As Dad was describing the interrogation "refinements" made by the Stasi in East Germany I cut him off with, "Okay, I think that's more than enough about torture," and he looked pleased at our discomfort.

Over the years Dad had been a regular at a series of theater district bars and restaurants, frequenting each one for about a year before suddenly moving on. He'd started at the blue-checkered-tablecloth restaurants with theater posters on the walls and leading ladies at the tables, then adopted a couple of second-tier places where character actors ate and the service was faster, and then switched again, to one of the nicer Bar and Grille joints where the crew guys had beer and burgers. The bartender would have a martini waiting for him at five o'clock every evening, and after the second one he drank for free.

But now he was staying closer to home and farther away from familiar faces. I didn't know for sure if he had actually been asked to move on from each of his old haunts, but I was pretty sure he had and pretty sure I knew why.

A few years earlier, when I'd been doing the play *Brighton Beach Memoirs* at the 46th Street Theater, I had lunch at the same nearby restaurant every Wednesday between shows. As far as I knew at the time, Dad was still a regular at one of the blue-checkered places around the corner. I only went there because I had a big crush on one of the waitresses, a former acting class partner of mine who was so talented I'd had to put my name on a waiting list to get a chance to work with her.

I'm not really a creature of habit, but I ordered the same thing from Sheri every Wednesday because when I'd come into the place the second time, she'd pointed at me and asked, "The usual?!" and before I could think about it, I pointed right back and said, "The usual!" like somebody who actually does that. I immediately wished that when I'd first come in I'd ordered a burger or an omelet—anything that might stand up to the pressure of being a "usual," but for some reason on that first fateful day I'd ordered the Wednesday special: extra-spicy, Cajun fried calamari that not surprisingly tasted like foreskins cooked in gasoline and that forever afterwards remained the Wednesday special, much to my intestine's annoyance. But I couldn't part with the utterly insane notion that by ordering this tongue-blistering concoction I had somehow increased my attractiveness in Sheri's eyes, and so needed to maintain the illusion of a decisive, iron-boweled squidetarian who ordered his revolting lunch every day with a mere flick of his finger. And so I did.

When I came in one hot summer day wearing shorts, Sheri looked down at my bare leg, spotted my old beach-umbrella, scar and said,

"Hey, sweetie, what happened to you here?" I took a long, slow sip of my lemonade and said, "Oh, that, yeah, I got mugged a few years back and the guy nicked me in the leg with a little pocketknife. It was really nothing, just a flesh wound. Didn't hurt at all." She paused for a moment and then smiled a smile that said, "I'm going to forgive you for that."

She could not have been sweeter. Or less interested. But over the months I was doing *Brighton Beach*, we struck up an honest-to-God friendship, and I found myself making mental notes onstage to tell her about how so-and-so did such-and-such. We were having such a fun, relaxed time at our lunches I was even considering ordering a grilled cheese sandwich sometime soon. But she sat down at my table very quickly one day, quicker than usual, and after a couple of pleasantries said, "Hey, I have to tell you something."

It was the first of many times I would have this same conversation over the years, but I knew right away what she was going to say.

"Your dad has been coming in here? And, um, well . . ." And, he'd been hitting on her. And she didn't give it much thought at first, but then he did it again. And then, when she'd said to him, "You probably don't know this but I'm actually friends with your son," he'd said, "So?" And when she'd said, "Well, you probably also don't know that I have a boyfriend," he'd asked, "Why is that a problem?"

I sank a little in my chair. I said, "Sheri, that's terrible. I am so sorry. I don't know why he . . . He's got problems. He doesn't seem to understand some things. I'm so sorry."

I forced myself to go back to Sheri's restaurant two more times after that, but eventually it was just too uncomfortable—did I lift my glass the way Dad did? Did my smile seem like a leer?—and so I moved on to a new place myself, just like Dad. Over the years, several other women friends approached me, always with the same scrunchy look on their faces, and after a while I learned to pre-empt the conversation with as much good humor as I could. I'd say, "Oh God, I know what you're going to say, and I'm so sorry," and they'd say, "Really?"

and I'd say, "Really," and we'd eventually laugh a bit about it, but it was never any fun.

So Dad had few options left when it came to restaurants. While I'm relatively sure he hadn't hit on either of the elderly female servers at the Indonesian place, he'd clearly already alienated them with the startlingly loud, cartoon Charlie Chan accent he hauled out for "jokes" whenever he ate there.

He did make a few attempts at graciousness. He toasted Nora. He asked her where she was from. He asked her "what it is" she "did again, darling?" He said, "Oh, that's wonderful, hon," when I told him about my next job. He limited himself to two glasses of wine.

Still I was nervous as we walked back to Dad's place and then said our good-byes in front of the building. He invited us in and just as I was about to say we had somewhere to be, a woman came out of the front door and said hi. Dad said, "Yasmine. How are you? This is my son Peter." She greeted us in an accent I couldn't place and shook our hands. She was youngish but looked tired and preoccupied, like seemingly everyone who lived in the building, and I remembered all the times Dad had talked about moving, all the much nicer places that people had found for him over the years. He'd told us that this place would be temporary when he first moved into it, but then he never moved out.

Nora and I made our excuses and headed up the block.

The usual mixed feelings came over me quickly, but Nora was incredibly great about it. She took my arm as we left, kissed me on the cheek, and with the gentlest of smiles she said, "I don't like him." I smiled back and said, "I peed all over his bathroom wall," and she whispered, "It'll still smell better than that godforsaken restaurant." We walked arm in arm as we headed to Times Square to catch the subway, talking about everything in the world but Dad, reacquainting ourselves with each other and normalcy.

In the fall of 1989, Times Square was like a twenty-four-hour, multi-denominational revival meeting. On the corner of Forty-eighth and Broadway we were damned to everlasting hellfire by an emaciated, smiling Southern Baptist preacher standing on the back of a pickup truck. He called Nora a "temptress," or at least he said the word "temptress" while he was looking at her, which I admittedly found very exciting. And only a block later we almost fell down from the sudden auditory assault of the "Mitzvah Mobile," a beat-up old mini-van with a giant menorah/speaker on its roof that was blaring klezmer music at seizure-inducing volume. A fervent young guy in a beard, black fedora, and tattered sports jacket appeared from out of nowhere in front of us and asked with great urgency, "Excuse me, are you Jewish?!" "Um, what?" I said. "No, no, not today," and he grabbed my arm as if I'd just said, "Don't be silly, the *Titanic* can't sink!"

Nora had to literally pry me away from the guy and we jumped back into the stream of buzzing matinee-goers and made our way down to Forty-second Street, where we got stuck in a logjam behind a slow-moving wall of seniors in matching blue windbreakers. The Black Hebrew Israelites were taking up the rest of the corner, in full force and high dudgeon, five very big guys in plastic breastplates and gold wristbands, the tallest one barking very, very loudly into a microphone and pointing at me. I faced Nora, put my hands in her coat pockets, and kept my eyes right on hers as he roared through huge, distorted speakers:

"So-called white man! Hey, so-called white man! So-called white man, if you don't believe in God, you shall be lost! You hear me? You shall be roasting on your roaster while you're toasting on your toaster as you're coasting on your coaster. The devil's gonna baste you like a Butterball turkey!"

"Ooo, you're going to be so juicy," she said, and kissed me. A couple of white-haired, windbreaker ladies clapped for us and giggled as I whispered, "Do I look especially sinful today or something?" and she said, "Well, yeah, you do, you kinda do, sugar," and we headed down into the Times Square station to catch the subway back home.

We huddled together against a pole and waited for a train that wasn't packed to the gills with shoppers and show-goers, and I noticed the word "PRAY" just behind Nora's head. I smiled but didn't say a word. We spent the rest of the day at home.

The next morning I wrote this letter:

Dear Dad,

I hate you and hope you choke on Babi Kecap.

I am genuinely sorry you have to work with actors. I know from experience that you're right—they do spend a lot of time thinking about money. Some of the actors you negotiate with might even be trying to pay off debts incurred through years of working for no money at all, or to put away savings for hard times to come. The nerve of these people is amazing, it's true.

I was reminded yesterday how much we owe you for our education in the finer points of torture. I think Alison's depression, Richie's arrest record, David's fondness for not speaking to people, and my habit of punching the pillow in my sleep all stand as testaments to the toughness it imbued us with, and the sense of security one can only develop growing up surrounded by guns.

I hope Miss Marple sticks a vial of peppers up your ass and breaks it.

Sincerely,
Peter

I left town soon after with the unsent letter in my suitcase to do a play in Cleveland, and Nora came to visit for the holidays. She had been raised unambivalently Jewish, so I decided I would treat her to a first-ever Christmas, and spent the day before her arrival buying a little Charlie Brown tree, some decorations, and a couple of drugstore stockings with our names on them. I was in serious need of company other than my co-miserable castmates and the Hitlerian director who'd made us all that way. I'd been bitching about the show to Nora for weeks and wracking up an enormous phone bill.

Nora's plane raced a blizzard across the Great Lakes, and by the time I pulled our rental car up to my little apartment the radio was predicting six to ten inches for Christmas Day. I turned the engine off and we sat for a little while in the driveway, listening, rapt, to an almost unbearably beautiful and sad Mendelssohn string concerto. She said it reminded her a little of Papa, my grandfather, who was still alive, of the way he walked, and I said, yes, yes, my God that's so true, and she closed her eyes. I sat there and drank her in for a moment. Hearing Nora say that she noticed Papa in this way, that she appreciated something so essential about him, made me feel the first intimations I can remember of true adult love. The sense of an emotional connection running from Nora to me to my grandfather was like a first glimpse at how it was that love could create families.

The car heater made us sleepy, and the cold outside was startling. As I pulled her bags from the trunk, Nora took a deep, foggy breath, smiled, zipped up her bright green, ankle-length, A-shaped down coat, and said, "Looks like a white Hanukkah, huh?" and I replied with a smile, "Hey, didn't I see you in Rockefeller Center last week?"

I wanted to grab the steam clouds left by my words and stuff them back in my mouth, but you know how that goes. Nora shifted her weight in the snow and asked if I'd just called her a Christmas tree. Before I could answer, she asked me if I knew we weren't eleven, that she wasn't a boy, and this wasn't a junior high gym class. That she didn't spend the last couple of days hoping I'd give her a good ribbing as soon as she got there. I replied that yes, I did know those things but that words sometimes came out of my mouth before I knew they were there and I would love to maybe rewind the clock and do the last two minutes over. She shifted her weight again, and after a pause said okay, but maybe I could do some thinking about why they were there in the first place, and I bit my tongue, grudgingly inhaled, and nodded yes. I crunched over to her and gave her a big hug and told her how much I really did love her coat and she said, "Don't," so I didn't, and I grabbed her bags.

On Christmas morning I snuck out of bed before dawn in my brand-new L.L. Bean union suit to hang the stockings, but quickly realized I didn't have any thumbtacks or nails. I rummaged as quietly as I could for something sharp or adhesive, and ended up tearing the baggage-claim sticker off my suitcase, cutting it in half with a dull kitchen knife, and pasting the little, red polyester stockings to the living room wall. But as soon as I did I realized I hadn't filled them with anything yet. I quickly and maddeningly discovered that even the weight of a candy cane was too much to ask of month-old baggage tape, and I ended up laying the stockings against the back of the sofa like wet laundry. I hung a couple of Rite-Aid ornaments on the tree, put her present under it, arranged some tinsel on the windowsill, wrapped a twig of mistletoe around the shower curtain rod, cued up a mixed tape, and crawled quietly back into bed, my heart jackhammering against my ribs.

The apartment was overheated and difficult to wake up in. I opened a couple of windows to relieve some of the stuffiness but Nora regarded each decoration with half-closed, sleepy eyes; few words; and a smile poised perfectly between pleasure, curiosity, and a couple of other things I couldn't quite name. I tried to keep quiet, too, but I ended up following her from room to room, pointing out missed details in the decorations and unheard lyrics in songs. She put a cautionary hand on my arm and I managed to dial the energy down a bit, but couldn't keep it there for long.

Nora rubbed her eyes and said she was going to jump in the shower. "Wait," I insisted, "you gotta hear this—it's Memphis Slim!

'I'll Be Home for Christmas.' Can you believe how much he's slowed it down? God, it kills, doesn't it?"

"It is good," she said. "Hey, I'm pretty hungry. Do you—"

"Oh! Wait!" I chirped. "'Run Run Rudolph'!"

She waited a couple of beats and smiled thinly. "Okay, I'm gonna shower. Do you want to get some breakfast soon?"

"Sure, yeah, there's a good place down the block. You've got a lot of candy canes here, though. Don't you want to spoil your appetite?"

"Why don't we leave that tradition for another time?"

"Okay, Scrooge. Go shower. I'll go after you. Hey!"

She tuned at the bathroom door.

"You sure you like your new coat? You can take it back."

I'd given her a coat, and now very much wished I'd gone for a necklace.

"No, my God, it's beautiful, thank you, really."

"Okay. I'm glad. You look fantastic in it, by the way."

"You're very kind. I'll be right out."

Those words in my mouth, the ones I didn't know were there—I needed to replace them. I needed new words, waiting there, ready to go at a moment's notice. It would be nice if the thing that came to me naturally was something I could be happy to have said. That would be good. I needed to think different thoughts, grow a whole new throatful of words.

I counted silently to myself. I figured twenty, maybe thirty seconds for Nora to get undressed, turn on the shower, pull the curtain back, and spot the mistletoe. Then it all depended on whether or not I deserved a third chance. Or was it a fourth? Nakedness would calm me down, though, I was sure of that. I'd be good. I swear. The water started. I counted. I heard her pull the curtain back, firmly. And then, and then . . . nothing. The sound of hands in water. Oh, well. Nuts. Maybe she just didn't see it.

And then I heard her scream. But not in the way I'd hoped.

The door flew open and Nora came falling out, naked, soaking wet, one eye closed, soap in her hair, pointing frantically towards the bathroom.

She said, "There's a, a, a squirrel!" I looked into the bathroom. There *was* a squirrel! A little dark gray squirrel, sitting on top of the shower curtain, mockingly calm and unrepentant, chewing lazily on a mistletoe berry and watching the naked shouting lady like she was a movie.

"Ho! A squirrel!" I said, and Nora shot me the "no shit" look of the century as she ran very fast to her open suitcase and grabbed something towelish.

The squirrel munched happily as I sized him up. How could he be so nonchalant? Cornered, outnumbered, outsized. If I were him I'd be completely frightened. Yet here he was, cool enough to eat his lunch, cool enough to unnerve me. What did he know that I didn't? I watched him for a moment longer.

Then I walked slowly into the bathroom and I said, "Okay, buddy, think it's time to go home now," but he kept chewing on his berries. So I paused, and then, as suddenly as I could, I slammed the door back against the bathroom wall and shouted, "Squirrel!" and he sprang with super-amazing-squirrel force from the curtain rod, flew across the room, and landed directly on my flinching head, digging his claws into my scalp with unmistakable malice aforethought. I screamed like a six-year-old girl and spun around as fast as I could, watching in the mirror as Rocky hung on effortlessly to the amusement park ride that was my noisy, hairy, careening noggin.

Nora cawed loudly with the most delicious laugh I've ever heard and held the edges of the doorway to keep herself from falling down with schadenfreudean delight. I came towards her, arms out, shouting, "Get him off! Get him off!" as Rocky rode my head like a champion rodeo squirrel. She said, "Get him off? How am I supposed to do that?" and I shook my head as hard as I could, like Eddie Van

Halen with a squirrel on his head, which made Nora hyperventilate, spitting out "No no no" with a laugh that was now nearing losing-bodily-fluids level, and simultaneously put a hand in front of her nose and another in front of her still-naked crotch, lurched towards the sofa, grabbed a big cushion, and cower behind it. I was on the verge of tears as Rocky and I flopped towards the living room carpet, but just as I was about to land he zipped into the air, taking small pieces of my brain with him, bounced off a desk lamp, knocking it over, and onto the windowsill where he paused in front of a little snowdrift that had formed there. I looked up from the floor just as he turned his back, shook his tail disparagingly, and leapt over the tinsel and snow back out into the frozen wilds of Cleveland.

I twisted my head to see Nora, also prostrate, crying and moaning with laughter, her naked tush bouncing on the carpet like someone had just put a quarter in it. I made my way over to her like a soldier under fire (just in case Rocky was waiting to pounce again through the window) and kissed the tears off her cheek. We strained our necks to kiss some more and soon she was on top of me and under me and alongside me, her mouth on my ear and my hand in her hair.

We laughed again quietly when we finished, spacey and loose. The air from the window cooled us and the sun squeezed into the room. We lay quietly, sweaty and still, touching each other's fingers and chuckling with the memory of our feisty and demonic new friend.

The breakfast place was closed. So was the other breakfast place around the corner. The snow was up to our eyeballs but we defiantly traipsed up the block, because it was inconceivable that there wouldn't be several restaurants of varying ethnicities within walking distance, open and ready for our business, Christmas Shmistmas.

Cleveland was completely shut down, of course, and we took the requisite New Yorker's offense. Two grumpy cans of vegetarian chili later we were huddled on the floor of the apartment, our backs against the couch, sucking on candy canes and talking.

We liked to talk a lot. But we were twenty-nine and bad at listening. Nora talked with her hands, feet, arms, shoulders, and waist. It was mesmerizing. She'd stop short in the middle of a sentence and cock her hips, flare her elbows, make a pepper-grinder motion with her hands, and you would know precisely what it had been like for her to watch *Born on the Fourth of July*. That is, if you were listening.

But I had a habit of sometimes hearing only every third word of Nora's, and Nora, who was often several mental steps ahead, would sometimes keep her segues to herself, jump from introduction to conclusion, then announce, "It's all about layering!" and I would have no idea what "it" even was, let alone why it was layered. We spent many hours picking through the verbal rubble created by our lack of understanding that we were two distinct, autonomous people, that we weren't each other.

I had been feeling better since my time in *Ghosts*. A little less angry, a little more clearheaded, a little more real to myself. But it was definitely a two steps up, one step back kind of thing. Or one step up and two steps back sometimes. Nora and I had been together for over a year now and I badly wanted it to keep going, but I hardly ever saw what I was doing wrong when I was doing it. I always had to look back to see it, like I was driving with a rearview mirror but no windshield.

We had almost redundantly similar temperaments; both of us given to brow furrowing, belly laughing, silently judging, secretly admiring, tearing up, and shutting down. We would talk past each other, connect intensely, be very sweet to each other, take offense, fight, crawl into corners, and start again.

We tried to take another walk outside but the morning's winter wonderland was now icy under a purple bruise of a sky, so we crawled back into our energy-sapping little cave and crashed from our candy binge, woke an hour later, wrapped ourselves in blankets, tore into a bag of chocolate kisses, and started yacking up a yack storm.

The subject was losing touch with people. I was telling Nora about the last time I'd seen Ben, and she said something like, yeah, she still missed Jane, her best friend from high school, but that it was harder to reconnect now that everyone was "so convinced about everything."

"Look, everybody I know is obsessive," she said, "about one thing or another. There are people out there filling their Day Planners (hand moves imaginary pen, frantically and precisely) with perfectly spelled, entirely legible little notes to themselves about, who knows? Buying new pens and Day Planners. Jane has made every day of the last eight years about her three kids, as well she should, but she thinks I'm crazy for doing the same thing with books and movies and my big, bad dramapalooza feelings. She thinks I get swept away too easily; I thrive on conflict. And it's true, I do. We take things personally. I catch my reflection sometimes and I can't . . . I mean, I am just shocked at how intense I look, how extreme my emotional reaction seems to be to the most everyday, nothing sort of event. But what am I going to do? I'm a sponge. You're a sponge. And how do you have a dependable, Day Planner relationship with someone like that? It's hard. It's very hard, I know. Anyway. So you were in the car with Ben?"

"Yes. But God that's—I think you're right. People's obsessions go in different directions. Imploders and exploders, or something. It's true. Jane sounds a lot like Ben. Yeah."

And I went on to tell her how Ben and I had been sitting in his car in front of my building. We'd had a great lunch, it had been great to catch up, but I was ready to go and he was sort of not letting me out. He was bringing up new subjects, asking me about work a couple of different ways. He kept saying things like, "Can you make a living with that?" I told him yes, maybe not the living he was thinking of, but yes. He asked me about my love life, and I told him I was having fun, which for some reason made him look kind of sad. He was clearly thinking about the future, feeling at a crossroads. I told Nora that he said, "Is that enough for you? You don't want to live the way our parents did, do you?" and I had said, no, I didn't, but I really had no idea what he was talking about.

So I asked him, and he said that for starters he didn't think he'd be doing any wife swapping soon. He laughed, pretty loudly, and that's how I found out about them. I said something like "Right, wow, I guess everyone was fucking each other back then," and then before I could ask more questions, he asked me if I knew anything about numerology, of all things. He said he'd gone on a retreat up in the Catskills with the Lubavitchers, the "Mitzvah Mobile" people, and told me how if you read some particular part of the Bible and you looked at the first letter of every line it spelled out "Shoa" or "Holocaust" or something.

Nora said, "Wow."

I said, "I know. I really could *not* believe it. Ben. The most rational—I mean, hyper, hyper-rational guy, ever. Maybe that's why he's doing it. Maybe he's found a hyper-rational way into the irrational or something. But now he's a born-again Jew. Full out, every holiday. Shavuos. It's crazy."

Nora said, "Wait. I mean your parents. I didn't know that."

"Oh, I know, me either," I said, "Until then. But that was a lot of years ago. It all made sense of course, as soon as Ben told me."

I told her that I'd asked Mom and she'd told me everything. She reminded me that she and Arthur had been classmates in college and they had even written a couple of songs together, that he was her first writing partner.

She told me more about the time Dad hit her and broke her nose, when I was three, what he'd been angry about. She said the Aaronsons lived in that same apartment complex in Brooklyn, that she hadn't seen Arthur in a couple of years, since they'd graduated from college, and that at some point that year they had begun to see them socially. They all drank a lot, except for Mom, and they would tease her about it. Then one night, she said, when they had been drinking, Liz and Arthur and Dad decided they should "switch partners."

Mom said that she asked Dad, "You mean you'd just give me away to someone else?" and he said, "Why not," or some such thing. Liz and Dad pressured her, and that's when Dad began using the argument that Mom was repressed, that there was obviously something wrong with her. She said, "Eventually, I'm sorry to say, I gave in." Arthur had had a crush on her in school, and he turned their involvement into a much more "emotional" affair. She thought that Dad and Liz were a lot more suited to each other than they were to their mates. At one point she said to me, "I'm sorry if you find this shocking, honey," and then she said Arthur was a sweet guy, calm and funny and a respite from Dad, but that she didn't know if she really loved him enough to want to marry him. She said that Arthur later turned into a good friend. She never really told him about the violence, but she wished she had. She never told anyone about it until after the split. I asked her again about David and Richard and I was relieved when she assured me Dad was the father.

On the night of the fight, Dad was pressing her for details about the sex and wouldn't let up. She didn't want to talk about it and, she said, "He got really, really angry, and tried to force it out of me, and I didn't want to tell him anything, and when I refused, he punched me. He punched me, and that was it. The rest you know."

When I finished telling her the story, Nora kissed me. I slumped down against the couch, and she put her head on my chest. "The poor thing," she said. "At that age. At that time . . . she must have felt so alone. I can only imagine how that made you feel, hearing about your parents from Ben like that."

"I don't . . . I wasn't surprised. It is weird to think that there was all this stuff happening in a parallel universe somewhere, but that's what childhood is, right? Did you know what was going on when your dad was in the hospital?"

She said, no, that her mother thought she was protecting her by not talking to her about it. She pointed out that either way, we get the message—I had clearly known my father was not available, that I had obviously picked up on the tension between my parents and their friends, on the fact that Mom felt so scared. And Nora had seen that her Mom was upset and forgetful, that things were different.

I said, "I wish I could go back in time and kiss you, talk to you about it. Parents are gods when you're that age. It must have been hard."

"Therapy helps," she said, smiling.

"Hey, it's getting late," I said, "and we have nothing to eat. We have to figure something out."

"I suppose we do. I think I like Cleveland," she said, and held me tight.

"Mid-afternoon bourbon, you say? What an excellent idea!"

I hopped up and into the kitchen. The whiskey had been an opening night gift from the stage manager, a thirty-year veteran who said he'd learned long ago not to waste anybody's time with homemade cookies or stuffed animals resembling characters from the play, a sentiment that at the time I thought was a little dark but that I was now starting to see the wisdom of. Nora and I stood by the window braving the cold in our floral, polyester, blanket togas and raised mismatched, plastic glasses to the eastern gray squirrels of Ohio.

We shook our heads as the bourbon warmed our stomachs. We kissed at the spicy residue on each other's lips and nuzzled each other's necks. We watched the sky darken. A sudden gust of cold air made her squeal and do a little tap dance. I said, "Let's have another shot!" and we did. And then the conversation went like this:

"I just don't know how she dealt with the guns all those years," Nora said quietly. "Especially with someone like that. Just being around them for ten minutes freaked me out."

I said, "I know, I'm sorry, that must have been weird. Hell, it's weird for us and we grew up with it. But it's the context, I think. There are lots of people out there who grow up around guns and it's no big deal for them. It's all about the owner."

"Yeah," she said, "but why does anyone own a gun in the first place? Really? Why would anyone own a gun, except to kill people or animals? They should just be banned, period, end of story." This is the moment I should have changed course. For some reason, even though I knew I was barreling ahead and wanted to slow down, or stop talking completely, I kept going. Years later I would wish that I'd just shut up and sat quietly with Nora for a while and let whatever was going on with me come to the surface slowly, or not at all. But I wasn't able to do that. That runaway train that had been heading my way for as long as I could remember, I was driving the damn thing, and I could see that I was driving it. But I didn't know how to stop it. I was in too big a hurry to get past everything. So I just kept going.

"Well," I said, "I don't know about 'banned, period.' I mean, I hate 'em, I hate guns. I don't like that my father owns them, and I believe in gun control, absolutely, but you know, the Second Amendment is there for a reason."

"Oh really? And what reason is that?"

I said, "It was, originally . . . it's to protect against tyranny."

"To . . . So, your father is keeping you safe from tyranny?" she replied heatedly.

"No, I—c'mon, you know what I mean."

Nora said, "No, I don't. This isn't 1789, and all the well-armed militias in Texas won't do Bo Diddley against a single Blackhawk. Guns are awful. Period. They exist to do harm to people."

"I know," I answered, "yes, I know. But the idea was that if the citizens of the country had weapons, then the government would be less likely to impose its will—"

Nora was aghast. She said, "You sound like some guy from my— Why are you defending guns, of all things? I can't believe it."

I said, "Hey, I'm not. I am not defending guns; I'm defending the right, just the right, to own guns. Not any kind of gun, not by anyone, just the right, and the reason it's there in the first place."

"Guns kill people and animals," she said. "Am I wrong? What is wrong with what I just said?"

I said, "Jesus, you're not even listening to me."

"Guns kill people and animals!"

"Oh, okay. Now I see. Great argument. What was I thinking?" I said, my sarcasm laden with contempt.

She shot back, "Don't fucking talk to me like that."

"I'm . . . look, I'm just saying, if you want to know . . . you can't just . . ."

"Yes I can," said Nora. "However you were going to finish that sentence, yes I can. I can say whatever I want to say."

"Yes, of course you can, I didn't mean—"

"Don't do that."

"What?" I said.

"Take a breath like that before you answer me. Make your voice softer like I'm a crazy person. Act like you have to calm yourself down to talk to me."

"I didn't mean to do that."

"Well you did it," she said

"Okay."

I got up.

She said, "Where are you going?"

"I'm just going to sit in the other room for a while."

"Oh, okay. Good. Fine. That was loads of fun. Next time why don't you just write out a little script so I know exactly what it is you want me to say."

"Hey I'm not the one—Look, I was just trying to say—"

Nora said, "I don't care what you were going to say. It's the way you say it. I don't . . . I don't celebrate Christmas, okay? All right? I'm a Jew. You could have asked me. This is all . . . it feels weird, I'm sorry. It was very nice of you to do, it was. But you could have asked me. And I don't like guns. Guns are sick and I can't believe you don't understand that."

"I don't understand? *I'm* not understanding something?"

She said, "What the . . . ? What, are you calling me stupid now?"

"No. No, I'm not, because you're not stupid, so why would you take a stupid fucking point of view just to pick a fight?"

"Fuck you, buddy boy. My point of view isn't stupid. You just don't want to hear it because something about it threatens you. I'm the one who's going in the other room."

I said, "It *threatens* me!? Wait, what?"

She walked into the bedroom and slammed the door shut.

"Fine," I said.

And then I kicked the door as hard as I could and my foot went right through my side of it and almost through hers. It got stuck for a couple of seconds, and as I struggled to pull it out, white dust and little bits of wood fell onto the teal, synthetic carpet.

13

You kicked the door in? Like we used to?" Rich had an eyebrow up. I was sitting with him, Alison, and David in David's Long Island living room during Thanksgiving, almost two years after I ruined everything with Nora that night in Cleveland.

"Yeah," I said. "Except she wasn't exactly used to things like that." When I heard her crying behind the door, it was like hearing Mom in the bathroom all those years ago. It made me sick to my stomach. I started therapy the day I got back to New York, but it was too late for Nora and me after that.

David said, "Well, if it makes you feel any better I see a lot worse than broken doors these days." He had recently been made a "domestic incident officer" for the Glen Cove Police Department. Alison told him how proud she was of him. He said, "I don't know, for some reason I have a niche for domestics. Most guys hate them, but some of them like DWIs, or narcotics. Everyone's got their thing. I talked this guy down in the ER the other day. Domestic, threatening violence to his girlfriend, and himself. And when it was all over, the psychiatrist told me my interaction with him was "masterful." That felt pretty cool."

"Holy. Shit," Ali said, squeezing a lens cap tightly, her fingers reddening, a camera cradled in the other hand. I wished I could snap a picture of her searching David's face. For years after the divorce, the four of us didn't have much contact, and that was just now starting to change. We were spending more time with each other, talking on the phone, seeing the occasional movie. I began to have fantasies of us becoming one of those sprawling Upper West Side mishpochas with keys to each other's apartments and a regular spot on the Sheep Meadow, but that was probably a ways off. We'd mostly spent the past decade apart, moving away from each other and inventing wholly separate new lives for ourselves. When we got together now it was sort of like the UN. We were like representatives of foreign countries just beginning to talk to each other.

"You ever have to do that before?" Rich asked, and we all turned to David. Everyone was nervous when it came to his work. We didn't know what was okay to ask and what wasn't.

"No. Not really. I mean we deal with suicides, but usually, you know, after the fact. Last year I had one, a mob guy. Blew his brains out. The body was in the living room downstairs and there was a huge hole in the ceiling right above it, that's how powerful the shot was. Went right up into the bedroom. I go up there and the damage is unbelievable. I'm walking around and I hear crunching under my feet, glass from the busted chandelier, I guessed. But then I look down and it's bone. Little pieces of skull."

Everyone was quiet. It was like someone had stilled the ocean.

I looked out the window and watched Dad pushing David and his wife, Kathy's, youngest daughter on a swing. She was laughing deliriously. I'd been thinking about Dad a lot lately, so much so that when I'd come across *Zulu* on TV recently I'd actually watched the whole thing for the first time since I was five. And it was a different kind of experience. I'd turned thirty-two a month before, the same age Michael Caine was when he played Gonville Bromhead. This time, as I'd watched him struggling to improvise his way through the Battle of Rorke's Drift, Gonville had seemed a little bit less like my dad than he had years before, and a little bit more like me. When I'd finished I'd sat on the couch for half an hour, wondering how I would respond to a surprise attack from four thousand Zulus.

A week or two later, on Thanksgiving, I turned off the TV again and got ready to leave. I was going to meet Dad for the ride out to David's. He was picking me up in his car in front of the Plaza so we could shoot right across the bridge to the expressway. I threw on a coat I wouldn't need on a warm November day, but was determined to wear anyway. It was a new coat, big, with lots of buttons and flaps and compartments—the kind of coat that says, "I'm just stopping off at Dean and DeLuca on my way to Nepal." As I caught my reflection in the dark and crackling TV screen, there was something about the way I was buttoning up the coat that reminded me of Gonville and I froze with my fingers at my neck.

I was suddenly hit with this painful, awesome bolt of what it must have been like to be Dad as a kid—a fat kid living in the toughest part of Brooklyn with crazy Communist parents and a brother in the navy during World War II.

I remembered how hard it was for me to learn anything about human nature growing up in a nut house, and I thought about how Dad's parents must have seemed like omniscient gods to him when all their dire predictions about evil people taking over the world started coming true. He was only eleven when his brother shipped out as a radioman aboard a submarine headed for the South Pacific, and fifteen in August of 1945 when Donald relayed the news of Japan's surrender to the mainland. Not a lot of use for ambiguity in that childhood. Dad must have felt afraid and impotent in the face of the drama going on around him every day, in his home and his neighborhood and in the world at large.

As a chubby child model, averse to athletics and all things physical, Dad wasn't exactly cut out for violence. And yet it was practically the only interest he'd ever had. Sometimes when I imagined what it was like to be him, it was hard for me to imagine him ending up any other way.

Dad has done so many bad things that anyone who hears about them doesn't see much point in measuring his badness against someone else's, but those people are not his children. The fact that his brother Donald beat four wives, and beat them worse and more often than Dad beat his, and that he made a monstrous ass of himself in public every day instead of just every few months meant a lot to me for a long time, and I think, to my dad. I remembered that twenty years ago Uncle Donald finally threw one punch too many, this one at Dad, and my father had booted him out of our lives.

I thought about how Dad probably liked Gonville not just because he proves that he's as tough as the other guys, but because he turns out just a little bit better than maybe he should have. Just a little. The big deal about Gonville's story isn't that he comes through in the clutch as a warrior, it's that he finds something in himself that his family of generals never warned him about. After the battle he tells the other officer that along with feeling exhausted and sick, he feels something else—he feels ashamed. My father was never very introspective, but he was always able to feel shame. That wasn't much, but it was some-thing. Some people didn't even feel that. Shame might be as close as my dad ever got to conscience.

As I took in my reflection on the blank TV screen, I wondered why I always overdressed when I visited my dad. I always wore a nice shirt, pressed pants, good shoes. I used to think that acting this way was self-preservation, a keeping of distance, but now, as I clomped down the warped old stairs of my walk-up, I thought maybe it was something else.

My father had lived through almost seventy New York winters without a hat. He had slept without a pillow for years, and I couldn't remember him ever seeing a doctor. He'd been camping out in a shit hole apartment forever. God knows what he was trying to prove. But what about me? What was I trying to prove, in this Range Rover of a coat? Did I want my father to see that I was not like him—that I didn't make a point of depriving myself of things, that I wasn't haunted by the ghosts of strangers who suffered at Stalingrad and Rorke's Drift? And then, as I flung open the front door of my building, it crashed hard into one of the garbage cans behind it, which didn't usually happen. I realized I was feeling hyped up, aggressive. It occurred to me that there might be something more than a desire to keep my dad at arm's length behind my Mr. Perfectly Put Together bit.

And I remembered that the really big deal about Gonville's story was that it was a lie. Part of it, anyway. There was no saluting of the Zulu warriors, or anything like it. That's the way the movie ends, but in real life, the British walked among the bodies of the fallen Zulus and stuck their bayonets into all the ones still breathing.

I heard the trash can fall over. I looked up to see that I had startled a Korean woman rocking back and forth behind a table covered with hats and scarves she was selling, and her movements reminded me distinctly of Floyd Patterson trying to bob and weave his way out of trouble in Las Vegas in 1965.

I suddenly realized that my hands were moving. That I was shadow-boxing, right there on Seventy-ninth Street I stopped and took a second to be freaked out a bit because I knew how this movie ended, but I let it play out in my mind. For weeks before Patterson fought Muhammad Ali, he kept referring to him by his old name, Cassius Clay, and everyone was expecting that when Ali got him in the ring, he would take care of poor old Floyd even more quickly than he had Sonny Liston the year before. But instead of a ferocious one-rounder, Ali treated the crowd at the fight to something even more frightening. All night long he battered Patterson right to the edge of unconsciousness, but when Floyd would start to droop, Ali would pull back, refusing to deliver the mercy of a final blow. The punches were only painful enough to stagger and humiliate Floyd, never enough to knock him out. Ali even went so far as to *hold Patterson up*, so he could deliver more punishment, and with every punch he repeated the same taunt to the old man, spitting it through his mouthpiece clearly enough for all the reporters at ringside to hear it, and never forget it: "What's my name! What's my name! What's my name!"

As I turned onto a windy Central Park West, I felt chilled by something colder than the air. It occurred to me that, by making a show for my father of how different I was from him, I may have been acting a whole lot like him. Was my refusal to share any trace of imperfect, scared personhood with him a small act of sadism? Was I holding him up on the ropes, purposefully extending the punishment of an old man into the later rounds?

And what was it with the wind on this street? It didn't make any sense. Buildings on one side, park on the other—it should be the opposite of a wind tunnel, but there were pretzel napkins and cigarette packs doing dogfights over my head. A Haitian nanny pushing a sour little prince in a stroller dropped her shoulder and forged ahead. I, on the other hand, surrendered immediately, turned from the wind, and was instantly slapped on the back of the head and then blinded. Something folded around my head, covering my face and flailing against itself, then suddenly tore off me and hovered in confusion. It was the back page of the *New York Post*. A teary-eyed Darryl Strawberry looked right at me, and the wind stopped for a second, so completely that I could hear the waxy sound of my lips parting to say something. But before I could the wind came back and sucked him into a vortex that took him all the way up past the Planetarium, to my mother's corner on Eighty-first Street.

For a moment I considered dropping by her place, but we weren't yet droppers-by in my family. We'd finally become visitors, but only by appointment. Still, it was at least possible to consider a spontaneous Hi, How Are Ya that day, and that felt like a lot. I was over at Mom's place maybe twice a month, and each time the hug at the door was a little fuller, and once we sat down she never got up, not even for the phone. She still wasn't in any danger of becoming the intrusive, guilt-tripping mother she swore she'd never be and I had always wished for, but there was an undeniable homey tug coming from Eighty-first Street, and it almost persuaded me to head up there for a visit. But I stuck with my plan and headed across town.

I turned left, into the park, where I imagined that I instantly made the transformation in the eyes of any observers, of which there were almost certainly none, from "that fuzzy-headed guy with nowhere to be" to "probably a painter." Aimlessness on the sidewalk is depression, but aimlessness in the park is soul. I saw a kid about thirty yards ahead of me who must have been heading for the boat pond, a very fat teenager carrying a remote-controlled aircraft carrier so big I could read the words U.S.S. *Truman* on its side from fifty yards away.

My father pulled his little Triumph Spitfire convertible up to the curb in front of the hotel—just yards away from the old southern border of GoodDadLand, I couldn't help but notice—at one o'clock on what had become a slightly rainy afternoon. He had the top down. I said something like, "Why don't we put the top up?" and he said, "Because we're Birkenheads," his standard answer to questions like that. I guess he heard the question as "Why aren't we as wimpy as everyone else?" whereas I'd meant it as "Hey, I have an idea—why don't we try going through the motions of sanity?" But I have to admit that, either way, his answer hit the nail on the head.

We drove for two hours on the Long Island Expressway with the top down. I was wearing a baseball cap, and the wind wanted to blow it off, so I had to hold it on my head. I didn't want to take it off because it was the only roof I had, but it wouldn't stay on by itself. I kept switching hands when my arms got tired, and then I decided to just stick with one arm until it went numb and I could forget about it. At least I had my big coat.

And that's when I started noticing the amazed and laughing children pointing at us from the back windows of station wagons. We were about a foot off the pavement in that car, and the noise made conversation impossible, which was just as well.

The ride in the rain put me in the unique position of being physically close to my father with no obligation to listen or speak, which meant I could actually listen to my own brain and hear what was really going on, and what was going on was a conversation I'd meant to have with him sixteen years before.

A voice spoke up, at least in my mind. It was tight and croaky, but I recognized it. It was me at fifteen, saying, "Hey, Dad—sometimes? I lie awake at night and I take these little mental trips into space. I sort of go to different places. Sometimes I try to get to the edge of the universe, and you know, really take in the emptiness, really feel the infinity. Do you ever do that? I mean, you must, right? Everyone does that. But do you get scared by it? Because I do—I get to where all the stars and planets stop, and I try to keep going into the rest of it, and I never really get too far without getting freaked out.

"Or sometimes I try to wrap my mind around something like Jupiter. You know, it's amazing—it's got like ten times the gravity of Earth, but it's a gas planet. It's just vapor, hydrogen, it's just a big ball of sky but it has weight and mass and gravity that's inescapable for anything that gets within a million miles of it. So, I'll lie there, and I'll *get* this, I'll *know* it, but no matter how hard I try I can't *feel* it. I can't make it real, and I'll spend the whole night trying to. Just lie there trying to feel the gravity of Jupiter. Does anything like that happen to you?" He doesn't say anything, even though this is an imaginary conversation, so I keep going, "Dad, sometimes I think that I'm just too afraid to be alive. I feel like my nerves are always moving and sparking, like little severed phone lines jumping around inside me. Do you feel like that? What was your dad like? Do you remember the time I got pulled out of that football game and you put your arm around my shoulder and told me it was just a game and everything would be okay? All those other dads were glaring at me and shaking their heads, and I remember thinking how lucky I was to have a father like you. God, sometimes I wish so much that you were all bad instead of almost good. Why am I so afraid to never talk to you again? I mean, even you would probably think that was the right thing to do—in fact, sometimes I'm pretty sure it's what you want me to do. Why did you break Mom's nose? What's your favorite song? What do I owe you? What do you owe me?"

By the time we got to David's house I felt like I would never be good at anything, because I didn't even have enough imagination to make an imaginary father talk to me. I mean, he was sitting right next to me, and . . . I didn't even imagine *him* exactly. I imagined very large or small versions of him, or photographs, or Albert Finney or Gonville. I thought, why can't I form a picture of this man in my mind? We pulled into my brother's driveway and I stepped out of the car with my hand still on my head, which David, who had opened his front door when he heard the car pull in, interpreted as a gesture of incredulity. In fact, I was frozen stiff, but excited to tell everyone the story of driving on the highway with the roof down, and my hat and the little kids pointing their fingers.

Now my siblings and I were sitting together, watching Dad through the window, and thinking about David walking across a floor strewn with pieces of skull. "Oh God," Rich muttered, almost to himself.

"Now that's a good name for a band," said David, "*Oh God.*" David didn't like the name of Richie's band, Into Another, whose new album we all loved, though Richie had summarily rejected all of our rave reviews. The songs he'd written were strange, funny, angry, beautiful, full of surprising chord progressions, shifts in tempo, shifts in tone and genre, even; and taken together, added up to a whole little world of Richieness. He'd written songs for a couple of bands before this one, too, all of which made very good records, all of which he had disowned the moment they were released, just as he'd done with this one, going into great detail about how he planned to destroy his guitars, kill his bandmates, and move to a shack in Montana.

But no one responded to David's comment about the name. I looked at David and Richard and saw that they were watching Dad. I remembered David crumpling to the floor under Dad's blows, and Richard falling down the stairs years before. And I wondered why, over all that time we were together as a family, my father had so often hit them, and Mom, but never Alison or me. Why he had spared us that particular violence. I don't think I'll ever really know, but my best guess is that as the oldest, I developed my conflict-defusing, Dad-distracting skills the earliest, that I learned at a young age to at least save my skin. And I think that Dad avoided hitting Alison because he avoided Alison. She told me once that she didn't have a single memory of him touching her in any way. Not a hug or a slap or a handshake. Mom said he wouldn't change her diaper. His aloofness was brutal.

I told the story about the Triumph and the ride in the rain. And when I got to the part about how I found it difficult to get a mental picture of Dad, there was another pause, and Alison finally broke it. She told us that years ago, just before the divorce, she'd found photographs in a closet, Polaroids of Dad with a naked woman wearing a dog collar and a leash. She said that, about a year before that, when she was eleven, she'd found his stash of porn, spread the pictures and magazines across Mom and Dad's bed, and written the word "disgusting" across the pillows in green toothpaste. We were all stunned, but she wasn't done. She said that Nana approached her a few days after the incident with the porn, put her hands up inside Ali's shirt, and said, "Oh look, I see you're developing. My God breasts are awful things. I wish I could cut mine off."

I decided to spend the night at David's and let Dad drive back to the city himself.

A week later we were all in Florida visiting Mom's parents. Near the end of a long day together we gathered in the living room, where Papa began a story about his father. Grandma quickly interrupted, "No, Ken, no," as Papa smiled in resignation. "No, no! You've told that before. They've heard it before. You're sitting in the Chair of Forgetfulness. You know what that is? That's Heracles. He saved people like you from the Chair of Forgetfulness."

Papa spoke softly. "Listen, my father came to this country, well, first to Canada, when he was thirteen years old, around 1884, that would be. He tramped the snow in Novia Scotia with snowshoes on his feet and a pack of writing materials on his back, which he sold to the farmers around there. His mother died when he was two years old and he was raised in Russia by his grandmother. He was self-educated, a very enthusiastic student of philosophy—Greek, Roman, German, American." Papa leaned forward in his chair. "We knew him as a very loving father. He was mild-mannered and gentle, he never punished his children by striking them." He looked directly at me. "He was a good man. He loved the spiritual and ethical principles of Judaism but he felt that they were obscured by observances. Of all the holidays he only celebrated Passover, which he thought of as a Jewish Fourth of July, a celebration of freedom. He loved being part of the chain of custom that had come down through thousands of years, Jews all over the world celebrating in the same way." His voice broke a little. "He made the most beautiful seder. You know, some people make a great contribution to the world, but most people, most people live their lives quietly, making their mark by the impact they have on those around them. Through their role as 'bearer of the torch,' by passing on humanity to their progeny. My mother had one of the most beautiful natural soprano voices I've ever heard. She learned all the arias sung by Alma Gluck and Tetrazzini on Victor Red Seal Records. I'll swear she sang them better! My earliest recollections are of my mother's beautiful coloratura voice, singing in our sunlit kitchen . . ."

After everyone else had gone to bed that night, the four of us kids sat around the kitchen table. We had started something that day at David's, and it wasn't going to stop.

"Do you think Dad is suicidal?" Alison asked, very quietly. "Do you think he would ever kill himself?"

David quickly said, "No, no he's not. I don't think so. He's an old man."

"I used to wonder about that, a lot," Ali said, "when we first moved into the city and he was coming up there all the time, to our neighborhood. You know, Mom looked out the window one day and saw him walking up and down the block, back and forth, with a paper bag in his hand."

"You remember that time he walked out into the street naked with a sword?" I said.

Alison said, "He wasn't naked. He wasn't. I know you remember it that way, but I asked Mom about it and she swears he wasn't. Not that it makes much difference. He was still carrying a sword, for God's sake."

"Are you sure?" I said.

"I'm sure," she said.

I couldn't believe I'd been carrying around such a vivid, yet false memory for so long. I had been doing a lot less bullshitting lately, had finally become more interested in accepting the truth than improving it, and I was worried that I might have remembered other things incorrectly. I asked about everything I could think of—David and the Jaguar, David and the baseball, Alison's party, England. It turned out that our memories were remarkably similar, down to the small details, and I noticed a real sense of relief in the room as we finally spoke them out loud. I felt like a lookout spotting land for the first time in years.

When I was done with my questions Rich asked me about the most recent addition to our now bulging storybook. Dad had recently surprised me with the information that he was going to be a father again. "He didn't look too happy the other night," I said, "when he told me about the baby." Alison said, "Oh God, that's so weird," and put her hands over her eyes. I said, "I hadn't seen him in almost a year. And then he drops this news." Rich asked how he told me.

"We were talking about something else. The usual stuff," I said.

"And then he says, 'Do you remember Yasmine?' and I have no idea who he's talking about but the name sounds familiar, and I say 'No,' but then I remember meeting this woman, a neighbor, for like, five seconds maybe, and I say, 'Wait, from the building?' and he says, 'Yep, that's her. On Friday she will be having my child.'"

"Ahh!!" Rich yelled. David and Alison both threw their heads back. We all moaned in unison. "I had no idea he was even seeing someone," I said. "But then again, you know, he's not." Yasmine had moved back to Portugal already. Dad said he would visit once or twice a year but that was about it. When I was done with the story David was smiling wearily, his cheeks puffed with fatigue. We all hugged each other good night and went off to bed exhausted.

When I got back to New York I asked Mom if she and I could have lunch at her place. As part of the divorce agreement, my mother had promised to give my father twelve and a half percent of her royalties from the next show of hers to open on Broadway. At the time of the divorce she'd been having a good run of it and this was no small concession, but he insisted, and she signed the papers under duress to cut herself free. Over the next fourteen years she did well—she had a couple of shows produced Off-Broadway, wrote a show with Jule Styne, the composer of *Gypsy* and *Funny Girl*, even had a couple of songs recorded by Frank Sinatra—but she also had some bad luck: shows closed out of town, collaborators died, projects fell apart at the last minute. So when *Jelly's Last Jam* was about to open on Broadway, it was cause for the kind of savoring that a good long wait makes for. But it came with a surprise.

Dad hadn't forgotten about their agreement, and he sent a letter asking for what he called "his" money. Mom had been keeping me up to date about the legal wrangling, and now, over lunch, she told me that Dad had rejected, out of hand, the latest compromise she had offered: to give the contested portion of her royalties to me and my siblings. Hearing this made me angry, but it also sobered me up, made me feel a bit more awake than I'd been a minute before.

After lunch we took out the photo albums and boxes of pictures. I asked her if I could have the picture of me at my junior prom. I wanted to burn it and bury the ashes in a sealed lead box in Antarctica, just to make sure no one would ever again see me in a powder blue tuxedo jacket and pink ruffled shirt.

I found pictures I'd never seen from her wedding to Jere in 1984. There was a great shot of them dancing together, looking at each other with palpable affection, and I smiled. Back when I was a kid, if a genie had asked me what I wanted most for my mother I would have said "dancing," and I would have meant what I saw in that picture. When we were all down in Florida, Jere and I watched through the front window as Mom came into the house with her father after a walk. Jere kept his eyes on her, leaned over to me, and said, "Look at how beautiful your mom is," and I had to grit my teeth to keep from throwing my arms around him. His voice was calm and even, and knowing that it was the last thing my mother heard at night made me breathe a deep sigh of thanks.

As I dug deeper into the trove, I came across other pictures I'd never seen, of David and Richard, Mom as a girl, childhood friends. I even found the shot of Martina she gave me that night in the park years before.

Mom handed me a big bag full of old clothes and book reports, handmade draydels and Christmas tree ornaments to take home, and we pressed our faces together tight when I left. The day had the feeling of a ritual about it, and as I walked west on Eighty-first Street my arms and legs felt loose, like I'd had an inside-out massage.

But I also felt a small hard stone of something in my throat that I couldn't seem to swallow, and halfway down the block I coughed it up. My left leg went completely rigid and the other buckled flat, and I dropped to one knee. I could feel every cold bump and bubble in the sidewalk through my jeans. I knelt there on the concrete for a long time, a hand on my bent left knee, looking straight ahead at a tiny sliver of Hudson in the distance.

It was the elbow patches. The jacket in the picture—the too-big man's sport jacket Martina was wearing back in 1977 on her bed. It had brown leather patches on the elbows. I was horrified but not surprised. *Of course he slept with her, of course,* I thought. I knew, but I didn't know. I turned around and headed back up to Mom's.

The last straw for Mom had come when Alison found the Polaroid photos in Dad's closet. As she stood in their bedroom thinking about what she was going to say to Dad, she looked up from the photos at one of his gun cases, holding a neat row of seven Martini-Henrys, and thought, "What in the world am I doing here?"

When she finally left my father, she left a lot behind. The police told her just to take the kids, go, and not to press charges. They said if she did press charges Dad would only spend a night in jail before being released, and he'd be angrier than he was before.

She had already told him she was leaving, but she wasn't going to move for another month, until her new apartment in the city was ready. Somehow, maybe because Dad seemed so calm and quiet, seemed outwardly to be taking it well, she'd convinced herself that it was safe enough to stay for those last few weeks. I was living in the city already, in a dorm room at NYU, and David had moved in with his girlfriend, so it was just Mom, and Alison and Richard, who were twelve and thirteen at the time.

Dad started sleeping downstairs, and Mom made sure she was never in the house with him alone. She timed her return from work every day for an hour after Richard got back from school, just to be sure, she told me. I asked her how she felt now about leaving Richard there alone with Dad back then, and she said, "I regret it more than anything I've ever done. I think about that now, about the danger he was in, and it hurts so deeply. I wish to God I could go back and fix it.

I must have been some kind of crazy from everything that was going on. I was really just focused on finding a place for us and moving out, and on getting through each day. I wasn't thinking clearly, that's all I can say. I'm just so thankful he never actually hurt Richard or Alison during that time."

School buses break down, like everything else, and on this particular evening, a flat tire on Richard's set the events in motion. I got the basic story a few days after it happened, but I never asked for further information about it. I locked the questions away somewhere until I was ready to hear the answers, which wasn't until I rang Mom's doorbell again ten minutes after I'd just left. That's when I heard myself ask her if she still had the police report somewhere.

When I asked to see the report, Mom reacted as if she'd been expecting it. No hesitation at all. She walked straight to the drawer where it was kept, didn't have to sort through anything, pulled it out, and said, "Here you go, sweetie."

It was stunning. Very Joe Friday, Just the Facts, Ma'am, but also handwritten and bleeding with feeling. Something about how hard the police officer had pressed his pen down on the paper, and the shortcuts he took in his writing, was very comforting to me. I was glad that Mom had told her story to someone who got upset about it. And I was glad that I asked for the police report instead of asking her to tell the story. It meant less pain for her and probably a clearer look at things for me. It's amazing how much more you can get from "Just the Facts, Ma'am" sometimes.

So here are the facts: Mom was upstairs, in her bedroom, brushing her hair. She'd just taken her clothes off and was about to change and take a walk, because she'd realized that Richard wasn't home yet. She didn't think Dad was either. He was barefoot, and the house was carpeted, so she didn't hear him come into the room. He just appeared behind her in the mirror. He was holding two long nylon dog leashes. Before she could put the brush down, he grabbed her by the neck and started to squeeze. He said, "Why can't you love me?" Just as Mom felt she was about to black out, she kicked him hard in the groin. She almost got away but he grabbed her by the hair and pulled her out of the bedroom and down the stairs to the kitchen. She managed to keep her feet on the stairs and didn't fall. When they got to the kitchen, he grabbed her by the shoulders and screamed, "Why can't you love me?" again. She wanted to say something but was too afraid to speak. He opened the door to the basement stairs and dragged her down them. She lost her footing near the bottom and scraped her knee on the concrete floor. He took her to the spot where the heavy bag usually hung; he had removed it already. He tied one leash around her wrists, and the other to the hook on the ceiling, so that her arms were held straight up over her head. He started yelling, "Why can't you love me?" over and over, not pausing for an answer anymore. He got behind her. He took his belt off and hit her back with it, five times. He grabbed her by the back of the neck with one hand, and started to unzip his pants with the other. When he was naked he turned her around to face him. Mom was screaming now. Dad demanded that she stop, but she couldn't. He lifted his hand to hit her, and she vomited on his chest. He stopped his hand, wiped his chest with it. He became flustered. Mom kept screaming and Dad kept telling her to stop. She told him she had a Valium that Barbara had given her (a lie) in her purse. He got the purse, unhooked Mom from the ceiling, and she put her hands (still tied together) into the bag. She closed them around her car keys, swung the purse hard at his head, and ran up the cellar stairs, out to the driveway, and into the car. She drove to Barbara's with her hands still bound together.

The first thing I felt was awe. At all of it. The kind I imagined you felt after an earthquake. Like someone had pulled on the fabric of everything years before and the wrinkle from that disturbance had not lessened with time and was just reaching me now.

After I read the report I spent the rest of the day with Mom, and we told each other secrets about our lives. I asked her about the affairs—hers and his—and she named names, and I asked what the fights with Dad were about, and I told her what it was like for me on the other side of the wall.

I spent the next week in a fever of anger, a low-grade but constant cooking of old things. I was completely immersed in the past, smelling it and hearing it, picking it up and turning it over and sorting it out.

The fever finally broke when I got calls from Alison and Richard, coincidentally or not, wanting to talk some more about Dad. We shared more stories, connected more dots, had slow, surprisingly easy, sensible conversations about the bad old days, and put together as complete a picture as we could of that dense, diseased time. I felt like I was breathing better than I had in years, like I was finally letting the air out of something big. Things around me—furniture, food, rain—almost felt like they'd gained more substance, had more heft. They seemed more tangible, perishable, and real.

It wasn't magic, it wasn't a cure-all—in fact, it was when depression began to seriously engulf me and my siblings. But that's what happens when you pull the wool from your own eyes. It was there for a reason, after all.

I told everyone I was going to go talk to Dad. Alison said, "I hate thinking of you being in that apartment with all those guns." I said, "Yeah, and that's the thing—whenever I think about some of the good times, when the guilt about spending so little time with him starts to get to me, when I think, 'Maybe I've blown things out of proportion all these years,' sometimes I try to imagine what that would be like, spending more time with him. But when I do, when I picture that moment, being in that apartment, the same damn thing always stops me."

"The guns," she said.

"The guns," I said.

"Me, too," she replied. "That picture of him surrounded by guns. The swords and knives and those Martini-whatevers. That's where everything stops."

About a week after the fever breaks, I'm heading downtown to see my father. I'm still afraid of him, and of myself, of what I might become or reveal myself to be, of what I might do to him or me if I open the dam inside. I've been having nightmares about him killing himself, about him appearing with a gun and shooting me, and of me grabbing his gun and beating him to death with it.

I know I won't be talking only to Dad. I'll be talking to imagined dads, gods and monsters, heroes and villains, the feared dad and the wished-for dad, even to the hope I still, incredibly, cling to that Dad will change.

I'm walking down Central Park West and thinking about Papa, something he said to me in Florida. We were talking about Hitler. He put his hand on my wrist and said, "The best way to not become a monster when you face a monster is to not believe in monsters."

And suddenly I'm standing under my father's window looking at a penny in the palm of my hand. I feel like I've just woken up. I have no memory of anything on the walk, but the sun is about where it was when I left and I'm breathing hard, so I must have been walking pretty fast.

There's about a wishing well's worth of pennies on the canvas awning in front of my father's window. The intercom in his building is behind the locked front door, so it's completely useless. The way I let Dad know I'm downstairs is by throwing a penny at his window, since there are no pebbles on the corner of Forty-fourth and Ninth. I take a little breath and spin the side of the penny off my finger at just the right speed to make a loud enough plink against the glass without breaking it.

Less than a second later Dad pulls the flag of St. George to the side, jerks his arm up in a little nervous wave, and disappears, the flag still waving after he releases it. It takes two deep breaths for the buzzer to sound and the front door lock to be released, and a few minutes later my father is Gonville again.

The eyes on the side of my head have been perusing his gun collection, and when I focus on him again I see spots on my father's face. Lots of them. Dark brown age spots, liver spots. His face seems rounder, and his neck is puffy, like he's taking steroids or something. I can see tiny creases below his ears, a dryness around his mouth, a rheumy fog in his eyes. There's a tank behind him—a little toy army tank on his dresser. His room, which had always felt like a lair to me, or a cave, looks instead like what it is: a tiny bedroom where an aging boy lives with his toys.

He asks me why Alison hasn't been in touch with him and I say, "Well, you did some terrible things, Dad. Terrible things."

He says, "Everybody spanked their kids back then."

I just look at him. He stares into the middle distance. His head looks like it's sinking into his shoulders.

Before I decide to, I start speaking and it's the easiest thing I've ever done.

"Dad? Dad. Bruce. Listen, I want to talk to you about this royalty thing. The royalties from Mom's show. She told me that you're asking for the twelve and a half percent from the divorce agreement, and I have to tell you, I know you can take it to court and maybe even win, but I don't think you're entitled to that money."

My father looks at me like I had always wanted to look at him, with easy gratitude, and he says, "So you think I'm legally right but morally wrong?"

I say, "Yes."

"Okay," he says. "Consider it done."

And we step across the equator. Only about six inches, really, but all of a sudden everything is spinning in a new direction.

Dad changes the subject, to lunch, and I let him. He picks up a loaf of dark bread and tells a story about it. He talks for a while but I only hear the sound of what's just moved through the room. Decades of gathering force have suddenly slipped from one track to another with the flick of a switch. I'm thrown by the abruptness of the moment, startled by its lack of crescendo. I've been thinking about it for so long I've forgotten there would be another moment right after it, and another one after that, and that the future will keep on becoming the past. The moment wasn't what I expected or feared, but what if it had been? There would still have been later to deal with.

So how am I going to do that? It crosses my mind to ask Dad what just happened, what "consider it done" really meant. Was it an apology? A guilty plea? A bully's cowardice? A father being gentle with his son? Yes, yes, yes, and yes, I decide. All of it and more, all at once. I don't ask. The look in his eyes tells me that whatever it was, it was all he could do. I remember that he and Mom met with a therapist once, many years ago, and that he'd stormed out of the room when he was asked about his childhood.

I remember him walking with his mother that morning in England, carrying his father's ashes into the field out back. His mother's gone now, too, dead for seven years, and her ashes are in this apartment somewhere. I scan the room. There are fading pictures of me and my brothers and sister as children on the walls and bookshelves and tables.

Dad's still talking. I try to watch him, see all of him, all the pieces. As little as I used to know him, I know him less now. And I will probably never know him again.

I look around at all the weapons. I wonder if my Portuguese half sister will ever see this place, or the seals at the Central Park Zoo. I tell my father I have to go, and when I leave he leans awkwardly forward and kisses me on the cheek.

I walk slowly down the one flight of stairs. I step outside, and the leafy fall smell that has been in the air all day is gone. The trees are bare. The sun is low, but there's probably an hour of it left, and I can still make it to the abandoned trainyard by the river. I've been promising myself that I would get over there before the new buildings go up. It's the only empty space left in Manhattan, a huge expanse of nothing, the rusty tracks overrun by tall, wild marsh grass.

I open my mouth and fill it with the new, clean air of winter. I turn to look back up at my father's window. The cross of St. George is waving, like someone has just let it go.

Acknowledgments

Many thanks to:
Wylie O'Sullivan, Farley Chase, Sydney Tanigawa, Jere Couture, Margo Lion, Ed Ugel, Jim Murphy, Susie Murphy, Kate Zeman, Bill Zeman, Rick Cleveland, Mary Cleveland, Dani Klein Modisett, Tod Modisett, Carol Locatell, Greg Prestopino, Bob Leonard, Gaby Salick, Matthew Arkin, Gary Martin, Nancy Donner, Mark Nelson, Ari Roth, Kate Shechter, Cordelia Richards, Chris Richter, Gordon Litwin, Anne Luzzatto, Chris Wall, Jamie Harman Birkenhead, Kathy Birkenhead, Carly Sommerstein, Eric Fuentecilla, Eric Rayman, the New York Historical Society, and the Maine Historical Society.

About the Author

Peter Birkenhead is a contributor to Salon.com, where he writes personal essays and cultural criticism. An essay about Oprah's endorsement of *The Secret* was the most-read piece on the site in 2007. He's also a contributor to *Marie Claire* magazine, and has written for *GQ*, the *Los Angeles Times*, the *Chicago Tribune*, and other publications. As an actor he has extensive stage and television credits. He lives in Los Angeles.